JUNIOR CYCLE

LESS STRESS
MORE
SUCCESS

Business Studies

Brian Fogarty

g GILL EDUCATION

Gill Education
Hume Avenue
Park West
Dublin 12
www.gilleducation.ie

Gill Education is an imprint of M.H. Gill & Co.

© Brian Fogarty 2020

978 07171 8668 6

Design by Liz White Designs
Print origination by Carole Lynch

At the time of going to press, all web addresses were active and contained information relevant to the topics in the book. Gill Education does not, however, accept responsibility for the content of views contained on those websites. Content, views and addresses may change beyond the publishers or authors' control. Students should always be supervised when reviewing websites.

For permission to reproduce photographs, the author and publisher gratefully acknowledge the following:

© Alamy: 11, 56, 65, 97, 230; © Competition and Consumer Protection Commission: 51; © iStock/Getty Premium: 3, 5, 8, 15, 19, 21, 25, 28, 31, 40, 42, 44, 46, 47, 53, 58, 60, 68, 75, 80, 85, 89, 101, 105, 106, 108, 111, 115, 117, 123, 124, 127, 128, 130, 135, 137, 140, 143, 147, 148, 151, 158, 164, 168, 174, 181, 186, 196, 203, 205, 215, 220, 224, 226, 231, 232, 235, 236, 239, 243, 250, 255, 256, 260, 263, 279; © Rolling News: 21, 62, 110, 209, 227, 266; © Shutterstock: 120, 153, 211.

The author and publisher have made every effort to trace all copyright holders, but if any have been inadvertently overlooked we would be pleased to make the necessary arrangement at the first opportunity.

The paper used in this book is made from the wood pulp of managed forests.
For every tree felled, at least one tree is planted, thereby renewing natural resources.

CONTENTS

Introduction

Business Studies should be an easy subject to relate to the real world around you – it relates to literally every product you see either at home or in school. Somebody somewhere invented each one and risked their time and money to invest in it. Thousands of hours have been spent designing it, improving it, producing it and marketing it in order to get you to like it enough to spend your money on it.

Regardless of what your favourite subject is at school, in the future you will either own or work for an enterprise of some kind, either publicly or privately owned. You'll also be a consumer all your life and perhaps an investor too.

Thanks to the globalised nature of our world and the rapid pace of technological change, there is no telling where you will work in the future, how you will work, or if all of the multiple careers you may have over your lifetime even exist yet.

Business Studies should not just be seen as a subject at school; business is part of your life and always will be. Business Studies is the most relevant, realistic and dynamic subject there is, and knowing this should help you to connect with it and absorb it.

Structure of this book

This book is based on the 37 learning outcomes contained in the Junior Cycle Specification. It contains 37 chapters that thoroughly address each of the learning outcomes, and also gives a detailed guide to the final examination, the classroom-based assessments (CBAs) and the assessment task.

Glossary of action verbs

This glossary defines each of the action verbs found in the 36 learning outcomes. Each action verb is described in terms of what the student should be able to do once they have achieved that learning outcome.

- **Analyse:** Study or examine something in detail; break it down in order to bring out the essential elements or structure; identify parts and relationships; and interpret information to reach conclusions.
- **Apply:** Select and use information and/or knowledge and understanding to explain a given situation or real circumstances.
- **Appreciate:** Recognise the meaning of; have a practical understanding of.
- **Assess:** Judge, evaluate or estimate the nature, ability, or quality of something.
- **Calculate:** Obtain a numerical answer showing the relevant stages in the working.
- **Classify:** Group things based on common characteristics.
- **Compare:** Give an account of the similarities and/or differences between two (or more) items or situations, referring to both/all of them throughout.
- **Complete:** Finish making or doing; bring to a successful conclusion.
- **Conduct:** Organise and carry out.

- **Consider:** Describe patterns in data; use knowledge and understanding to interpret patterns, make predictions and check reliability.
- **Construct:** Develop information in a diagrammatic or logical form; not by factual recall but by analogy or by using and putting together information.
- **Debate:** Argue about a subject, especially in a formal manner.
- **Describe:** Develop a detailed picture or image of, for example, a structure or a process, using words or diagrams where appropriate; produce a plan, simulation or model.
- **Develop:** Progress or improve to become more mature, advanced, or elaborate.
- **Devise:** Plan, create or formulate a procedure or system by careful thought.
- **Determine:** Ascertain or establish exactly by research or calculation.
- **Differentiate:** Recognise or ascertain what makes something different.
- **Discuss:** Offer a considered, balanced review that includes a range of arguments, factors or hypotheses; opinions or conclusions should be presented clearly and supported by appropriate evidence.
- **Distinguish:** Make the differences between two or more concepts or items clear.
- **Evaluate (data):** Collect and examine data to make judgements and appraisals; describe how evidence supports or does not support a conclusion in an inquiry or investigation; identify the limitations of data in conclusions; make judgements about ideas, solutions or methods.
- **Evaluate (ethical judgement):** Collect and examine evidence to make judgements and appraisals; describe how evidence supports or does not support a judgement; identify the limitations of evidence in conclusions; make judgements about ideas, solutions or methods.
- **Explain:** Give a detailed account including reasons or causes.
- **Examine:** Consider an argument or concept in a way that uncovers the assumptions and relationships of the issue.
- **Identify:** Recognise patterns, facts, or details; provide an answer from a number of possibilities; recognise and state briefly a distinguishing fact or feature.
- **Investigate:** Observe, study, or make a detailed and systematic examination in order to establish facts and reach new conclusions.
- **Interpret:** Use knowledge and understanding to recognise trends and draw conclusions from given information.
- **Justify:** Give valid reasons or evidence to support an answer or conclusion.
- **Monitor:** Observe and check the progress of something over a period of time; keep under systematic review.
- **Predict:** Give an expected result of an event; explain a new event based on observations or information using logical connections between pieces of information.
- **Prepare:** Make something ready for use or presentation.
- **Present:** Promote or propose an idea; deliver or illustrate evidence; show something for others to examine.
- **Propose:** Put forward a plan or suggestion for consideration.
- **Recommend:** Put forward something with approval as being suitable for a particular purpose.
- **Relate:** Associate, giving reasons.
- **Suggest:** Propose a solution, hypothesis or other possible answer.
- **Understand:** Have and apply a well-organised body of knowledge.
- **Use:** Apply knowledge or rules to put theory into practice.

STRAND 1
Personal Finance

Managing My Resources

Exploring Business

Using Skills For Business

Managing My Resources

1 Resources, Needs and Wants

Main Learning Outcome

1.1 Students should be able to review the personal resources available to them to realise their needs and wants and analyse the extent to which realising their needs and wants may impact on individuals and society.

aims By the end of this chapter you should:
- be able to list your financial, physical and other resources
- know how to differentiate between needs and wants
- understand how your need for resources can impact on other people.

Resources

A resource is anything that individuals or households can draw on in order to function effectively and achieve their objectives. There are several different kinds:

Financial resources

- Income from a full-time or part-time job, pocket money, occasional gifts of money, Jobseeker's Allowance, pension, savings.
- Financial resources allow you to purchase the goods and services you need, gain independence from others and invest in your professional and personal development.

Physical resources

- House, furniture, car, computer, internet connection, school bag, mobile phone, sports equipment, musical instruments, books, etc.
- Physical resources improve your everyday quality of life whether at work, at school or at home.

Personal abilities and experience

- Academic qualifications, work experience, foreign languages, involvement in sport or fitness, computer skills, leadership and communication skills, artistic or musical talent, culinary skills, travel experience, organisational skills, time management, problem-solving abilities, readiness to work to deadlines or under pressure, good work–life balance.
- Your personal abilities and experience play a part in making you the person you are, help you to withstand the challenges that life will throw at you, and prepare you for the opportunities that await you.

The people around you

- Spouse, partner, parent(s), children, friends, mentors, teachers, managers, employees, colleagues, classmates, neighbours, community.
- Even the most driven person cannot do it all by themselves. They need love, security, encouragement, support, advice, and even occasional criticism from those around them.

top tip

It is important to remember that even though your resources are scarce, if you work at expanding and improving them, they can become less scarce. So can the resources of a company or a country. This is one way we improve our lives – by expanding our resources.

Regardless of how many resources we have, nearly all of us would be happier with more. We therefore say that our resources are relatively **scarce**, since our demand for them is usually always greater than their supply.

Needs and wants

Demand for resources can be broken down into needs and wants.

Needs

These are the items you cannot do without and which should be given priority, e.g. food, shelter and clothing. Our needs are finite, but the cost of them can still be very high. Our basic needs should come first.

Wants

Anything else you might wish to consume once your needs have been satisfied, e.g. an iPhone. Wants tend to be unlimited or infinite. We sometimes think that we need something, e.g. a designer jacket, when, in fact, we just want it and may be better off saving the money for future needs, e.g. education.

Factors that influence needs and wants

- **Age:** As you leave education and enter the world of work, your needs and wants change, e.g. desire for travel. If you start a family, they change again, e.g. childcare needs. As you move into retirement, your priorities change yet again, e.g. the need for more health care.

- **Income:** When our incomes are low, we worry most about essentials, e.g. paying the rent. As we grow richer, we worry less about paying for our needs and shift our focus to our wants, e.g. an expensive car.
- **Prudent lifestyle:** Once their needs and a few wants are satisfied, some people don't feel a strong urge to spend the rest of their income.
- **Hobbies and pastimes:** The particular interests we develop will influence what we need or want to buy, e.g. skiing equipment.

- **Environmental consciousness:** We may wish to avoid harmful products or reduce our carbon footprint, e.g. a preference for locally grown food.
- **Influence of peers:** Many of us tend to want the same things that our friends, neighbours and colleagues want, e.g. the latest gadget.
- **Media:** We are often influenced by what we see in advertisements or trends set by celebrities and influencers, e.g. a brand of sunglasses.

Impact on society

How you use your resources to meet your needs and wants is a decision usually best left to you. However, your decisions can have a wider impact, so society sometimes intervenes in how you spend your resources.

- **Societal decisions:** Decisions regarding infrastructure such as roads, hospitals and schools are bigger than any one individual. Usually the government makes these decisions for the good of society in general.
- **Redistribution of wealth:** In general, governments tax those who earn more and use the revenue to support those who struggle to pay for their basic needs.

> **exam focus**
>
> A constant theme in the exam is the interaction between people and their personal goals of making money and society's need to look after the good of everybody.

- **Value Added Tax (VAT) rates:** There are higher VAT rates on luxury goods that are deemed by the government to be wants, e.g. chocolate, and lower VAT rates or even no VAT at all on goods that are considered to be needs, e.g. baby food.
- **Negative effects of individual decisions:** When individuals consume substances such as illicit drugs or alcohol, it negatively affects other people and society at large. The government bans or heavily restricts such products.
- **Encouraging desirable behavior:** The government can provide extra resources in the form of grants in order to promote cycling, solar panels, etc.

- **Social costs:** The costs paid by society as a whole as a consequence of individual decisions, e.g. noise pollution and litter from a nightclub in a residential area.
- **Impact on the environment:** An individual may not cause much damage to the environment, but all individuals taken together certainly can, e.g. the carbon footprint caused by total imports into a country. Governments pass laws to change individual behaviour for the good of all.
- **Pensions:** Governments often have compulsory pension schemes because many individuals would not otherwise invest in a pension.
- **Rights and responsibilities:** In general, individuals have a right to use their own resources as they see fit. However, individuals also have a responsibility to use their resources in a way that doesn't impose costs on society (social costs) or the environment (environmental costs).

Question 1, NCCA Sample Questions
'Irish mobile phone usage highest in the western world, global stats reveal.'

Irish Independent, August 27 2015

Explain **one** social cost and **one** environmental cost of using a mobile phone.

Answer
Social cost

Many people constantly use their phones, e.g. in restaurants, on trains and in workplaces. This can reduce our enjoyment of face-to-face communication.

Environmental cost

People upgrade their phone every year or so, usually replacing their old one long before it has stopped working. Very few phones are recycled. All this mobile phone production and waste uses up the world's scarce resources.

Sample Question
Indicate in each case whether the item is a need or a want. Tick (✓) the correct box below.

	Need	Want
Games console		✓
Shoes	✓	
Holiday		✓
Food	✓	

2 Household Income and Expenditure

Main Learning Outcome

1.2 Students should be able to identify and classify sources of income and expenditure, compare options available to best manage financial resources, evaluating the risks associated with each option and making informed and responsible judgements.

By the end of this chapter you should:
- understand the various sources of household income
- know how to differentiate between different types of expenditure
- be able to prioritise and reduce spending where necessary.

One of the most basic yet vital skills we all have to master in life is how to make ends meet. This means understanding the sources of our income, becoming prudent about our expenditure and learning the benefits of saving.

Sources of household income

Income is any money received by a household, whether earned (e.g. wages) or unearned (e.g. Jobseeker's Allowance). It can be divided into regular and irregular income.

Types of regular income

Regular income is steady income you can depend on that is received on a weekly or monthly basis.

- **Pocket money:** Parents may give their children a set amount of pocket money every week, e.g. €20 in exchange for doing household chores.
- **Basic wages:** The money earned by an employee for a normal working week, e.g. €23 an hour for a 39-hour week.
- **Salary:** An annual fixed amount received from your employer in return for work performed, usually paid in monthly instalments, e.g. a nurse who is paid a salary of €43,000 a year.
- **Child Benefit:** On the first Tuesday of every month, the government pays €140 to all parents in the country in respect of each of their children under the age of 18.
- **Jobseeker's Allowance:** A weekly payment made by the government to people who are unemployed and looking for work, e.g. €203 a week for a person aged 26 or over.

- **Pension:** A regular payment received by a retired person, usually less than the wage they were paid when they worked.
- **Rental income:** A landlord who has a rental contract with a tenant can have a steady amount of rent coming in every month.
- **Benefit in kind (BIK):** Any non-cash benefit or perk given by an employer to an employee, such as:
  — a company car
  — a free parking space
  — use of a phone/computer/tablet
  — health insurance
  — subsidised meals
  — gym membership.

Types of irregular/additional income

Income that varies from week to week or which may only be earned occasionally.

- **Self-employment:** Self-employed people work for themselves, so may not have a regular basic wage. They earn money if their services are required, e.g. the services of a window cleaner may not be required every week. Many self-employed people reach a point where they can be reasonably confident of earning enough money every week, but their incomes can still vary a good deal.
- **Casual work:** Employment is on a one-off basis, or on a daily basis when the need arises, with no guarantee of regular work, e.g. babysitting.
- **Overtime:** Employees work in excess of their normal hours, normally getting paid a higher rate per hour.
- **Commission:** Employees earn a percentage of the price of each item they sell in order to encourage them to sell more, e.g. 1% of the price of every house sold.
- **Bonus:** An extra payment made to employees for reaching a target in order to encourage them to sell more, e.g. a bonus of €1,000 if they sell 20 cars in one week.
- **Interest on savings:** If you have money on deposit in a bank or other financial institution, you will earn interest on your savings, e.g. the bank pays 2% interest on €3,000 savings.
- **Dividends:** A share of profits made by a company paid to the shareholders.
- **Gifts:** You may receive gifts of cash from relatives, e.g. on your Confirmation, at Christmas or on your birthday.
- **Inheritance:** Somebody passes away and leaves you money or other assets in their will.
- **Occasional rental income:** Some rental income varies from week to week, e.g. a holiday home rented out occasionally using Airbnb.

- **Winnings:** You win a prize, e.g. in a raffle or lottery.
- **Grant:** A sum of money paid by the government or a private organisation for a particular purpose that usually does not have to be repaid, e.g. an educational grant.
- **Sale of assets:** Sometimes you can make money by selling something you no longer need or want, e.g. a set of golf clubs or a second car.

Example 1: Income of the Dunphy family

Income of the Dunphy Family					
	Jan.	Feb.	Mar.	Apr.	Total Jan.–Apr.
Income	€	€	€	€	€
Rory salary	1,200	1,200	1,200	1,200	4,800
Denise wages	1,100	1,000	1,100	1,200	4,400
Child Benefit	280	280	280	280	1,120
Dividends	55		90		145
Total income	2,635	2,480	2,670	2,680	10,465

- The rows show each of the Dunphy family's four sources of income. The total amount for January to April for each source of income appears on the right of the table.
- The columns show how much income the Dunphy family received each month. The total amount of income for each month is at the bottom of the table.
- The Dunphy family's total income for January to April was **€10,465**.

Types of expenditure

Expenditure refers to all money spent by a household. It can be divided into fixed, irregular and discretionary expenditure.

Fixed expenditure

The same amount is paid out each week or month. The amount paid does not depend on how much the item is used, e.g. mortgage repayments, rent, car loan repayments, insurance, TV licence, Local Property Tax, etc.

Irregular expenditure

The amount paid varies from week to week or month to month depending on how much of an item is used, e.g. groceries; clothing; utilities such as gas, electricity and heating; petrol or diesel; bins; repairs; etc.

Discretionary expenditure

This is spending on non-essential items, e.g. holidays, presents, home improvements, entertainment, eating out, concert tickets, etc.

Example 2: Expenditure of the Dunphy family

Expenditure of the Dunphy Family					
	Jan.	Feb.	Mar.	Apr.	Total Jan.–Apr.
Expenditure	€	€	€	€	€
FIXED					
Mortgage	770	770	770	770	3,080
Car loan	250	250	250	250	1000
Motor tax		385			385
Subtotal	1,020	1,405	1,020	1,020	4,465
IRREGULAR					
Groceries	630	590	600	610	2,430
Diesel	85	80	95	80	340
Telephone	70	65	70	65	270
Subtotal	785	735	765	755	3,040
DISCRETIONARY					
Entertainment	150	140	140	160	590
Presents		40	100	75	215
Subtotal	150	180	240	235	805
Total Expenditure	1,955	2,320	2,025	2,010	8,310

- The rows show how much the Dunphy family spent on each item. The total amount for January to April for each item of expenditure appears on the right of the table.
- The columns show how much the Dunphy family spent each month.
- The subtotal rows show how much the Dunphy family spent on fixed, irregular and discretionary expenditure.
- The three subtotal rows are added at the bottom of the table to give the total expenditure for each month and for the four-month period.
- The Dunphys spent a total of **€8,310** between January and April.

Current expenditure

This is day-to-day spending on items that are used quickly and then need to be purchased again, e.g. bread, milk, washing powder, petrol or diesel and phone credit. Most items of current expenditure involve small amounts of money, but when added together they make up a large part of our spending.

Capital expenditure

This is one-off spending on items that usually last longer than a year, e.g. house, car, dishwasher, computer. Capital expenditure usually involves a larger amount of money, a longer-term commitment and therefore more careful decision-making.

top tip

Current and capital expenditure are also examined in Chapter 30, but for governments rather than for individuals. The basic idea is the same, but the sums of money involved are different.

Financial cost and opportunity cost

The financial cost of an item is the money you pay to buy it, e.g. €1,000 for a television.

The opportunity cost of an item is the other items you have to do without in order to buy it, e.g. the laptop you could have bought instead of the television.

Managing financial resources

Managing financial resources involves organising your income and expenditure in order to avoid the risk of running out of money.

- In the short term, you can borrow on the strength of your future ability to repay the loan.
- In the long term, however, your expenditure cannot exceed your income.
- It is good to learn prudence at an early age and to realise that, ultimately, you must earn in order to spend and that borrowing too much will get you into trouble.
- Remember that every time you overspend, you are transferring onto your future self the burden of earning that money back.

There are many steps you can take to try and ensure that you always have enough income to pay for your needs and wants.

Record income and expenditure

Monitor what you are earning and spending in a notebook or on a spreadsheet or with one of the many free budgeting apps available. (For more on this, see Chapter 12.)

Make extra money

- **Take a second job:** This is something many people have to do when their first job doesn't pay well, e.g. they wait on tables in the evenings, work in a petrol station at weekends, etc.
- **Ask for a raise:** All your boss can say is no. You'll never know if you don't ask.
- **Find a better-paying job:** If you can possibly earn more elsewhere, think about moving.
- **Get promoted:** It will mean more responsibility, but also more money.
- **Do overtime:** If there are extra hours going, work them and save the money.
- **Sell something:** You may have something of value that you can sell to raise much-needed funds, e.g. sell that coat you never wore on eBay.
- **Rent out a room:** You may have a spare room in your house that you can turn into cash.
- **Get an extra qualification:** Study at night to improve your CV.

Prioritise your spending

You should rank your expenditure in order of importance.

- **Fixed**: Pay your mortgage, rent, car loan, etc. before anything else.
- **Irregular**: Once fixed expenditure has been covered, think about food, clothes and utility bills, etc.
- **Discretionary**: Only when all other bills have been paid should you consider a holiday or home renovations. Even then, give consideration to saving for future fixed and irregular expenditure instead.

Reduce spending

Examine your expenditure and look for ways to cut back.

- **Reduce discretionary spending:** Invite friends over for dinner in order to eat out less; take a packed lunch to school or work; consider staying in budget hotels and flying on budget airlines; shop in charity shops – don't buy branded items just for the label; cycle if possible; read newspapers for free online or at the library; make rather than buy presents, etc.
- **Shop around:** Look for cheaper deals for your insurance and utilities, e.g. switch your electricity or gas provider; always haggle for discounts; research online to find the cheapest prices; shop at discount supermarkets, etc.
- **Reduce waste:** Turn off lights; install a programmable thermostat; buy in bulk where possible, e.g. to cook food and freeze meals in big batches; cycle or walk to school or work, etc.
- **Develop a habit of saving:** Starting with your next pocket money, save as much as you can. It starts with little steps.

- **Avoid false economies:** Sometimes you think you're saving when you're not. Spending €60 on a pair of jeans that will last for three years is smarter than spending €30 on a pair that will only last one year.

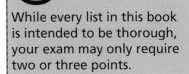

While every list in this book is intended to be thorough, your exam may only require two or three points.

- **Don't impulse buy:** Don't buy on the spur of the moment; always make a list before shopping; and never be pressured by a salesperson.

- **Pay off debts:** Whenever you have spare cash, pay off debts and reduce your interest payments.

- **Spread payments over the year:** Schedule bills in monthly instalments to avoid paying large amounts that will drain your bank balance, e.g. €200 a month may be better than €2,400 in one go.

- **Seek advice:** If you get into trouble, seek help, e.g. from the Money Advice and Budgeting Service (MABS).

Question 12, Junior Cycle Final Examination 2019

Name a source of income associated with each of the following people:

Retired person	Pension
Employed person	Wages
Unemployed person	Jobseeker's Allowance

Question 15, Junior Cycle Sample Paper, State Examination Commission (SEC)

In January 2018 the government introduced a scheme giving grants for solar panels for home use. Seán and Maureen O'Mahony were considering landscaping their back garden this summer but have now decided to take advantage of the grant scheme and install solar panels in their home. Using the above information explain what is meant by opportunity cost.

Answer

- When you have a choice between two options, the opportunity cost is the option you don't choose and therefore have to do without.
- Since Seán and Maureen have decided to install solar panels, the opportunity cost of doing so is landscaping their back garden.

Question 1, Junior Cycle Sample Paper (SEC)

Using the below graphic identify one example each of fixed, irregular and discretionary expenditure. Write your answers in the table below.

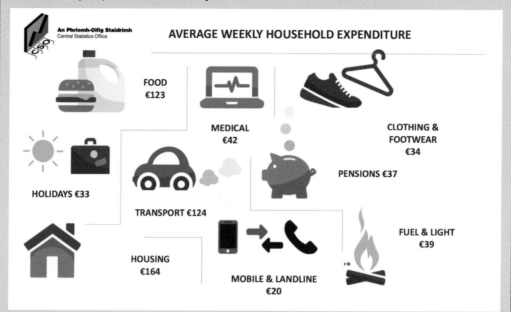

Fixed Expenditure	Irregular Expenditure	Discretionary Expenditure
Example: Housing: €164 Pensions: €37	Example: Food: €123 Medical: €42	Example: Holidays: €33

3 Your Personal Financial Lifecycle

Main Learning Outcome

1.3 Students should be able to construct a personal financial lifecycle to identify financial needs at different life stages.

> **aims** By the end of this chapter you should:
> - understand the needs and wants people have at different stages of the personal financial lifecycle
> - be able to suggest suitable sources of income at each stage of the lifecycle.

Introduction

- As we move through life, our financial needs and wants change from one stage to the next.
- Our capacity to earn income and the source of that income will also change as we grow and mature.
- A **personal financial lifecycle** can be constructed to examine these stages and the challenges each one presents as we attempt to plan for our futures.
- Note that while the personal financial lifecycle probably describes the pattern of most people's lives most of the time, real life is usually much too complicated and unpredictable to be reduced to any kind of list or formula.
- The age at which the stages described on the following page begin and end can vary widely from person to person:
  — some people stay in education longer than others
  — some people start working at an earlier or later age than others
  — some people marry and/or have children; others live a different life
  — many people will change jobs and move house more than once in their lives
  — some people choose to retire early; others continue working.

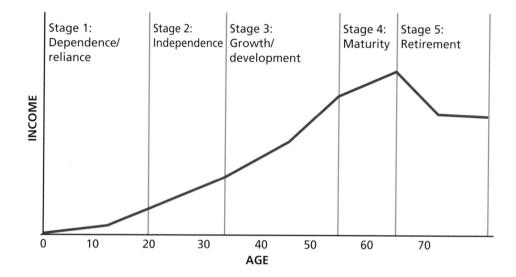

Stage 1: Dependence/ reliance

top tip

- At this stage, we live at home with our parents or guardians.
- As children, we have little if any income of our own, apart from a little pocket money or money received as a gift, e.g. at Christmas or First Communion.

> To better understand the importance of the financial lifecycle, you don't have to look beyond the experiences of your own family for supporting examples. You, your parents and your grandparents clearly have very different needs and wants.

- We depend almost entirely on our parents for all our financial needs. Since we do not earn money ourselves, we sometimes take the support of our parents for granted.
- The government helps by giving parents €140 a month in Child Benefit for each child up to the age of 18, provided the children are in full time education and/or have a disability.
- Children are also entitled to two years of the ECCE Scheme, which provides three hours a day of free pre-school; and free GP care up to the age of six.
- In our teens, we begin to earn money through part-time jobs, and we start to understand the meaning of money. If we want something, we have to work for it or do without.
- Some people start working as soon as they leave school; most people go on to third-level education.

Sources of finance at the dependence/reliance stage

- Support from parents or guardians
- Child Benefit payments
- Gifts from relatives
- Pocket money
- Wages from part-time job or casual work
- Grants and scholarships

Needs and wants at the dependence/reliance stage

- Food and clothing
- Accommodation
- Crèche place
- Medical costs
- School and college expenses
- Mobile phone
- Holidays and presents
- Toys, books and games

Stage 2: Independence

- At this stage, those of us who aren't already in the workforce leave college and take up our first full-time jobs.
- We grow in confidence and gain more independence from our parents. We are now fully responsible for ourselves; we must earn our own incomes and learn to use them wisely.
- We may move out of our parents' houses and find places of our own to live. This can be a hard time because of high rents and the difficulty in getting a mortgage.
- In our twenties, many of us buy our first car; some of us manage to buy our first house.
- For many, it is a time to enjoy themselves and travel the world before settling down and starting a family.
- Many people in their twenties either do not earn enough to save, or may view money as there to be spent and enjoyed.
- Others prefer to accumulate wealth for their future, e.g. save a deposit for a house, start paying into a pension.
- This stage can also have its setbacks. Job security can be very uncommon: some people lose their jobs and have to move back in with their parents. Others will change careers or go back to college, forcing them to rethink their finances.

Sources of finance at the independence stage

- Support from parents or guardians
- Income from part-time job or casual work
- Grants and scholarships
- Wages or salary from full-time job
- Jobseeker's Allowance

Needs and wants at the independence stage

- Food and clothing
- Accommodation
- Medical costs
- College expenses
- Household expenses
- Entertainment, holiday and travel expenses
- Presents, books, and pastimes
- Car-running expenses

Stage 3: Growth/development

- As we grow in experience and ambition, the wages we can demand begin to rise.
- Many of us begin to earn enough that we can afford to save and build up our wealth, by investing in property or shares while continuing to pay into a pension.
- At this stage, we no longer feel the urge to continue to live as we did at the independence stage. It's time to settle down. For many, the focus turns to marriage and children.
- Our sense of responsibility continues to develop. We place our children's needs before our own.
- In some cases, an elderly parent may have to move into our home and must also be provided for.
- A large percentage of our income is spent on mortgage repayments or on rent.

Sources of finance at the growth/development stage

- Wages, salary or Jobseeker's Allowance
- Car loan, mortgage loan
- Dividends
- Rental income
- Child Benefit

Needs and wants at the growth/development stage

- Food and clothing
- Accommodation
- Medical costs
- Household expenses
- Child-rearing costs
- School and college expenses for children
- Pension contributions
- Support for elderly parents
- Entertainment, family holidays
- Presents and pastimes
- Car-running expenses

Stage 4: Maturity

- We eventually reach the peak of our careers and our incomes reach their maximum.
- We continue to pay into our pensions, and our wealth continues to accumulate.
- As our children grow up, we face many expenses and devote much of our time and energy to helping them to find their place in the world.
- As we prepare for retirement, some may choose to work less by job-sharing or even retiring early.

Sources of finance at the maturity stage

- Wages, salary or Jobseeker's Allowance
- Child Benefit, if children still qualify
- Dividends
- Rental income
- Savings
- Borrowings

Needs and wants at the maturity stage

- Food and clothing
- Accommodation
- Medical costs
- Household expenses
- School and college expenses for children
- Support for adult children
- Pension contributions
- Entertainment, holidays
- Presents
- Car-running costs

top tip

It is important as you grow older to try to diversify your sources of income. Getting paid a wage is not the only way to make money.

Stage 5: Retirement

- At this stage, most of us leave the world of work and retire. From then on, we rely on a pension for most of our income.
- The more wealth we have built up over our lives, the more comfortable our retirement will be.
- With more time on our hands, retirement is a chance to do things we had postponed all our lives, e.g. to travel and to take up new interests.
- However, many continue to hold a part-time job and there are some who never stop working at all.
- For many, retirement is a time to watch our children develop and mature, and to welcome grandchildren.
- By now, those of us who bought a house when we were younger have our mortgage paid off.
- Some thought should be given to making a will and the passing on of our assets after we are gone.
- Due to illness and old age, some retired people must move in with their children and depend on them for care and support.

Sources of finance at the retirement stage

- Private pension, state pension
- Salary or wages (if still working)
- Rental income
- Dividends
- Endowment policy
- Sale of assets
- Lifetime savings
- Borrowings

Needs and wants at the retirement stage

- Food and clothes
- Household expenses
- Holiday and travel expenses
- Medical costs
- Nursing home care
- Entertainment
- Holidays
- Presents for children and grandchildren

Sample Question 1

At what stage are you most likely to receive the following types of income? Please enter your answers in the box provided.

Income type	Stage
Pension	*Retirement stage*
Jobseeker's Allowance	*Independence stage* *Growth/development stage* *Maturity stage*
Pocket money	*Dependence/reliance stage*
Rental income	*Growth/development stage* *Maturity stage*

Sample Question 2

Each stage in the Personal Financial Lifecycle brings different needs. Suggest one need that may be associated with each stage.

Stage	Need
Dependence/reliance stage	*School books*
Independence stage	*First car loan*
Growth/development stage	*Child-rearing costs*
Maturity stage	*School and college expenses for children*
Retirement stage	*Health care costs*

4 **Personal Taxation**

 Main Learning Outcome

1.4 Students should be able to explain key personal taxes and charges and suggest the occasions when and why they might arise.

> **aims** By the end of this chapter you should:
> - be able to differentiate between direct and indirect taxes
> - be able to contrast progressive and regressive taxes
> - have an understanding of the main taxes collected by the Irish government.

Introduction

Almost everybody in Ireland is liable for at least some taxation. If it did not collect tax, the government would not have money to provide services such as health care or infrastructure such as motorways. The **Revenue Commissioners** is the state body that collects tax on behalf of the government.

Direct and indirect taxes

- **Direct taxation** is a tax on income. It is paid directly to the government by those on whom it is imposed, e.g. PAYE, PRSI, USC, capital gains tax, capital acquisitions tax.
- **Indirect taxation** is a tax on spending. It is collected by the retailer and passed on to the government, e.g. VAT, excise duty, customs duty, stamp duty.

Progressive and regressive taxes

- A **progressive tax** takes a greater percentage of your income as your income rises, e.g. you normally pay income tax of 20% on the first €35,300 of your income and 40% on the rest.
- A **regressive tax** takes a greater percentage of your income as your income falls, e.g. if you buy a carton of fruit juice, the VAT rate is 23%, regardless of your income.

Imposition and incidence of a tax

- The **imposition of a tax** refers to the person on whom the tax is officially levied, e.g. a food importer is charged tax on their imported goods.
- The **incidence of a tax** refers to the person who ends up paying the tax, e.g. the food importer adds the tax to the selling price, so it is the consumer who ends up paying it.

Key personal taxes and charges

Pay As You Earn (PAYE)

top tip

Also called income tax, this is a tax on income that you earn from employment.

- It is a direct tax, deducted from your wages by your employer.
- A single person pays 20% on the first €35,300 of their income and 40% on the balance.
- A married couple with one income pays 20% on the first €44,300 of their income and 40% on the balance.
- A married couple with two incomes pays 20% on the first €70,600 of their income and 40% on the balance.

> On Budget Day each year, the major newspapers publish articles and case studies online detailing the new tax changes. You should talk about them the next day in class with your teacher and discuss how they affect people in different ways.

Example 1

Noel is single and earns €40,000 a year. He must pay:

● 20% on the first €35,300	= € 7,060
● 40% on the balance of €4,700	= € 1,880
● Total PAYE payable	= **€ 8,940**

Example 2

Simon and George are a married couple. Simon earns €70,000 a year. George is not currently employed. They must pay:

● 20% on the first €44,300	= € 8,860
● 40% on the balance of €25,700	= € 10,280
● Total PAYE payable	= **€ 19,140**

Example 3

Pat and Margaret are a married couple. Pat earns €40,000 a year, Margaret earns €50,000. They must pay:

● 20% on the first €70,600	= € 14,120
● 40% on the balance of €19,400	= € 7,760
● Total PAYE payable	= **€ 21,880**

Self-employed taxes

If you are self-employed, you must calculate and submit your preliminary tax payment to the Revenue by 31 October each year or by 15 November if paying online.

Tax credits

Reductions in the PAYE payable that has already been calculated, for example:

- If you are married, you can share your tax credits with your spouse.
- It is up to you to apply for the tax credits to which you are entitled.

PAYE tax credit	€1,650
Single person tax credit	€1,650
Married person tax credit	€3,300

Pay Related Social Insurance (PRSI)

A deduction from wages that helps to fund social protection payments.

- It is a direct tax, deducted from your wages by your employer.
- It is paid into the Social Insurance Fund, which is used to fund Jobseeker's Benefit and other social protection payments.
- PRSI is charged at 4% on all earnings over €352 a week.

Example 4

Maeve earns €500 a week. She must pay:

- 0% on the first €352   =   € 0.00
- 4% on the balance of €148   =   € 5.92
- Total PRSI payable   =   **€ 5.92**

Universal Social Charge (USC)

A tax payable on all gross income.

- It is a direct tax deducted from your wages by your employer.
- If your income is €13,000 or less, you pay no USC.
- If your income is above €13,000, you pay the rates identified in the table.

0 to €12,012	0.5%
€12,012 to €19,874	2%
€19,874 to €70,044	4.5%
Over €70,044	8%
Over €100,000 (self-employed only)	11%

Example 5

Ava earns €50,000 per year. She must pay:

- 0.5% on the first €12,012   =   €   60.06
- 2% on the next €7,862   =   €   157.24
- 4.5% on the balance of €30,126   =   € 1,355.67
- Total USC payable   =   **€1,572.97**

Value Added Tax (VAT)

A tax you pay when you purchase goods and services.

- VAT is an indirect tax, which is included in the price you pay for goods and services at the till.
- The seller is responsible for submitting the tax to the Revenue every two months. They pay the difference between the VAT they collect on their sales and the VAT they pay on their purchases.
- The standard rate of VAT is 23%. This applies to most goods and services.
- The reduced rate of VAT is 13.5%. It applies to coal, heating oil, cleaning and maintenance services, and to some other products and services. This rate also applies to tourism-related activities, e.g. restaurants and hotels.
- A rate of 4.8% is charged on the agriculture sector, e.g. livestock.
- The zero rate of VAT applies to tea, coffee, milk, bread, books, children's clothes and shoes, oral medicine, disability aids and other necessities.

Deposit Interest Retention Tax (DIRT)

A tax on interest earned on deposit accounts (see Chapter 5).

- It is a direct tax and is charged on interest earned on savings accounts in banks, building societies, credit unions and An Post.
- Exemptions and reductions apply to people aged over 65, people with disabilities, non-residents with accounts in Ireland, charities and others.
- It is charged at a rate of 35%.

Example 6

Sean has €5,000 on deposit in his bank account. He earns €87 in interest. He must pay:

- 35% of €87 = **€30.45**
- The remaining €56.55 is added to his account.

Stamp duty

A tax on documents transferring ownership of property or shares.

- It is an indirect tax that applies to residential properties such as houses, apartments or sites, and on non-residential property.
- Stamp duty is also charged on property leases, on transfers of shares and on ATMs and credit cards.
- Transfers of property between spouses and civil partners are exempt from stamp duty.
- Stamp duty is charged at 1% up to €1 million and 2% on the balance.

Example 7

Suzanne buys a house for €1,200,000. She must pay:

- 1% of the first €1,000,000   =   € 10,000
- 2% of the balance of €200,000   =   € 4,000
- Total stamp duty payable   =   **€ 14,000**

Local Property Tax (LPT)

LPT is charged on the market value of residential properties.

- LPT is an indirect tax. Each homeowner pays LPT based on their own assessment of the market value of the property.
- LPT is based on market value bands. The first band covers all properties worth up to €100,000. Bands then go up in increments of €50,000.
- LPT is charged at 0.18% for properties valued €1 million and under. The tax is based on the mid-point of the relevant band.
- For properties valued over €1 million, LPT is charged at 0.18% up to €1 million and 0.25% on the amount of the value over €1 million.
- LPT doesn't apply to development sites or farmland.

Example 8

Jaclyn's house is valued at €450,000, which places is it in the €400,000–€450,000 band. LPT is charged at 0.18% on the mid-point of band, i.e. €425,000. Jaclyn must pay:

- 0.18% of €425,000 = **€765**

Capital Gains Tax (CGT)

Charged on profits earned from the sale of assets.

- The difference between the sale price of an asset and its original purchase price is considered taxable income.
- CGT is a direct tax.
- Exemptions include the sale of your main residence, winnings from lotteries, betting or prize bonds, and gains made from life assurance policies.
- The standard rate is 33%.
- The first €1,270 of gains every year are exempt.

Example 9

Myra and Donald sold shares in Apple Inc. for €75,000 that they bought five years ago for €40,000, making a profit of €35,000. They must pay:

- 33% of (€35,000 – €1,270) = **€11,130.90**

Capital Acquisitions Tax (CAT)

A tax on gifts from other people or inheritances from people who have died.

- CAT is direct tax and is charged at 33%.
- Gifts and inheritances can be received tax-free up to a certain amount, depending on how closely you are related to the other person.
- You are entirely exempt from CAT on gifts or inheritances from a spouse or civil partner, compensation awards and retirement lump sums.
- The first €3,000 received in a year is exempt from CAT.

> **top tip**
>
> Money given to children for support, maintenance or education is also exempt if they are under 18 years of age, or up to 25 if they are in full-time education, or at any age if they have a physical or intellectual disability.

Customs duty

A tax charged on certain goods imported from outside the EU, e.g. ordering a suit from the United States.

- Customs duty is an indirect tax.
- It is normally calculated as a percentage of the value of the goods.
- The rate depends on the type of goods and the country of origin.
- It is intended to discourage EU consumers from buying certain goods from outside the EU so that they will buy them from domestic sellers instead.

Excise duty

A tax payable on alcoholic drinks, tobacco products, petrol, diesel, kerosene and other fuels.

- Excise duty is an indirect tax and is included in the price you pay at the till.
- Because people generally cannot do without some of the taxable goods, excise duty is a very reliable source of revenue for the government.
- It is also used to discourage the consumption of harmful goods and to fund public services needed to deal with their consequences, e.g. hospitals.

Motor tax

A tax on cars and other vehicles.

- Motor tax is an indirect tax.
- Motor tax is collected by local authorities.
- The amount due depends on the car's CO_2 emissions, or on engine size in the case of older cars.
- Every car must display a current tax disk as proof of payment.

Vehicle Registration Tax (VRT)

A separate tax you must pay when you first register a motor vehicle.

- VRT is an indirect tax.
- Once a vehicle is registered and VRT paid, a registration number is issued.
- Usually this is done by a car dealership, but you can also do it as an individual.
- The amount of VRT payable depends on the level of CO_2 emissions from the car.
- There are reduced rates for electric and hybrid vehicles.

Sugar Sweetened Drinks Tax (SSDT)

Charged on drinks containing added sugar, e.g. flavoured waters, carbonated drinks, etc.

- The SSDT is an indirect tax.
- It is designed to reduce the consumption of drinks with added sugar and to persuade manufacturers to reduce the amount of added sugar in their products.

Carbon tax

Levied on electricity, natural gas and solid fuel.

- It is an indirect tax, imposed in response to the problem of climate change.
- It is intended to help fulfil Ireland's legally binding targets on reducing greenhouse gas emissions by 2030.

Sample Question 1

Nora earns an annual salary of €53,000. She pays PAYE at 20% on the first €35,300 and 40% on the remainder. Calculate Nora's tax liability.

Answer

- 20% on the first €35,300   = € 7,060
- 40% on the balance of €17,700   = € 7,080
- Total PAYE payable   = € 14,140

Sample Question 2

What do the following acronyms stand for?

PAYE	Pay As You Earn
PRSI	Pay Related Social Insurance
USC	Universal Social Charge
CAT	Capital Acquisitions Tax

5 Saving and Borrowing

Main Learning Outcome

1.5 Students should be able to identify reasons for saving and borrowing money, relate the reasons to determining appropriate sources of finance with respect to their purpose, costs and risks.

aims By the end of this chapter you should:
- have an understanding of the reasons why people save and why people borrow
- be able to outline the main options available to savers and borrowers
- understand the importance of matching the source of borrowing with its use.

Over our lifetimes, we will hopefully be savers more often than borrowers. There are multiple reasons to save and to borrow, and many different ways of doing each. It is wise to always consider your options and to seek advice, and it is very important to remember that every penny spent also has to be earned some time.

Some important saving and borrowing terms

- **Annual Equivalent Rate (AER):** The rate of interest a saver earns in a year after accounting for the effects of compound interest, by showing what the interest rate would be if it was paid and compounded once each year. It allows consumers to easily compare their savings options.
- **Annual Percentage Rate (APR):** The annual rate charged for borrowing that tells you the total yearly cost, including any fees or charges. By law, lenders must publish the APR in their advertisements, so that consumers can easily compare their borrowing options.
- **Arrears:** To be in arrears on a loan means to be behind in your repayments.
- **Borrowing:** You are given a sum of money on the condition that you will repay it at a later date, usually with interest.

- **Compound interest:** As interest is added to a savings account, interest is then calculated on the new amount, so that the saver is earning interest on the principal and also on the interest.

> **Example 1: compound interest**
>
> Alan saves €1,000 and is paid 5% interest at the end of Year 1.
>
> At the start of Year 2, he has €1,050 (€1,000 plus the 5% interest).
>
> At the end of Year 2, he gets 5% of €1,050, which is €52.50, so he starts Year 3 with €1,102.50.
>
> At the end of Year 3, he is paid interest of €55.13, giving him a total of €1,157.63.
>
> As we can see, after the first year Alan didn't just receive interest on the principal, he also received interest on the interest.

- **Collateral/security:** Something of value that the lender can easily value and sell if the borrower is unable to repay a loan, e.g. the deed to your house as collateral on your mortgage. Collateral should be worth more than the loan it secures.
- **Credit rating:** An estimate of your ability to repay your loans. It is based on your financial history, e.g. unpaid loans in the past.
- **Deposit Interest Retention Tax (DIRT):** A tax on the interest earned on savings (see Chapter 4).
- **Direct Debit:** An arrangement made with your bank to allow companies such as phone or internet providers to take varying amounts from your bank account each month in payment of your bill.
- **Fixed rate:** A fixed rate loan loan means that the interest rate doesn't change over the life of the loan even if the European Central Bank (ECB) changes its rate (see Chapter 35). Fixed rates are slightly higher than variable rates because they give the borrower certainty about how much they will have to pay.
- **Instalment:** When you borrow money, you usually pay it back a little at a time, e.g. €120 a month. Each payment is called an instalment.
- **Interest:** The price you pay to borrow money or the reward you receive for saving money.
- **Guarantor:** A person who guarantees to pay a borrower's debt in the event that the borrower cannot pay, e.g. a bank may require a young person to nominate a guarantor on a loan, usually a parent.

top tip

One of the ways banks make money is to charge a higher rate from borrowers than it pays on savers.

- **Liquidity:** Refers to the ease with which you can turn something into money (see Chapter 26). Some illiquid (opposite of liquid) investments pay a higher rate of interest in return for you being unable to withdraw your money at short notice.

- **Non-priority debt:** Debt that is less important than priority debt, but still must be paid to avoid legal action, e.g. credit card debt.
- **Principal:** This is the initial amount saved or the original amount borrowed. It does not include the interest earned or owed.
- **Priority debt:** Refers to debts that carry serious imminent consequences if not repaid, e.g. your house may be repossessed if you do not make your mortgage repayments.
- **Saving:** Income that is not spent.
- **Simple interest:** Means that interest is only calculated as a percentage of the principal and that there is no compounding.

> *Example 2: simple interest*
> Louise saves €1,000. At the end of Year 1, she received 5% interest, so now she has €1,050.
> At the end of Year 2, she is again paid 5% of €1,000, to bring her up to €1,100.
> At the end of Year 3, she again gets paid 5% of €1,000, so she finishes with **€1,150.**

- **Standing order:** An instruction to your bank to make payments each month of the same amount to the same recipient, e.g. to make mortgage payments.
- **Variable rate:** A variable rate loan means that the rate of interest can change during the lifetime of the loan, usually as a result of a change in the ECB rate (see Chapter 34).

Saving

Reasons people save

- To accumulate money to purchase an expensive item, e.g. an engagement ring.
- To earn interest on their savings.
- Because they lead a prudent lifestyle. Once their needs and wants are satisfied, they don't feel the urge to spend the rest of their income.
- To build a good credit rating to help them borrow in the future.
- To ensure they have money for any unplanned expenses that arise, e.g. a household appliance breaks down. This is known as saving 'for a rainy day'.
- To prepare for retirement, i.e. paying into a pension.
- To accumulate a deposit for a house.
- To be ready for investment opportunities that may arise, e.g. a sought-after house comes up for sale.

Ways to save

Banks

In Ireland, there are several commercial banks that you can deposit money with, e.g. AIB, Bank of Ireland, Ulster Bank. Banks offer a range of savings options:

Demand deposit accounts
- You can save and withdraw as much as you like, when you like.
- You are given a low, variable rate of interest.

Notice deposit accounts
- You earn a higher variable rate of interest than a demand deposit account.
- You must give advance notice to make a withdrawal, e.g. seven days.

Fixed-term deposit accounts
- You earn a fixed rate of interest that is higher than the rate paid for notice deposit accounts.
- There may be a minimum opening balance, e.g. €15,000.
- You are not permitted to withdraw your money for a considerable period of time, e.g. two years.

Junior saver/Student accounts
- Aimed at recruiting younger customers.
- You can save and withdraw as much as you like, when you like.
- You are given a low, variable rate of interest.
- The bank may ask for a parent's approval to open the account.

Building societies

You can also save with a building society, e.g. EBS or Permanent TSB. If you save with a building society, it may increase your chances of obtaining a mortgage from them at a later date.

An Post

Offers a number of savings options including:

- five-year savings certificates
- four-year national solidarity bonds
- three-year savings bonds
- prize bonds
- six-year instalment savings accounts
- regular deposit accounts
- current accounts

Credit union

Saving with a credit union is another option:

- A credit union is a co-operative (see Chapter 14) whose members can borrow from pooled deposits at low interest rates.
- Credit unions are often based in one locality or associated with one profession, so when you save, you are enabling your neighbours or colleagues to borrow, e.g. St Raphael's Garda Credit Union Ltd.
- Most impose a cap on how much you can save on deposit, e.g. €15,000.

Investing

As an alternative to saving your money in a bank, you could invest it by buying an **asset** in the hope that it will rise in value over time, e.g. land or property, shares, government or corporate bonds, or even gold or artwork. Some questions to ask before investing:

- Do I understand what I'm investing in?
- How much money can I afford to invest?
- How easily can I convert the asset back into money if I need to?
- What is the risk associated with the investment?

Borrowing

Reasons why people borrow

- People wish to purchase something that they are unable to pay cash for. Borrowing means that instead of having to save up for something before buying it, **you can buy it now and save up for it afterwards**.
- **Borrowing spreads payments over time**. Even if you have the cash, it can still make sense to borrow if the rate of interest is low.
- **To buy a house.** Hardly anyone has the money to buy a house for cash – most of us pay for it over thirty or forty years by means of a mortgage.
- **To buy a car** or to make home improvements.
- **To start a business.** Usually a detailed business plan is required before the loan is released (see Chapter 22).
- **To pay for college.** Individuals take out loans for college with the expectation that they will be able to begin repaying the loan when they graduate and find a job.
- **To get to the next pay cheque.** If you know you're getting paid in a few days, there may be little harm in buying groceries on your credit card and paying back the cost of the groceries when you get paid.
- **To take advantage of an investment opportunity**, e.g. a local business is advertised for sale and the only way to buy it is to borrow the money.
- **For Christmas and back to school.** Certain times of the year can make big demands on people's finances, forcing them to borrow money.
- **For holidays.** People sometimes borrow money to go on that trip of a lifetime.

Applying for a loan

Questions to ask before borrowing money

- What methods of borrowing are available?
- Is a deposit required?
- What is the APR?
- Can I afford the repayments?
- How much do I need to borrow?

- How long does the agreement last?
- What is the total amount payable on the loan?
- Is security required?

Questions a bank will ask before lending you money

- What is the purpose of the loan?
- Have you sufficient financial resources with which to repay the loan?
- How much do you wish to borrow?
- For how long is the loan required?
- Can you provide security?
- What is your credit rating?

Before you can borrow

- You should be 18 years of age.
- You must have a history of saving money.
- You must have a good credit rating.
- Depending on the loan, you may need to have collateral.
- Ultimately, you must be able to repay the loan with interest and on time, i.e. have proof of a steady income.

Ways of borrowing

Short term (less than one year)

Credit card

- A credit card is a convenient, cashless way of paying for goods and services.
- The card is presented at the time of purchase, and a receipt is given.
- The holder receives a statement at the end of the month and has 25 days to pay part or all of the balance.
- A high rate of interest is charged on the outstanding amount.

Bank overdraft

- The bank gives permission to a current account holder to withdraw more money from the account than is actually in it.
- It is a flexible form of finance.
- No security is needed.
- Amount available is usually small.
- Interest is only charged on the amount overdrawn, even though the account holder may be allowed to overdraw more.
- It must be cleared for at least thirty days in the year.
- The bank can recall the overdraft at any time, and there are penalties for those who exceed their limit.

Moneylender

- A moneylender is an individual or company whose main business is to lend money, often to people who are unable to get loans from banks or building societies.
- They must hold a licence to trade in moneylending, and the Central Bank of Ireland regulates their activities.
- The rate of interest is often quite high.

Medium term (up to five years)

Medium-term loan

A variable-rate loan of up to five years. Its features include:

- an agreed period of time
- an agreed amount
- repayment by instalments agreed in advance.

> *Example 3: five-year loan*
>
> Paul wishes to buy a computer for €2,000. He takes out a five-year loan, repayable monthly, at an APR of 7%.
>
> Each year, he pays back €400 (€2,000 ÷ 5).
>
> His interest payments are:
>
> - €2,000 @ 7% = € 140
> - €1,600 @ 7% = € 112
> - €1,200 @ 7% = € 84
> - €800 @ 7%   = € 56
> - €400 @ 7%   = € 28
> - Total interest = € 420
>
> In total, Paul pays the bank €2,000 + €420 = **€2,420**.

exam focus

Don't forget that you can still get partial marks for a wrong answer, provided you show your workings.

Leasing or renting

- The customer never has ownership.
- A deposit is paid, followed by a number of instalments, which are fixed for the duration of the agreement.
- At the end of the agreement, the item leased is returned. The deposit is returned to the customer, provided the item is in good condition.
- Usually cheaper than hire purchase.
- No security is required, and no capital is tied up in the asset.

> *Example 4: renting*
>
> Look again at the example above. Now consider: if it cost Paul €500 a year to rent a computer instead, his total cost would be:
>
> - 5 × €500 = **€2,500**.
>
> However, he would never own the computer.

Hire Purchase (HP)

A form of credit that allows customers to have the immediate use of an item while paying for it over an agreed period of time in instalments.

- Payment consists of an initial deposit and an agreed number of instalments.
- Ownership is only transferred after the last instalment.
- Hire purchase carries a high rate of interest.
- The customer is entitled to a written contract containing:
  — the cash price
  — the amount of the deposit
  — the number of instalments
  — the amount of each instalment
  — the total hire purchase price
  — the procedure for ending the contract
  — the APR.

> ### Example 5: hire purchase
>
> Let's consider Paul again. Paul can buy his computer on hire purchase by paying a deposit of €500 and 36 monthly instalments of €50 each.
>
> He pays:
>
> - Deposit   =   €   500
> - 36 × €50   =   €   1,800
> - Total cost: =   € **2,300**
>
> Buying the computer on hire purchase would seem to be the cheapest of the three options. However, it's worth remembering that Paul does not own it until he makes the very last payment.

Long term (longer than five years)

Mortgage

A variable-rate loan taken out to buy a house or property.

- Usually it is repaid over a period of fifteen to thirty years.
- The longer the time period, the smaller each instalment is, but the greater the total amount repaid.
- The deeds of the property are used as collateral/security.
- A type of life assurance policy called a mortgage protection policy (see Chapter 6) is taken out on the value of the mortgage to cover the bank in the event of the death of the lender.
- The size of the mortgage depends on:
  — the level of the borrower's earnings
  — the value of the house being bought.

Example 6: mortgage

Una applies for a mortgage. She earns €60,000 a year, has savings of €30,000 and wishes to purchase a house for €230,000.

The bank requires a deposit of 10% of the value of the house:

- Una's savings of €30,000 are more than 10% of €230,000.

The bank will lend up to 3.5 times the applicant's salary:

- $3.5 \times €60,000 = €210,000$
- €30,000 + €210,000 = €240,000, which is greater than the value of the house.
- The bank approves Una's mortgage.

Matching sources with uses

If you borrow money for longer than you need it, you pay more interest than you need to. This is why, when borrowing money, it is best to ensure that you use:

- short-term sources of finance for short-term needs
- medium-term sources for medium-term needs
- long-term sources for long-term needs.

Example 7: short-term finance

If you require €200 until next week, it makes no sense to borrow the money for a year, since you will be paying more interest than you should. It would be better to borrow the money for a week and then pay it back.

Conversely, if you take out a short-term loan to buy a long-term asset, you are repaying the loan before earning the money to do so, and are likely to run short of money.

Example 8: long-term finance

The reason a mortgage is over 30 years is because most people take that long to earn enough to pay it back.

If you attempt to pay your mortgage too soon, you risk being short of funds when you need them at a later stage.

Matching Sources with Uses					
Short term		**Medium term**		**Long term**	
Sources	**Uses**	**Sources**	**Uses**	**Sources**	**Uses**
Credit card	Groceries	Term loan	Car	Mortgage	House
Bank overdraft	Petrol	Rent/Lease	Household appliances		Second home
Moneylender	Electricity	Hire purchase	Furniture		
	Rent		Electronic devices		

Question 3, Junior Cycle Examination 2019

Suggest a suitable source of finance to make the following consumer purchases.

Purchases	Source of Finance
House	*Mortgage*
Car	*Car loan*
Groceries	*Credit card*

Question 9, Junior Cycle Sample Paper (SEC)

SOLAS Ltd is considering purchasing a new electric or hybrid sales vehicle.

(a) Tick (✓) the most suitable source of finance that might be used to purchase this vehicle.

Short term	
Medium term	✓
Long term	

(b) State one reason for your choice.

Answer

You should always try to match sources with uses. Cars normally last one to five years, therefore you should pay for it over the same time span.

6 Insurance

 Main Learning Outcome

1.6 Students should be able to identify appropriate types of insurance for particular personal needs and consider costs, benefits and risks.

 By the end of this chapter you should:

- understand the various types of insurance that are available
- be able to outline the principles of insurance
- know what factors affect the size of your insurance premium and the steps you can take to reduce it.

Introduction

Insurance is a contract agreed between an insured person and an **insurer** (insurance company) in which the insured person pays a fee, called a **premium**, to the insurance company in return for a guarantee of **compensation** if loss or damage occurs.

Example 1

Gerry wishes to insure his car against the risk of accident.

He pays a premium to an insurance company, e.g. €600.

The insurance company agrees to compensate Gerry for the cost of repair if he gets into an accident.

During the year, Gerry reverses into a tree and causes €6,000 of damage to his car.

Gerry claims on his insurance and, after assessing the damage, the insurance company pays Gerry €6,000. Gerry can then use this money to repair his car.

If he has no accidents during the year, the insurance company simply keeps the €600 premium.

How insurance works

- For a relatively small premium, the insured person is protected from the financial consequences of an accident. The risk of an accident occurring isn't reduced, just the financial cost, e.g. Gerry pays €600 in order to avoid the risk of paying €6,000 or greater.
- The insurance company makes money by collecting premia from a large number of people, while only a small percentage will suffer accidents and claim compensation. This is called **pooling of risk**.

> **Example 2**
>
> If 100,000 people each pay an average premium of €600, the insurance company has revenue of €60,000,000.
>
> If one in 20 (5,000 people) suffer an accident, and if the average compensation is €8,000, then the insurance company pays out 5,000 × €8,000 = €40,000,000.
>
> The insurance company is better off by €20,000,000. Even after it has paid its other costs, e.g. wages, rent, it can still make a profit.

Types of insurance

- **Motor insurance**
  - **Third party insurance** – which is compulsory by law – covers all parties involved in a car accident except the insured person.
  - **Third party, fire and theft insurance** covers the third party for any damage caused in an accident, and also covers the insured person's car if it's damaged by fire or stolen.
  - **Comprehensive insurance** covers all persons and all cars involved, even if the insured person is at fault. This is the most expensive, but also the most popular, form of motor insurance.
- **Home insurance:** Covers loss or damage to a house and its outhouses.
- **Contents insurance:** Covers damage to the contents of a building whether caused by fire, water, accident or theft.
- **Mortgage protection insurance:** Usually required by a bank when they grant a mortgage to protect them in case the insured person cannot repay the mortgage.
- **Personal accident insurance:** Covers losses due to accidents, e.g. a broken ankle.
- **Health insurance:** Covers the costs of medical treatments.

top tip

Insurance is an example of a topic that comes to life if you discuss at home how many different types of insurance your parents have purchased. Then it is no longer just a chapter in a book but something that is a reality for every household, including yours.

- **Serious/critical illness cover:** Protects against loss of income resulting from illness.
- **Travel insurance:** Covers the risk of accident while abroad. It is particularly important in countries where medical costs are higher than at home.
- **Life assurance:** Can be taken out for two reasons:
  - A **whole life policy** pays out when the insured person dies.
  - An **endowment policy** pays out when the insured person reaches a certain age, e.g. 60, or if they die before reaching that age.

Insurance premiums

Factors that affect the size of premiums

- The risk of a claim, which will be influenced by:
  - age, e.g. young drivers cause more accidents
  - driver permit or full licence
  - location of a house, e.g. risk of flooding
  - previous claim history
  - dangerous pastimes, e.g. skydiving
  - health history, e.g. high blood pressure.
- The value of the item being insured, e.g. a diamond necklace.
- The level of cover required, e.g. comprehensive insurance costs more than third party insurance because it covers more risks.
- The number of people insured, e.g. the more people there are sharing the risk, the lower the premium for each one.
- The other costs faced by the insurance company, e.g. wages, rent.
- The level of competition within the insurance industry.

How to reduce your premium

- Pass your driving test and get a licence.
- Regularly service your car.
- Install speed-limiting technology on your car that prevents you from exceeding the speed limit.
- Have a good driving record by driving carefully, never drinking and driving, and avoiding penalty points.
- Install smoke alarms and burglar alarms in your house.
- Have the electrical circuits in your house professionally checked and upgraded.
- Store expensive items in a bank rather than at home.
- Take daily exercise, go for regular checkups, adopt a balanced diet and don't smoke.
- Avoid dangerous pursuits, such as parachuting, or only engage in them under expert supervision.
- Shop around when purchasing insurance.

Principles of insurance

These are the legal rules that the insurance business is founded on.

Insurable interest

The insured person must benefit from the existence of the item and suffer from its loss, e.g. I can insure my own house, but I cannot insure my neighbour's house.

Utmost good faith

The insured person must disclose all material facts to the insurer, even if doing so increases their premium. Otherwise, the contract can be declared void and compensation withheld, e.g. when asked if you are a smoker, you must tell the truth.

Indemnity

The insured person cannot profit from insurance. They are only entitled to enough compensation to return them to the same position they were in immediately before they suffered the loss, e.g. Conor bought a car last year for €35,000 which is now only worth €25,000. If it is written off in an accident, he only deserves €25,000 in compensation.

Subrogation

After paying compensation, the insurance company is entitled to take over any property left and can exercise any legal rights the insured party has against any third party that was involved.

Contribution

If an item is insured with more than one insurance company, each only has to pay according to their proportion of the total risk covered.

Other insurance terms

- **Actuary:** A person who works for an insurance company who calculates the risk and therefore the premium.
- **Assessor:** A person who works for an insurance company who calculates how much compensation should be paid as a result of a claim.
- **Claim form:** A form that the insured person fills out when making a claim.
- **Days of grace:** A short period of time after the premium is due in which the insured person can renew their policy without coverage lapsing.
- **Deduction:** When your premium is reduced due to a factor that lowers your risk, e.g. non-smoker. It is the opposite of loading (see following page).
- **Exclusion clause:** When an insurance policy doesn't cover a specific risk, e.g. playing rugby.
- **Insurance agent:** A person who works for a particular insurance company and sells insurance policies on its behalf.

- **Insurance broker:** A person who works for themselves who helps the insured person to shop around for the best insurance policy for them.
- **Insurance policy:** The contract between the insurer and the insured, giving details of what is covered.
- **Loading:** When a sum is added to your premium because of a specific additional risk, e.g. a younger driver.

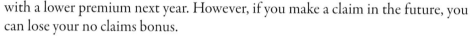

- **Named driver:** A person who is added to another person's car insurance policy, e.g a son or daughter. They have the same cover as the main driver.
- **No claims bonus:** If you take out car insurance and don't suffer any accidents, the insurance company rewards you with a lower premium next year. However, if you make a claim in the future, you can lose your no claims bonus.
- **Non-insurable risk:** A risk that an insurance company will not cover because its likelihood cannot be accurately assessed or because the compensation if it did occur would be too great, e.g. war, recession, a meteor strike.
- **Over-insurance:** insuring a property for more than it is worth.
  — In the event of a loss, the insurance company will not pay more than the current value.
  — Otherwise, this would be a breach of the principle of indemnity, and the insured person would be making a profit.

top tip

You can go to the major insurance websites and learn a lot about insurance simply by looking at the questions they ask when applying for insurance and experimenting with various answers to see how the premium changes.

- **Policy excess:** This is an amount the insured person pays towards a claim on their insurance, even if they aren't to blame for any loss or damage, e.g. you pay the first €300 of any claim, and the insurance company pays the rest.
- **Proposal form:** A form that you fill out when applying for insurance. This can often be completed online.
- **Renewal notice:** A letter from an insurance company reminding you to renew your insurance.
- **Surrender value:** The amount the insured person will get from a life insurance company if they decide to discontinue a policy.

- **Under-insurance:** insuring an item for less than its value in order to save money.
  - In this case, the **average clause** applies, meaning that compensation is received in proportion to the fraction of the loss suffered.
  - Formula:

$$\frac{\text{Insured value of the item}}{\text{Current value of the item}} \times \text{Loss suffered}$$

Example 3

Breda's house is valued at €400,000, but she has only insured it for €300,000. A fire causes damage of €10,000.

Compensation:

$$\frac{€300,000}{€400,000} \times €10,000 = €7,500$$

Question 4, Junior Cycle Examination 2019

Gerard is 21 years of age and has recently passed his driving test. He has now purchased an old car and needs to insure it.

Outline two factors that the insurance company will take into account when calculating the cost of Gerard's car insurance.

Answer

- Gerard is an inexperienced driver and therefore at a greater risk of getting into an accident. This will make his premium higher.
- Older cars do not have the same safety features as newer models. The age of Gerard's car will also result in a higher premium.

Question 11, Junior Cycle Sample Paper (SEC)

Tom and Michelle have been renting an apartment for the last five years. They currently have insurance for the contents of their apartment, valued at €25,000. They have been reviewing their insurance requirements to save some money. They have received a quote for contents from BE Insurance Ltd as follows:

> €6.50 per €1,000.
> There is also a discount of 25% for online applications.

They decide to accept the quote and apply online.

Calculate the cost of Tom and Michelle's contents insurance.

Answer

- €25,000 ÷ 1,000 = 25
- 25 × €6.50 = €162.50
- 25% of €162.50 = €40.63
- €162.50 − €40.63 = **€121.87**

Exploring Business

7 Rights and Responsibilities of Consumers

 **Main Learning Outcome**

1.7 Students should be able to distinguish between and appreciate their rights and responsibilities as consumers.

 By the end of this chapter you should:
- be able to outline the rights of consumers in Ireland and the legal obligations of retailers
- know your rights when buying online
- understand the characteristics of responsible consumers.

Consumer rights

- A **consumer** is any person who purchases goods or services from a seller for personal use and not for resale.
- A **right** is something you are legally entitled to.
- A **responsibility** is something that you have a duty to deal with.

In the past, it was your responsibility to be aware of faults in a product before you bought it. This rule was known as *caveat emptor*, Latin for 'Let the buyer beware.' Today, there are a number of laws in place to protect the consumer.

The Sale of Goods and Supply of Services Act 1980

- **Goods must be of merchantable quality**: Goods should be of reasonable quality, taking into account what they are meant to do, their durability and their price, e.g. the stitching in a jacket should not come apart after three days of normal wear.

- **Goods must be fit for their intended purpose**: They must do what they are reasonably expected to do, e.g. a toaster should toast bread.

- **Goods must be as described**: The consumer should not be misled into buying something based on an inaccurate description, e.g. a consumer should not be charged extra for meals on an all-inclusive cruise.
- **Goods should correspond with the sample:** The goods should match any sample that the consumer was shown, e.g. a tablet sold in its packaging should be the same as the one on display.

exam focus

The four rules above form the backbone of Irish consumer law. You should know them by heart going into your exam. And going into a shop.

- When you buy goods **on sale** you have the same rights as when you pay full price for the goods.
- Signs reading 'No Refunds' or 'No Exchanges' cannot take from your rights. Your contract is with the retailer who sold you the product. If there is a problem, the retailer is responsible for solving it. They cannot tell you to contact the manufacturer.
- A **guarantee** or **warranty** is an undertaking to repair or replace a product within a set period of time after it has been purchased, e.g. seven years. A seller does not have to offer a guarantee, but if they do, it is legally binding.
- When buying a **service**, you are entitled to expect that:
  — the supplier has the necessary skill
  — the service is provided with care and diligence
  — any materials used are sound and reasonably fit for the purpose
  — any goods supplied are of merchantable quality.

The Consumer Protection Act 2007

- It is illegal to make misleading claims about goods, services or prices or to engage in unfair, aggressive or misleading commercial practices.
- It is illegal to sell goods that have a false or misleading description, e.g. claiming that toothpaste whitens teeth if it does not.
- It is illegal to leave out important information about a product or service, e.g. that a car was previously crashed.
- It is illegal to make false claims about ingredients, performance and the weight of products, e.g. bread advertised as gluten-free must be gluten-free.
- Previous prices, actual prices and recommended prices of goods must be stated accurately. If a retailer advertises a product's previous price in a sale, the product must have been for sale at that price for 28 consecutive days within the previous three months.
- It is illegal to harass or unduly influence a consumer, e.g. intimidating an older person into having their driveway resurfaced.

Other consumer laws

Food labelling

All food labelling should include:

- the name of the product
- the selling price and the price per unit
- a list of the ingredients
- the net quantity
- special storage conditions or conditions of use
- the use by date
- the best before date
- the country or place of origin
- nutritional information.

Financial products

Advertisements for financial products should state the **annual percentage rate** (see Chapter 5), which includes the total cost of borrowing, not just the interest rate. This is so the consumer can easily compare products.

Redress

If you discover a fault with a product, you should always return the goods as promptly as possible. The longer you wait, the fewer rights you have, since you may be deemed to have accepted the item. If your complaint is valid, you are entitled to your choice of the **3 Rs**:

- a full **refund**, if the fault is a major one. If you delay in returning or if the fault is less serious, you may still be entitled to a partial refund
- a **replacement** for the faulty product, provided one is available
- **repair**, if repair is possible.

The seller may offer you a **credit note**, which entitles you to buy something else in the shop to the value of the credit note. You may choose to accept a credit note, but you are not obliged to.

You don't have grounds for complaint if:

- the seller told you about a defect before you bought the item, e.g. a scratch on a phone screen
- you examined the item before you bought it and should have seen the defect, e.g. a shirt with no buttons
- you bought the item knowing that it wasn't fit for what you wanted it to do, e.g. a jacket that is obviously not waterproof
- you damaged the product yourself, e.g. you dropped it while unpacking it
- you made a mistake when buying the item, e.g. you thought a dress was size 8 but it was size 10
- you changed your mind after buying it, e.g. you bought green paint for your hall but now you don't like it. Many shops will still take back the product provided it is in saleable condition, but this is a gesture of goodwill and not a legal requirement
- you received the item as a gift – however most shops will treat you as if you are the purchaser provided you have proof of purchase, e.g. a gift receipt.

Online shopping

Distance selling means buying an item online, over the phone or from a mail order catalogue.

- If you buy a product online from inside the European Union (EU), you are protected by the EU's **Consumer Rights Directive (CRD)**. With most goods, if you change your mind within 14 days of the delivery date, you can send back the item and obtain a refund. However, you may have to pay for return postage.

exam focus

Given that more and more consumers buy online, your consumer rights on the internet are likely to be a constant source of exam questions.

- If the product is faulty when you receive it, your rights are the same as if you bought it in a shop.
- Goods should arrive within 30 days, unless otherwise agreed.
- If you buy a product from outside the EU, the Consumer Rights Directive does not apply, only the website's own returns policy. Even then, it may not be possible to enforce. For this reason, you should be careful buying from websites outside the EU.
- When shopping online, only shop from reputable websites. Look for the padlock symbol, and for websites that have 'https' in their address, not simply 'http'.

Characteristics of a responsible consumer

- Shop around for the best deal.
- Only buy luxuries once necessities have been paid for.
- Be fully familiar with consumer rights.
- Avoid **impulse buying**, i.e. buying goods without planning to, or on the spur of the moment.
- Avoid **false economies** where you think you're saving money, but in the long run you're spending more, e.g. better to spend €100 on a pair of shoes that last two years than €50 on a pair that wear out after six months.
- Only buy from sellers you can trust, whether online or otherwise, and be wary of entering credit card details online.
- Keep antivirus software on laptops and computers up to date, don't shop while connected to public Wi-Fi networks, and change passwords on a regular basis.
- Be aware of the consumer agencies that can help if you encounter a problem (see Chapter 8).
- Act promptly when you discover a problem, and make a complaint in an appropriate way (see Chapter 8).
- Hold onto receipts for a reasonable period of time.
- Use all products in accordance with instructions, and read and store instruction manuals carefully.
- Dispose of packaging and products in an environmentally friendly manner.

Question 16, Junior Cycle Examination 2019
Explain three things a good consumer should do when buying goods online.

Answer

- Check if the business they are buying from is located inside the EU. If so, this strengthens their rights in the event of an issue later.
- Shop around and refrain from impulse buying, just as they should when buying items instore. Don't choose the first item they see.
- Never enter bank details on a public Wi-Fi network, and use services such as PayPal, which allow individuals to pay online without revealing their bank details to prevent them from being stolen.

Question 16 (b), Junior Cycle Sample Paper (SEC)

'Online spending overtook face-to-face spending in March.'

Irish Examiner, April 2018

(i) State two benefits for consumers when shopping online.

Answer

- Consumers can avail of a much wider variety of goods online than they can purchase in Ireland.
- Consumers can read customer reviews online before making their purchase.

(ii) The European Consumer Centre Ireland (ECCI) encourages consumers to be safe when shopping online and offers helpful tips. State two ways consumers can shop online safely.

Answer

- Consumers should have up-to-date virus protection software installed on their computers.
- Consumers should only use websites that they trust. Look for the padlock symbol, and only shop on websites that have 'https' in their address, not simply 'http'.

8 Agencies That Help Consumers

➡️ **Main Learning Outcome**

1.8 Students should be able to compare the services provided by consumer agencies and financial institutions to assist and support customers.

aims By the end of this chapter you should:
- understand the steps involved in making a consumer complaint
- be able to outline the role of the various bodies that exist in Ireland to protect and inform consumers.

Making a consumer complaint

- Identify the problem and know your consumer rights.
- If you have a written contract with the seller, read it carefully.
- Make sure that you have a receipt, cheque stub or credit card statement as proof of purchase.
- Return to the seller with the faulty product as soon as possible after you notice the problem.

top tip

It is rare for a case to get as far as a courtroom. 99% of problems are solved in a matter of minutes when the customer returns to the shop.

- If you complain by phone, make a written record of the call, the name of the person you spoke to and what was said.
- Begin by making your complaint informally. Explain the problem calmly and clearly. In the vast majority of cases, your complaint will be resolved straight away.
- If it is not, ask to speak to a manager. Again, explain your problem as calmly and clearly as you can.
- If your complaint is still not resolved, put it in writing. Keep a copy of what you wrote and only send photocopies of receipts. Keep the originals.
- If there is still a problem, seek the help of an outside agency, such as the Competition and Consumer Protection Commission (CCPC)or the Financial Services and Pensions Ombudsman (FSPO).
- If you are still not satisfied and feel you have a case, approach a solicitor with a view to taking legal action.

Consumer agencies

The Competition and Consumer Protection Commission (CCPC)

Coimisiún um
Iomaíocht agus
Cosaint Tomhaltóirí | Competition and
Consumer Protection
Commission

- This is an independent statutory body with two broad roles:
  - — it enforces **competition law** so that Irish consumers have choice and low prices
  - — it enforces **consumer laws**:
    - ○ The Sale of Goods and Supply of Services Act 1980
    - ○ The Consumer Protection Act 2007
    - ○ EU consumer law.
- Provides Irish consumers with information and advice to help them to make informed decisions.
- Investigates firms that break the law and takes civil or criminal enforcement action where necessary.
- Ensures that firms comply with product safety standards.
- Supports a culture of business compliance by helping businesses to understand and obey the law.
- Tries to influence public debate, promote competition and further the interests of consumers.
- Provides personal finance information and education to consumers.

The Small Claims Procedure

This is also known as the Small Claims Court.

- Provides a cheap, fast and easy way for consumers and businesses to resolve disputes without the need to employ a solicitor.
- The fee is €25, and the value of a claim cannot exceed €2,000.
- If the dispute cannot be resolved before it goes to the Small Claims Court, both sides give evidence before a judge, who then makes a ruling.

Consumer Association of Ireland (CAI)

- An independent, self-funded and non-profit body that aims to protect and strengthen the rights of Irish consumers.
- Supports consumers' right to information, fair dealing, protection, education and safety.
- Offers advice and support to consumers.
- Publishes *Consumer Choice*, a monthly magazine about consumer issues.

Advertising Standards Authority of Ireland (ASAI)

- An independent agency set up by the advertising industry.
- Aims to ensure that all advertisements are legal, decent, honest and truthful.
- Maintains a code of standards that is enforced through the commitment and cooperation of advertisers, agencies and the media. Members are prohibited from publishing advertisements in breach of the code.
- The ASAI deals with complaints from members of the public and can order ads to be withdrawn.

The National Standards Authority of Ireland (NSAI)

- Ireland's official standards body.
- Ensures minimum standards in the quality and safety of goods and services, e.g. the thickness of insulation in houses.
- Works to improve the performance of Irish business and protect consumers.

The Office of the Ombudsman

- Examines complaints from members of the public who feel they have been unfairly treated by any of the following:
  — government departments, e.g. the Department of Education and Skills
  — local authorities, e.g. Cork City Council
  — the Health Service Executive (HSE) and charities and voluntary bodies that work on its behalf
  — public hospitals
  — publicly funded third-level education bodies, e.g. UCD
  — public and private nursing homes.
- If a person has complained to any of the above and is still unhappy, then they should contact the Ombudsman.
- For no fee, the Ombudsman will examine the complaint in a fair, independent and impartial way.

Commission for Communications Regulation (ComReg)

- Responsible for regulating the electronic communications sector, which includes phone companies, TV and radio stations. It also regulates the postal sector.
- Regulates prices, assigns frequencies and issues licenses.
- Facilitates competition, protects consumers and encourages innovation.
- Deals with complaints from the public about communications providers.

The Citizens Information Board

- A statutory body which provides information, advice and advocacy on a range of public and social services.
- It operates a website containing extensive information on all public services and on Irish citizens' entitlements.
- It also funds and supports the **Money Advice and Budgeting Service (MABS)**, the government's money advice service.
- It funds and supports a website (www.assistireland.ie) that provides information on technology and appliances for older people and people with disabilities.

The Citizens Information website, www.citizensinformation.ie, is an extremely good source of information on all of the public services provided by the Irish government.

- A series of Citizens Information Centres are located around the country, and a phone service is also available.

Financial Services and Pensions Ombudsman (FSPO)

- A free, independent, fair and impartial service that deals with complaints against pension providers and providers of financial services.
- It tries to resolve disputes in a way that is fair, transparent and accessible to all sides.

Central Bank of Ireland

- Regulates more than 10,000 firms providing financial services in Ireland and overseas including:
  — all banks and credit institutions that lend money to the public
  — mortgage brokers
  — money lenders
  — credit unions
  — bureaux de changes
  — insurance companies
  — investment firms
- Aims to ensure financial stability, consumer protection and market integrity.

Trade Associations

- Many retailers are members of trade associations, such as the Irish Hotels Federation (IHF) or the Society of the Irish Motor Industry (SIMI).
- Consumers can complain to a trade association if they are not happy with the standard of service provided by one of its members.

Mediation

- Both parties involved in the dispute agree to use a neutral third party to help to solve their disagreement.
- Normally, decisions made in mediation are not legally binding, but, if both sides agree, then they can be made binding.

Arbitration

- Both parties involved in the dispute agree to go to an arbitrator to resolve issues.
- The decision of the arbitrator is legally binding.

Question 16, Junior Cycle Examination 2019
Your friend Deirdre (@deirdre22) has ordered a book online from a business in the European Union. Forty days have passed and the book has not arrived. Write a tweet to @deirdre22 to let her know what agency she should go to for help.

Answer
The Competition and Consumer Protection Commission (CCPC) have a very good website where you can find help, www.ccpc.ie. #bestofluck

Question 16 (a), Junior Cycle Sample Paper (SEC)
(ii) Name one agency that could assist you if you need further support [with a consumer issue]. State one function of this agency.

Answer

Agency	Consumer Association of Ireland (CAI)
Function:	• Exists to protect and strengthen Irish consumers' rights. • Supports consumers' rights to information, fair dealing, protection, education and safety. • Offers advice and support to consumers.

9 Ethics and Sustainability

⇨ **Main Learning Outcome**

1.9 Students should be able to debate the ethical and sustainability issues that arise from their consumption of goods and services and evaluate how they can contribute to sustainable development through consumer behaviour.

aims By the end of this chapter you should:
- understand the meaning of ethics, sustainability and interdependence
- be able to outline the ethical obligations of businesses
- be aware of what we can do as consumers to behave in an ethical and sustainable manner.

Introduction

Whenever we consume goods and services, in addition to the trade that takes place between retailer and consumer, there are also consequences beyond ourselves, particularly in relation to ethics and sustainability.

Ethics

The study of right and wrong. Being an ethical consumer means:
- buying products that do not harm society or the environment
- avoiding or boycotting harmful products or companies that produce them.

Sustainability

Meeting the needs of the present without compromising the ability of future generations to meet their needs. The goal is to find a balance between our social, environmental and economic needs. This is called the **Triple Bottom Line** of people, planet and profits.

exam focus

This idea of a balance between the needs of individuals, society and environment is a theme that runs through the Junior Cycle Business Studies course.

Sustainable development

Economic development that is conducted without depletion of natural resources.

Sustainable consumption

Only buying products and services that have the least possible impact on the environment so that future generations can meet their needs too.

Interdependence

This concept means that we need one another, not just at a family or a local level, but globally too. You need, and are needed by, people you have never met and will never meet, e.g. you need the person who made the shoes you are wearing; in return, they need you to respect the environment. Your unborn grandchildren need you to leave them a habitable planet.

Your ecological footprint

The ecological footprint is a metric that measures how much nature we have and how much nature we use (i.e. the supply of and demand on). Since we only have one planet, we must learn to live in a way that sustains it.

Climate change

Describes the recent and ongoing human-driven changes in global and regional climate patterns, causing increases in global average temperatures and a rise in sea levels.

Climate justice

Global warming is not just an environmental issue, but also an ethical, political and economic issue, since it is the poorest who stand to suffer most from climate change.

Fairtrade

A global organisation that works in partnership with farmers and workers in the developing world to provide them with better prices, decent working conditions, local sustainability and fair terms of trade. Fairtrade goods carry the Fairtrade Mark, which means they were produced according to international Fairtrade standards.

Living wage

A wage that enables people to afford adequate food, shelter and other necessities. The goal of a living wage is to give workers a basic but decent standard of living.

Consumerism

A culture in which too much attention is given to buying and owning things, e.g. a new phone, a faster car, a bigger handbag.

Consumerism can harm the environment in the following ways:

- more pollution from the factories that produce the goods we demand and the trucks and planes that transport them to us
- clearing of forests to create cropland
- a build-up of plastic in our oceans
- rising temperatures and sea levels.

Ethical obligations of businesses

Just as individuals have ethical responsibilities, so too do businesses. Ethical businesses are mindful of their obligations to their stakeholders, i.e. those who are impacted by their business.

Customers

- To provide products and services that do not harm customers in any way.
- To give value for money to the buyer.

Employees

- To pay fair wages.
- To provide good working conditions.
- To treat employees with respect and encourage intrapreneurship (see Chapter 15).

Investors

To maximise the return on their investment and grow the value of the business.

Community

- To produce as little noise, pollution and traffic disruption as possible.
- To pay all due taxes, which are needed to fund services in the local community.
- To obey all laws under which it operates.

Environment

- To use safe, quiet and clean production processes.
- To produce safe and healthy products.
- To only use packaging that can be recycled.

What can we do as consumers?

There are countless steps that we can take as consumers and as citizens to be ethical and to contribute to sustainable development.

Buy less

Before you buy anything, ask yourself if you really **need** it or if you just **want** it. Most of us have too many clothes, eat too much and live in houses filled with things we rarely use. Less consumption would mean less waste and a smaller carbon footprint.

top tip

Many of the steps listed here are not only good for society and for the environment, but are also kind to our pocket and to our health.

Buy Fairtrade

This would translate into better prices, improved working conditions and more sustainable production methods for growers of crops.

Buy Irish

This would boost Irish jobs, while also reducing the carbon miles of the goods that we purchase.

Buy local

Support local small businesses, independent coffee shops, bookshops and farmers' markets. You'll reduce carbon miles, keep money in the local economy, and support and sustain farming in your community.

Buy second-hand

Donate clothes, furniture, books and toys you no longer need to your local charity shop. Try to buy things there too. You'll be saving money, helping those less fortunate than you and caring for the environment all at the same time.

Research

Before you buy, find out where products are made, whether fair wages are paid, what kind of production process is used, where the ingredients come from. It only takes a minute to Google it or to ask.

Eat less meat

Huge amounts of greenhouse gases are generated from cattle, millions of acres of forest have been destroyed to make way for farmland, and large volumes of water are needed to produce meat. Happily, major advances are underway in the development of lab-grown meat, and there is a huge range of plant-based meat alternatives available.

Cut down on plastics

- Stop using plastic straws.
- Carry a reusable shopping bag.
- Don't buy packaged fruit; buy it loose.
- Carry a reusable water bottle/coffee cup/travel mug.
- Save packaging – and money – by buying in bulk where possible.

Drive less

- Try to walk or cycle to work or school where possible.
- If it's too far, try to take public transport or carpool with friends.
- If you must use a car, try to opt for an electric or hybrid vehicle.

Save energy

- Take the stairs instead of lifts and escalators.
- Turn lights off when you're not using them.
- Only use a washing machine on a full load.
- Try to air dry your clothes rather than using an electric dryer.
- Use energy-efficient light bulbs and a more energy-efficient boiler.
- Consider installing solar panels.
- Get your bills and bank statements emailed to you.
- Freeze leftover food. This will save time, food, money and the planet all in one go.
- Properly insulate your house.
- If buying online, try to bundle your orders to save on packaging and delivery costs.
- Consider flying less. Aeroplanes burn enormous amounts of fossil fuels and contribute to global warming.

Spread the word

Encourage people you know to be ethical and to practise sustainability.

Question 17, Junior Cycle Examination 2019
Consumers can act ethically by purchasing a reusable coffee cup. Explain one other step a consumer could take to be more ethical in their purchasing decisions.

Answer
Consumers should do some research before they buy clothes to try to ensure that the workers who made them are treated ethically and paid appropriately. There is usually extensive information available online.

Question 16 (b), Junior Cycle Sample Paper (SEC)
(iv) As consumers, whether purchasing online or instore, we have ethical responsibilities. State two ethical responsibilities that we have as consumers.

Answer
- We should consider the working conditions of the people who make what we buy, and refrain from purchasing from companies that do not treat their workers as they should.
- We should try to buy locally in order to reduce the carbon miles of the items that we buy, e.g. apples from Ireland instead of from the other side of the world.

10 Globalisation and Changing Technology

Main Learning Outcome

1.10 Students should be able to discuss and evaluate how globalisation and developments in technology impact on consumer choice and behaviour.

> **aims** By the end of this chapter you should:
> - understand what globalisation is and the reasons for it
> - be able to outline the advantages as well as the challenges of globalisation.

Globalisation (see Chapter 33) means that the economies and societies of different countries have increasingly merged into a single global economy and society, allowing for greater trade in products and services, ideas and other aspects of culture.

Reasons for globalisation

Advances in human technology since the Industrial Revolution

- The development of oil extraction, electricity generation and modern steelmaking has led to an age of spectacular mass production.
- The invention of cars, buses and subways has facilitated the growth of cities and their suburbs.
- The development of rail, sea and air transport allows people and goods to be moved around the world easily and efficiently.
- The invention of the telephone, cinema and television made the world a smaller place and inspired millions to dream of more affluent lifestyles, e.g. seen on movies and television shows.
- The development of computers, the internet and smartphones have made global communications and access to information instant and economical, and rendered location less relevant, e.g. WhatsApp.

Deregulation of markets

- Since the Second World War, the **World Trade Organisation (WTO)** has steadily reduced barriers to trade around the world, eliminating tariffs, quotas, etc.
- Since 1957, the growth of the European Union (see Chapter 34) has integrated the economies of Europe into a single economy.
- Other trade blocs such as the **North American Free Trade Agreement (NAFTA)** have reduced trade barriers in other parts of the world.
- The collapse of the Soviet Union in 1991 brought millions of people into the global economy. India joined the WTO in 1995 and China followed in 2001.

Global brands

The emergence of global companies and global brands that can be marketed worldwide with little or no modification, e.g. Louis Vuitton, Pepsi, Hyundai. When global companies treat the world as one market, it speeds up the process of globalisation.

A list of firsts

Probably nothing better illustrates how profound and rapid technological progress has been than to look at just some of the inventions of the two centuries:

- The first oil well was drilled in 1859.
- The first plane flew in 1903.
- The first TV broadcast took place in 1928.
- The first man walked on the moon in 1969.
- The first email was sent in 1971.
- The first text message was sent in 1992.
- The first iPhone was released in 2007.
- The first photo was posted to Instagram in 2010.
- Apple became the first company worth US$1 trillion in 2018.

Advantages of globalisation

- **Choice:** Consumers gain access to a wider range of goods and services, e.g. television channels, holiday destinations, food and drink. Likewise, firms can source raw materials from anywhere in the world.
- **Competition:** Increased competition from foreign companies, e.g. Lidl and Aldi, results in lower prices and more innovation.

top tip

Ireland is often described as one of the most open economies in the world, with very few restrictions on trade with other countries. Therefore, we are one of the countries that has embraced globalisation the most.

- **New markets:** Exporters can market their goods and services anywhere in the world, e.g. medicine exported from Ireland to Chile. Even small independent retailers can build a global presence online.

- **Work and collaboration:** With an internet connection, there are more and more jobs that can be performed anywhere, even in rural Ireland. Colleagues around the world can collaborate on projects using cloud computing.

- **Sharing of learning:** Institutions of education and research can collaborate globally, e.g. Trinity College Dublin and the Chinese Academy of Sciences. Discoveries made anywhere can be shared everywhere.

- **Greater access to knowledge:** The internet has brought truly profound advances, many of them free. At any moment on your phone you can access an inconceivable number of songs, movies, TV shows, newspapers and magazines, as well as instant weather, traffic, shipping and aircraft data, endless hours of free lectures, tutorials and debates on every conceivable topic.

- **Economies of scale:** Companies benefit from global economies of scale, which ensures a lower average cost as output increases, leading to lower prices for consumers, e.g. you can buy a bottle of Coca-Cola as cheaply as you can because billions of bottles are produced every day, bringing down the individual cost of each bottle.

- **Expansion:** Companies that have reached saturation in their home countries can continue to expand by selling their goods around the world, e.g. Starbucks coffee.

- **Outsourcing:** Some or all of the production process can be outsourced to wherever is cheapest or most convenient, e.g. Nike hires firms in China, Indonesia, Taiwan and elsewhere to make its shoes.
  - This brings jobs and investment to those countries and raises their standard of living.
  - It also enables Nike to sell their shoes at lower prices.

- **Emigration:** In times of recession, globalisation has enabled Irish people to find work in other countries, to explore the world and to bring Irish culture wherever they go.

- **Immigration:** When people come to Ireland from abroad, they bring their language, culture, traditions and ideas. In turn, they benefit from adopting our values, finding work and opportunity in our economy and raising their families in their new country.

- **Mutual understanding:** Globalisation proves that people have much more in common than they have to divide them.

We help one another when we trade and cooperate, reducing the risk of conflict and war.

- **Foreign Direct Investment:** Many transnational companies have located in Ireland, bringing investment, employment and an injection of skills and ideas.

top tip

A transnational company is one that does business in several countries, e.g. Coca-Cola.

- **Global consciousness:** More people than ever think in terms of a single global community rather than their own narrow local self-interest, e.g. for Ireland's economy to flourish, we need to care about a healthy and sustainable planet.

- **A better world:** We have seen huge reductions in extreme poverty and infant mortality, and major improvements in literacy, life expectancy, access to education and health care, largely thanks to the technological and economic improvements associated with globalisation.

Challenges of globalisation

- **Competition:** While it can deliver lower prices and increased innovation, global competition can also lead to job losses, bankruptcy and an unending quest for efficiency.

- **We are all self-employed:** Even if we officially work for a company or the government, globalisation forces us to think and act like we work for ourselves. This requires independence, self-reliance and adaptability. In a globalised world, where permanent jobs are less common than they were, we are forced to become entrepreneurial in how we market ourselves. This has been called the 'gig' economy.

top tip

In a globalised world, the skills and characteristics of entrepreneurs found in Chapter 15 start to become very important indeed.

- **Relentless technological change:** Many of the jobs of today will be performed by computers in the future, creating unemployment and uncertainty and threatening job security.

- **Decline of local cultures:** Just as a society is a collection and a connection of individual people, our world is a collection and a connection of unique places and communities. This can be lost in a globalised world.

- **Cultural change:** Irish culture has been strengthened by immigration, but it can be a challenge for some to adjust to the rapid pace of change and to the decline of old certainties.

- **Exploitation of workers:** When there is a large supply of unskilled labour, transnationals can get away with paying low wages or providing poor working conditions.

- **Large transnationals:** It can be a challenge for Irish firms to compete against major transnationals with bigger advertising budgets and a lower cost base, e.g. Supermacs vs. McDonalds.
- **No loyalty:** Transnational companies may relocate elsewhere if there is a cost saving to be made, leaving workers laid off and factories idle. For this reason, it can be dangerous to become over-reliant on transnationals.
- **Environmental damage:** Unsustainable consumption of natural resources has led to rising global temperatures and sea levels, with potentially drastic climate change to come.
- **Increased inequality:** Even with the decline in extreme poverty, the growing gap between rich and poor is viewed negatively by many, with calls for greater redistribution of wealth from the developed to the developing world.
- **Lack of regulation:** Even the most powerful governments cannot control the world economy. Some of the largest companies in the world have more power than most countries do, and it can prove difficult to tackle global issues without global cooperation.

Question 16 (c), Junior Cycle Sample Paper (SEC)
'The internet and globalisation have greatly increased the power that companies hold around the world.'

Adapted from www.governmenteuropa.eu

(i) What is meant by the term globalisation?
(ii) State one way Ireland benefits from globalisation.

Answer
(i) Globalisation means that partly thanks to advances in technology, the world is shrinking and the economies and societies of the world have merged into one economy and society.
(ii) Due to our low rate of corporation tax and our membership of the EU and the euro, we have become a prime location for transnational companies.

Using Skills for Business

 11 Employment and Wages

⟹ **Main Learning Outcome**

1.11 Students should be able to interpret a wage slip and calculate personal tax liability arising from employment.

aims By the end of this chapter you should:
- understand the layout of a wage slip
- be familiar with the various methods of calculating pay
- be able to calculate a person's tax liability.

Payslip/wage slip

- A payslip or wage slip is a document you receive each time you are paid, detailing your gross pay, your deductions and your net pay. You are legally entitled to receive a payslip.

- An **electronic payslip** (or **ePayslip**) means that you do not receive a hard copy. Instead, you are either emailed your payslip or given a login and password to a secure website where it can be viewed, downloaded or printed.

exam focus

There are quite a few calculations in this chapter, so if figures are not your strong suit, it will take repeated and patient study.

Sample payslip

PAYSLIP					
Employer:		FORTFIELD OPTICIANS LTD			
Employee name:		Zara G. Kearney			
Payroll number:		901497758			
PPSN:		75456016BP			
Payment period:		Week number 24			
Date:		13 June 2019			
Payment details:		**Deductions:**			
Basic pay	780	PAYE	308.80		
Overtime	120	PRSI	56.40		
Commission	300	USC	48.20		
Bonus	200	Health	25.00		
		Pension	32.00		
		Trade union	18.00		
Gross pay	1,400	**Total deductions**	488.40	**Net pay**	€911.60

Explanation

- **Employer:** The name of the company or organisation that has issued the payslip.
  — Fortfield Opticians Ltd.
- **Name:** The name of the employee.
  — Zara G. Kearney.
- **Payroll number/employee number:** Many organisations assign a number to each of their employees.
  — Zara's payroll number is 901497758.
- **PPSN:** This is the employee's Personal Public Service Number, used when accessing a wide range of government services.
  — Zara's PPSN is 75456016BP.
- **Payment period:** The week number in which the payslip was issued.
  — This is Zara's payslip for week number 24.
- **Date:** The date the payslip was issued.
  — Zara's payslip was issued on 13 June 2019.
- **Basic pay:** The amount that you earn for a normal working week.
  — Zara is paid €20 an hour for a 39-hour week. Therefore, her basic pay is:
    $39 \times 20 = €780.$

- **Overtime:** If you work extra hours in addition to your normal hours, you get paid more at a higher rate per hour.
  — Zara is paid €30 an hour for each hour of overtime. If she works four hours overtime, she receives:
  $4 \times 30 = €\mathbf{120}$.
- **Commission:** You are paid a percentage of the price of each item you sell in order to encourage you to sell more. Commission can only be paid in jobs where it is possible to count how many items you sell.
  — Zara is paid 10% of the value of what she sells.
  — If she sells €3,000 of lenses and frames in a week, Zara is paid commission of €300.
- **Bonus:** You may be paid extra for reaching a target, again to encourage you to sell more.
  — Zara is paid an extra €200 because she told 30 frames in a week.
- **Gross pay:** This is your total pay before any deductions have been taken away.
  — Zara's gross wage for this week is €1,400.
- **Deductions:** Amounts taken away from an employee's gross pay. There are two categories:
  — **Statutory deductions** are amounts taken from an employee's pay that are required by law.

  > Zara's statutory deductions:
  > PAYE (Pay As You Earn) €308.80.
  > PRSI (Pay Related Social Insurance) €56.40.
  > USC (Universal Social Charge) €48.20.

  — **Non-statutory deductions** are amounts taken from an employee's pay that are not required by law. They are deducted and paid to other organisations at the request of the employee and are a convenient way to pay certain bills.

  > Zara's non-statutory deductions:
  > Health insurance €25.
  > Pension contribution €32.
  > Trade union membership fee €18.

  — Zara's total deductions are €488.40.
- **Net pay,** also called **take-home pay**, is the amount that you receive after deductions. Zara's net pay is:
  — Gross pay (€1,400) – Deductions (€488.40) = €911.60

Other terms

- If you are paid a **salary**, you are paid an annual fixed amount by your employer in return for work performed, usually in monthly instalments.
- If you are paid a **wage**, the amount you are paid depends on the number of hours worked or the number of items produced. Wages are usually paid weekly.
- **Health insurance** (see Chapter 6) is a non-statutory deduction whereby an employee can pay their health insurance premium in instalments directly out of their pay.
- **Pension contribution** is a non-statutory deduction whereby an employee pays into their retirement fund directly from their pay.
- Under the **Cycle to Work Scheme**, employers can pay for bicycles and bicycle equipment for their employees and the employee pays back through a non-statutory deduction from their pay over a 12-month period.
- If an employee is a member of a **trade union** (see Chapter 17), they can pay their membership fees by means of a non-statutory deduction from their pay.
- **Paypath** means that your wage or salary is paid electronically into your bank account, without the need for cash or cheques. You are still legally entitled to receive a payslip.
- The **minimum wage** is the lowest hourly wage permitted by law, e.g. €9.80 per hour for adults over 20 years of age. Those under 18 are only entitled to 70% of the adult minimum wage.
- **Flexitime** is when employees can start or finish work at times that suit them as long as they complete their working week.
  - It facilitates employees to drop off and pick up children from school or avoid rush hour traffic.
  - It is particularly suited to jobs that may not involve dealing directly with the public, e.g. graphic designer, translator.

Ways to calculate basic pay

Time rate

You are paid by the hour for a normal working week. Additional hours (overtime) are paid at a higher rate, e.g. time-and-a-half, double-time or even triple-time.

Example 1: time rate

Adrian is paid €12 per hour for a basic 39-hour week, time-and-a-half for the first five hours overtime, and double-time for any further overtime. If he works 47 hours in a particular week, he is paid as follows:

- 39×12 =   € 468
- $5 \times 12 \times 1.5$ =   € 90
- $3 \times 12 \times 2$ =   € 72
- Gross pay   =   **€ 630**

Piece rate

You are paid per item made or produced. It is only possible to use a piece rate for jobs in which the number of items made can be counted.

Example 2: piece rate

Charlotte works in a craft shop making handmade greeting cards. She is paid €4 for each one. If she makes 86 cards in a particular week, she is paid as follows:

- $86 \times 4 = €344$.

How to calculate taxes

The amount of tax that is deducted from your wages (see Chapter 4) will depend on a number of factors.

- Your **gross pay,** e.g. people who earn €30,000, €50,000 and €80,000 are charged different amounts of tax.
- The **tax rates**, e.g. PRSI is charged at 4% of gross income.
- The **tax bands**, which indicate the point at which you begin paying tax at a higher rate, e.g. USC is charged at at 0.5% on the first €12,012 and at increasing rates thereafter (see Chapter 4, page 23).
- Your **marital status** and whether your spouse is working, e.g. the PAYE tax bands are different for single and married people, and different for single-income and dual-income married couples.
- The **tax credits** you are entitled to that reduce your tax bill, e.g. single person tax credit, incapacitated child tax credit, home carer tax credit.

Examples of how tax is calculated

Example 3

Dave earns a basic wage of €32,000.

Total gross pay:			€32,000
PAYE: ● €32,000 @ 20%		€6,400	
Tax credits: ● PAYE tax credit ● Single person tax credit	€1,650 €1,650	€3,300	
PAYE due:		€3,100	
PRSI: ● €32,000 @ 4%		€1,280	
USC: ● €12,012 @ 0.5% ● € 7,862 @ 2.0% ● €12,126 @ 4.5%	€60.06 €157.24 €545.67	€762.97	
Total deductions:			€5,142.97
Net annual pay:			€26,857.03
Net monthly pay:			€2,238.09
Net weekly pay:			€516.48

Explanation

- As you can see, you calculate the PAYE first, and then deduct the tax credits to find the PAYE due.
- Since Dave earns less than €35,300, he is taxed at the lower PAYE rate of 20%.

top tip

There are a number of tax calculators online that allow you to enter your gross pay and other details and work out how much tax you have to pay.

Example 4

Tessa earns a basic salary of €60,000 and earns a bonus of €7,000.

Salary:			€60,000
Bonus:			€7,000
Total gross pay:			€67,000
PAYE: • €35,300 @ 20% • €31,700 @ 40%		€7,060 €12,680	
Total PAYE:		€19,740	
Tax credits: • PAYE tax credit • Single person tax credit	€1,650 €1,650	€3,300	
PAYE due:		€16,440	
PRSI: • €67,000 @ 4%		€2,680	
USC: • €12,012 @ 0.5% • € 7,862 @ 2.0% • €47,126 @ 4.5%	€60.06 €157.24 €2,120.67	€2,337.97	
Total deductions:			€21,457.97
Net annual pay:			€45,542.03
Net monthly pay:			€3,795.17
Net weekly pay:			€875.81

Explanation

Since Tessa earns more than €35,300, part of her income is taxed at the higher PAYE rate of 40%.

Example 5

Kate and Paul are married. Kate earns a basic salary of €67,000, while Paul does not currently work.

Total gross pay:			€67,000
PAYE: • €44,300 @ 20% • €22,700 @ 40%		€8,860 €9,080	
Total PAYE:		€17,940	
Tax credits: • PAYE tax credit • Married person tax credit	€1,650 €3,300	€4,950	
PAYE due:		€12,990	
PRSI: • €67,000 @ 4%		€2,680	
USC: • €12,012 @ 0.5% • € 7,862 @ 2.0% • €47,126 @ 4.5%	€60.06 €157.24 €2,120.67	€2,337.97	
Total deductions:			€18,007.97
Net annual pay:			€48,992.03
Net monthly pay:			€4,082.67
Net weekly pay:			€942.15

Explanation

- Because Kate and Paul are married, they are each entitled to a married person tax credit.
- Because only one of them is working, they do not begin paying the 40% higher rate of PAYE until Kate's income reaches €44,300. This is because it is assumed that Kate is using her income to support Paul.

Example 6

Ruth and Oliver are married. Ruth earns €53,000 while Oliver earns €35,000.

Ruth's salary:			€53,000
Oliver's salary:			€35,000
Total gross pay:			€88,000
PAYE:			
• €70,600 @ 20%		€14,120	
• €17,400 @ 40%		€6,960	
Total PAYE:		€21,080	
Tax credits:			
• Ruth PAYE tax credit	€1,650		
• Oliver PAYE tax credit	€1,650		
• Married person tax credit	€3,300	€6,600	
PAYE due:		€14,480	
PRSI:			
• €88,000 @ 4%		€3,520	
Ruth's USC:			
• €12,012 @ 0.5%	€60.06		
• € 7,862 @ 2.0%	€157.24		
• €33,126 @ 4.5%	€1,490.67	€1707.97	
Oliver's USC:			
• €12,012 @ 0.5%	€60.06		
• € 7,862 @ 2.0%	€157.24		
• €15,126 @ 4.5%	€680.67	€897.97	
Combined USC:		€2,605.94	
Total deductions:			€20,605.94
Net annual pay:			€67,394.06
Net monthly pay:			€5,616.17
Net weekly pay:			€1,296.04

Explanation

- Because Ruth and Oliver are married and both working, they do not begin paying the 40% higher rate of PAYE until their joint income reaches €70,600; double the cut-off for a single person.
- Married couples are not obliged to have their tax assessed jointly, although most do. If they wish, they can also be taxed as two individuals. Their USC is still calculated separately.

Question 18, Junior Cycle Examination 2019

Mary's position with Ryanair earns her a monthly wage of €7,000 and she earned overtime of €600 in May. She pays PAYE at the rate of 40% and has a monthly tax credit of €275. She pays PRSI at 4% and USC at 5.5%.

Using the details above, complete Mary's payslip for 31/05/2019.

Payslip				
Employee Name:	Mary Brennan	**Date:**		31/5/2019
Earnings		**Deductions**		
Basic Wage	€7,000	PAYE		€2,765
Overtime	€600	PRSI		€304
		USC		€418
Gross Pay	€7,600	**Total Deductions**		€3,487
		Net Pay		€4,113

PAYE workings box:
7,600 @ 40% = 7,600 x 0.4 = 3,040
3,040 – 275 = 2,765

PRSI workings box:
7,600 @ 4% = 7,600 x 0.04 = 304

USC workings box:
7,600 @ 5.5% = 7,600 x 0.055 = 418

Question 13, Junior Cycle Sample Paper (SEC)

Complete the following wage slip showing gross pay, total deductions and net pay.

Employee No. 15		Gráinne Dwyer	Week 20	Date: 19 May 2018
PAY:	€	**DEDUCTIONS:**	€	T and M Motors Ltd
BASIC	544.00	PAYE	77.07	
OVERTIME	168.00	PRSI	28.48	
		USC	22.71	
		CYCLE TO WORK SCHEME	15.00	NET PAY
GROSS PAY	712.00	TOTAL DEDUCTIONS	143.26	568.74

Main Learning Outcome

1.12 Prepare and analyse a budget, determine the financial position, recommend appropriate action and present the analysis in tabular and graphic formats.

aims By the end of this chapter you should:
- know why a household should prepare a budget
- be able to prepare a household budget
- understand how to analyse a budget and recommend an appropriate course of action.

A budget is an estimate of income and expenditure for a set period of time in the future. Budgets are prepared by organisations of all sizes, by governments, by individuals and by households.

Why a household should prepare a budget

- To keep track of income and expenditure each month and give a clear picture of your finances so that you can live within your means.
- To avoid overspending and impulse buying. When you know how much you have to spend each month, you are more likely to mind your money and less likely to buy things on the spur of the moment.
- To identify periods in which you may need to borrow, e.g. coming up to Christmas.
- To highlight areas in which you are spending too much so that you know where to cut back, e.g. entertainment.
- To anticipate periods in which you have surplus funds so that you can decide how to best use them, e.g. to pay off debts.
- To help you to save for the future, e.g. for a holiday.

How to prepare a household budget

In Chapter 2, we saw the income and expenditure tables for the Dunphy family. We now combine them into one table, called a household budget.

Example 1: The Dunphy family

Household Budget of the Dunphy Family					
	Jan.	Feb.	Mar.	Apr.	Total Jan.–Apr.
Income	€	€	€	€	€
Rory salary	1,200	1,200	1,200	1,200	4,800
Denise wages	1,100	1,000	1,100	1,200	4,400
Child Benefit	280	280	280	280	1,120
Dividends	55		90		145
Total income	2,635	2,480	2,670	2,680	10,465
Expenditure					
FIXED					
Mortgage	770	770	770	770	3,080
Car loan	250	250	250	250	1000
Motor tax		385			385
Subtotal	1,020	1,405	1,020	1,020	4,465
IRREGULAR					
Groceries	630	590	600	610	2,430
Diesel	85	80	95	80	340
Telephone	70	65	70	65	270
Subtotal	785	735	765	755	3,040
DISCRETIONARY					
Entertainment	150	140	140	160	590
Presents		40	100	75	215
Subtotal	150	180	240	235	805
Total expenditure	1,955	2,320	2,025	2,010	8,310
Net cash	680	160	645	670	2,155

- At the bottom, the total expenditure for each month has been subtracted from the total income to give the **net cash**, the difference between what the Dunphys expect to earn each month and what they will spend. Net cash can be either positive or negative.

- In the 'total' column, the total net cash is found by adding the net cash for each one of the four months together:
  — €680 + €160 + €645 + €670 = **€2,155**.

- The net cash can also be found by subtracting the total expenditure for the four months from the total income:
  - €10,465 – €8,310 = **€2,155**.

Opening and closing cash

- Let us suppose that the Dunphy family had €1,000 in the bank at the beginning of January. This is called their **opening cash**.
- From the opening cash, we can work out the **closing cash** for January and also for the following three months:

	Jan.	Feb.	Mar.	Apr.	Total Jan.–Apr.
	€	€	€	€	€
Total income	2,635	2,480	2,670	2,680	10,465
Total expenditure	1,955	2,320	2,025	2,010	8,310
Net cash	680	160	645	670	2,155
Opening cash	1,000	1,680	1,840	2,485	1,000
Closing cash	1,680	1,840	2,485	3,155	3,155

- Since the Dunphy started January with an opening cash of €1,000, we can add the opening cash to the net cash of €680 to calculate the closing cash for January of €1,680. This is how much the Dunphys expect to have in the bank at the end of January.
- Of course, it must also be how much they have the very next day at the start of February. Therefore, the opening cash for February is the same as the closing cash for January, i.e. €1,680.
- The process repeats itself to give a closing cash for February of €1,840, a closing cash for March of €2,485 and a closing cash for April of €3,155.

Method

- The closing cash for each month must be the opening cash for the next.
- The net cash for each month is found by subtracting the total expenditure for that month from the total income for that month.
- The closing cash for each month is found by adding the net cash for that month to the opening cash for that month.
- The closing cash can be either positive or negative.

top tip

It's like starting the second day of a golf tournament on 5 under. If your score on the second day is 3 under, you finish the second day and go into the third on a total of 8 under par (5 + 3). Your opening score added to your score that day equals your closing score, which then becomes your opening score the next day.

- If it is negative, you are not only dipping into your savings, you are spending money you do not have.
- This can be financed by borrowing in the short run, but in the long run you can only spend what you earn (see Chapter 2).

The total column for the four months works differently

- The net cash is found by subtracting the total expenditure for the four months from the total income for the four months.
- The opening cash is the same as the opening cash for January. This is because the total column covers the period of time from January to April. Since January to April begins on the same day that January begins, it must start with the same opening cash.
- For the same reason, the closing cash must be the same as the closing cash for April. Since the total column covers the period of time from January to April, which finishes on the same day that April finishes, it therefore has the same closing cash.

Example 2: The Grehan family

You are required to prepare a household budget for the Grehan family for the months January to March. Their opening cash is €1,400.

Income

- Patrick Grehan's salary is €1,500 in January, but he will get a €500 pay rise at the beginning of February.
- Belinda Grehan's wages are €2,100 a month. She expects to earn €300 in overtime in February.
- Child Benefit is €140 a month for each of their two children. The older child will be 18 at the end of February and will no longer qualify for Child Benefit.

Expenditure

- The rent is €1,500 a month. This is due to rise to €2,000 a month from February 1st.
- The last instalment of the car loan of €450 a month will be paid in March.
- Motor tax of €413 is due in March.
- The Grehans expect to spend €850 a month on groceries, except for April when they will spend €1,000.
- Diesel will cost €250 a month.
- Telephone expenses will be €85 a month.
- The Grehans are booking a summer holiday in Croatia to the value of €4,500. They must pay a deposit of €3,000 in February and the balance in April.
- The Grehans expect to spend €120 a month on presents, except for March when they will spend €20 extra.

Household Budget for the Grehan Family					
	Jan.	Feb.	Mar.	Apr.	Total Jan.–Apr.
Income	€	€	€	€	€
Patrick salary	1,500	2,000	2,000	2,000	7,500
Belinda wages	2,100	2,400	2,100	2,100	8,700
Child Benefit	280	280	140	140	840
Total income	3,880	4,680	4,240	4,240	17,040
Expenditure					
FIXED					
Rent	1,200	1,200	1,400	1,400	7,200
Car loan	450	450	450		1,350
Motor tax			413		413
Subtotal	1,650	1,650	2,263	1,400	6,963
IRREGULAR					
Groceries	850	850	850	1,000	3,550
Diesel	250	250	250	250	1,000
Telephone	85	85	85	85	340
Subtotal	1,185	1,185	1,185	1,335	4,890
DISCRETIONARY					
Holiday		3,000		1,500	4,500
Presents	120	120	140	120	500
Subtotal	120	3,120	141	1,620	5,000
Total expenditure	2,955	5,955	3,588	4,355	16,853
Net cash	925	(1,275)	652	(115)	187
Opening cash	1,400	2,325	1,050	1,702	1,400
Closing cash	2,325	1,050	1,702	1,587	1,587

- In this example, we can see that in both February and April, the Grehans expect to spend more than they earn.
- This gives a negative net cash figure of €1,275 in February and a negative net cash of €115 in April. A negative figure is denoted by brackets.
- However, in neither month will they need to borrow money since they expect to have sufficient opening cash to cover the deficits.

Deficits and surpluses

A negative net cash figure is called a **deficit**. There are several steps that a household can take to deal with deficits:

- reduce discretionary expenditure, e.g. go on a cheaper holiday
- shop around and save on household costs, e.g. groceries
- try to earn extra money, e.g. by working overtime
- reduce waste, e.g. turn off lights.

A positive net cash figure is called a **surplus**. A surplus can be used to:

- increase spending, e.g. on overdue home renovations
- save, e.g. for a deposit on a house
- pay off debts, e.g. a car loan. This will reduce the amount that is spent on interest.

Example 3: The Norris family

Here is a partially completed budget for the Norris family for the months January to March. Their opening cash is €580. Based on the following information, you are required to fill in the estimates for April to December, and also for the full year from January to December.

- Donal is due a 10% increase in wages from July 1st.
- Sorcha will receive a bonus of €700 in May.
- Child Benefit is due to decrease at the end of April by €20 a month.
- The Norris family's rent will go up by 10% from September 1st.
- Household expenses will stay unchanged until October, when they will increase to €750 a month.
- Telephone and internet bills will fall by 15% from May 1st.
- The Norris family also expect to spend a further €4,000 on home renovations in October.
- They will spend €300 on presents in December.
- All other income and expenditure will remain the same.

Household Budget for the Norris Family					
	Jan.	Feb.	Mar.	Total Jan.–Mar.	Estimate Apr.–Dec.	Total Jan.–Dec.
Income	€	€	€	€	€	€
Donal wages	1,500	1,500	1,500	4,500	14,400	18,900
Sorcha wages	1,400	1,400	1,400	4,200	13,300	17,500
Child Benefit	140	140	140	420	1,260	1,680
Total income	3,040	3,040	3,040	9,120	28,960	38,080
Expenditure						
FIXED						
Rent	1,300	1,300	1,300	3,900	12,220	16,120
Car insurance	100	100	100	300	900	1,200
Motor tax	187			187	0	187
Subtotal	1,587	1,400	1,400	4,387	13,120	17,507
IRREGULAR						
Household expenses	650	650	650	1,950	6,150	8,100
Petrol	150	150	150	450	1,350	1,800
Telephone and internet	60	60	60	180	468	648
Subtotal	860	860	860	2,580	7,968	10,548
DISCRETIONARY						
Home renovations		2,000		2,000	4,000	6,000
Presents	100		70	170	300	470
Subtotal	100	2,000	70	2,170	4,300	6,470
Total expenditure	2,547	4,260	2,330	9,137	25,388	34,525
Net cash	493	(1,220)	710	(17)	3,572	3,555
Opening cash	580	1,073	(147)	580	563	580
Closing cash	1,073	(147)	563	563	4,135	4,135

- In this example, you are given the Norris family's spending plans for January to March and required to work out their budget for the remainder of the year.
- Note that the closing cash of €563 in March will become the opening cash for April to December, since April begins the next day.
- At the end of February, not only will the Norris family have a deficit of €1,220, but they will also have negative closing cash of €147. Unlike the Grehan family in Example 2, this will require them to borrow.

Revised budgets

Quite often when we plan, something then changes that forces us to adjust or revise it.

- You planned to cut the grass today, but now it's raining so you must wait until tomorrow.
- You planned to go to the cinema, but your parents have announced that they're going out for dinner, so you have to babysit your little brother.
- Your earned €50 babysitting, which now enables you to buy a set of wireless headphones.

Household budgets sometimes need revision also. This can happen for many reasons:

- We get promoted, giving us a higher income and allowing us to spend more.
- We experience a fall in income and have to cut back on proposed spending.
- Interest rates go up, increasing the cost of our mortgage.
- The cost of electricity falls, allowing us to spend more on something else.

Example 4: The Walczak family

- Filip and Iwona Walczak had drawn up their budget for October to December. They have opening cash of €800.
- After preparing it, Filip was told that he had been successful at an interview and was being promoted. In light of this, the Walczaks decided to revise their budget.

You are required to fill in the revised budget, taking the following factors into account:

- Filip's income will increase by 25% from November 1st.
- The Walczaks decide to buy a second car. This will mean:
  — a doubling of motor tax in November
  — a second car insurance payment of €600, due to be paid in November
  — an increase in petrol costs of €200 a month.
- Household expenses will increase to €1,200 a month.
- Light and heat will increase by €100 a month.
- Spending on birthdays will increase by 20%.
- Spending on entertainment will increase to €350 a month.
- All other income and expenditure will remain the same.

Explanation

- As a result of Filip's pay increase, the Walczaks dramatically increased their planned spending.
- Their planned closing cash has decreased from €3,230 to just €836.
- A major reason for this was the decision to buy a second car.
- Insurance and petrol costs will each increase by €600 and motor tax by €385.
- It is just as important to be able to handle an increase in income as it is to take the right steps when income decreases.
- Note that in a revised budget, the opening cash does not change.

Revised Household Budget for the Walczak Family							
	Original Budget				Revised Budget		
	Oct.	Nov.	Dec.	Total Oct.–Dec.	Oct.	Nov.	Dec.	Total Oct.–Dec.
Income	€	€	€	€	€	€	€	€
Filip wages	1,500	1,500	1,500	4,500	1,875	1,875	1,875	5,625
Iwona wages	1,700	1,700	1,700	5,100	1,700	1,700	1,700	5,100
Child Benefit	140	140	140	420	140	140	140	420
Dividends		225		225		225		225
Total income	3,340	3,565	3,340	10,245	3,715	3,940	3,715	11,370
Expenditure								
FIXED								
Mortgage	700	700	700	2,100	700	700	700	2,100
Car insurance	550			550	550	600		1,150
Motor tax		385		385		770		770
Subtotal	1,250	1,085	700	3,035	1,250	2,070	700	4,020
IRREGULAR								
Household expenses	770	770	770	2,310	1,200	1,200	1,200	3,600
Petrol	200	200	200	600	400	400	400	1,200
Light and heat	350	200	170	720	450	300	270	1,020
Subtotal	1,320	1,170	1,140	3,630	2,050	1,900	1,870	5,820
DISCRETIONARY								
Birthdays	130		240	370	156		288	444
Entertainment	260	260	260	780	350	350	350	1,050
Subtotal	390	260	500	1,150	506	350	638	1,494
Total expenditure	2,960	2,515	2,340	7,815	3,806	4,320	3,208	11,334
Net cash	380	1,050	1,000	2,430	(91)	(380)	507	36
Opening cash	800	1,180	2,230	800	800	709	329	800
Closing cash	1,180	2,230	3,230	3,230	709	329	836	836

Question 1, Junior Cycle Examination 2019

The graph below shows Joan Murphy's monthly budget:

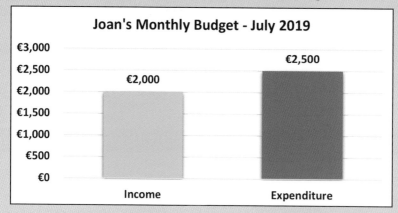

(i) Calculate the difference between Joan's income and expenditure. State if it is a surplus/deficit.

(ii) What advice would you give Joan based on your answer?

Answer

(i) A deficit of €500.

(ii) • Reduce discretionary expenditure, e.g. eating out.
   • Earn extra money, e.g. work overtime.
   • Shop around for cheaper deals, e.g. online.
   • Avoid impulse buying by sticking to a shopping list.

Question 14, Junior Cycle Sample Paper (SEC)

Complete the following extract from the Quinn household budget for three months.

Months	July	August	September	Total
Net cash	520	(300)	450	670
Opening cash	375	895	595	375
Closing cash	895	595	1,045	1,045

13 Recording Income and Expenditure

Main Learning Outcome

1.13 Students should be able to monitor and calculate income and expenditure data, determine the financial position, recommend appropriate action and present the analysis in tabular and graphic formats.

aims

By the end of this chapter you should:
- be able to enter income and expenditure in an analysed cash book and correctly balance it
- know to how to present data in various graphical formats.

In this chapter, we learn about the steps necessary to monitor income and expenditure as it is in progress.

Cash book

A lot of money can flow into and out of a family's bank account every month, but without a system for organising and analysing the information, it remains just a list of figures.

A cash book is a way of recording income and expenditure that tells us how much money was received, how much money was spent, and how much money is left over at the end of the month. It is completed using a **T-account**:

- To draw a T-account, follow the example below with a **debit side** (**DR** for short) on the left that will be used for income (money in) and a **credit side** (**CR** for short) on the right that will be used for expenditure (money out).

DR			Bank A/C			CR
Date	Details	Total	Date	Details	Total	

Example 1: The Hynes family

The Hynes household had the following income and expenditure for the month of March:

March 1	Opening balance	€350
March 2	Received Child Benefit	€280
March 3	Paid for diesel	€45
March 5	Received wages	€1,100
March 6	Paid for groceries	€165
March 7	Paid rent	€850
March 8	Paid for diesel	€50
March 10	Paid for home heating oil	€350
March 14	Paid for NCT test	€55
March 16	Paid for doctor's appointment	€60
March 18	Paid for diesel	€90
March 19	Received wages	€1,100
March 21	Paid for groceries	€125
March 26	Paid for medicines	€90

- Draw a T-account and enter the Hynes family's **opening balance**, i.e. the amount they had in their account at the beginning of the month. This goes on the **debit** side. From the list of the Hynes family's transactions, their opening balance on March 1st was €350.

DR			Bank A/C			CR
Date	Details	Total	Date	Details		Total
Mar 1	Balance	350				

- Next, enter the Hynes family's income and expenditure. On the **debit side**, enter all their income (money in). On the **credit side**, enter all of their expenditure (money out).

DR			Bank A/C			CR
Date	Details	Total	Date	Details		Total
Mar 1	Balance	350	Mar 3	Diesel		45
Mar 2	Child Benefit	280	Mar 6	Groceries		165
Mar 5	Wages	1,100	Mar 7	Rent		850
Mar 19	Wages	1,100	Mar 8	Diesel		50
			Mar 10	Oil		350
			Mar 14	NCT test		55
			Mar 16	Doctor		60
			Mar 18	Diesel		90
			Mar 21	Groceries		125
			Mar 26	Medicines		90

How to balance an account

- Next, **balance** the account to find out how much money the Hynes family still has to spend at the end of March, i.e. the closing balance, which will then become the opening balance for next month.

DR			Bank A/C			CR
Date	**Details**	**Total**	**Date**	**Details**		**Total**
Mar 1	Balance	350	Mar 3	Diesel		45
Mar 2	Child Benefit	280	Mar 6	Groceries		165
Mar 5	Wages	1,100	Mar 7	Rent		850
Mar 19	Wages	1,100	Mar 8	Diesel		50
			Mar 10	Oil		350
			Mar 14	NCT test		55
			Mar 16	Doctor		60
			Mar 18	Diesel		90
			Mar 21	Groceries		125
			Mar 26	Medicines		90
			Mar 30	Balance c/d		950
		2,830				2,830
Apr 1	Balance b/d	950				

- Add up the figures on the debit side and on the credit side of the account to get a total figure for each side.
- In the Hynes family example, the total on the debit side is €2,830 and the total on the credit side is €1,880.
- Calculate the difference and add it to the smaller side. The difference is called the balance '**carried down**', or **c/d** for short.
- In the Hynes example, the balance c/d is €2,830 – €1,880 = €950. It must be entered on the credit side.
- Next, total both sides on the highest line that is vacant on both sides. The totals on the debit and credit sides must appear on the same line, with double red lines beneath. In this case, the total on each side is €2,830.
- Finally, enter the balance again on the line just below the totals on the bigger side, but this time call it the balance '**brought down**', or **b/d** for short.
- The balance b/d tells us how much the Hynes family had in their bank account at the end of March: €950.
- Its position on the debit side tells us that it is a positive balance, i.e. that more has come into the Hynes account on the debit side during the month of March than has gone out of it on the credit.
- If the balance b/d had appeared on the credit side, it would mean they had overdrawn their account.

Analysed Cash Book of the Hynes family

DR						CR						
Date	Details	Total	Wages	Child Benefit		Date	Details	Total	Groceries	Fuel	Medical	Other
Mar 1	Balance b/d	350				Mar 3	Diesel	45		45		
Mar 2	Child Benefit	280		280		Mar 6	Groceries	165	165			
Mar 5	Wages	1,100	1,100			Mar 7	Rent	850				850
Mar 19	Wages	1,100	1,100			Mar 8	Diesel	50		50		
						Mar 10	Oil	350		350		
						Mar 14	NCT test	55				55
						Mar 16	Doctor	60			60	
						Mar 18	Diesel	90		90		
						Mar 21	Groceries	125	125			
						Mar 26	Medicines	90			90	
						Mar 30	Balance c/d	950				
		2,830	2,200	280				2,830	290	535	150	905
Apr 1	Balance b/d	950										

Analysed cash book

- An analysed cash book functions exactly the same as a cash book, but with one extra feature – the income and expenditure is broken down (analysed) by category, in order to show separate totals for how much was earned and spent in each category.

- For example, the Hynes family spent €290 on groceries, €535 on fuel, €150 on medical expenses and €905 on other expenses. An analysed cash book makes this breakdown much easier to see than an ordinary list of transactions.

- The only columns that are balanced are the total columns.

Example 2: The Adebayo family

The Adebayo family had the following income and expenditure for the month of September:

Sept 1	Opening balance	€120
Sept 3	Received Child Benefit	€420
Sept 4	Paid for groceries	€45
Sept 5	Received wages	€700
Sept 6	Paid babysitter	€30
Sept 8	Paid mortgage	€700
Sept 9	Paid for petrol	€55
Sept 10	Withdrew from ATM	€130
Sept 12	Paid dentist fees	€70
Sept 14	Paid for groceries	€50
Sept 19	Paid babysitter	€30
Sept 20	Received wages	€700
Sept 22	Withdrew from ATM	€60
Sept 27	Paid for groceries	€25
Sept 28	Paid for babysitter	€30

You are required to record the transactions in an analysed cash book and to balance it. Find the solution on the next page.

Solution

Analysed Cash Book of the Adebayo family

DR									CR
Date	Details	Total	Wages	Child Benefit	Date	Details	Total	Groceries	Petrol	Babysitting	Other
Sept 1	Balance b/d	120			Sept 4	Groceries	45	45			
Sept 3	Child Benefit	420		420	Sept 6	Babysitter	30			30	
Sept 5	Wages	700	700		Sept 8	Mortgage	700				700
Sept 20	Wages	700	700		Sept 9	Petrol	55		55		
					Sept 10	ATM	130				130
					Sept 12	Dentist	70				70
					Sept 14	Groceries	50	50			
					Sept 19	Babysitter	30			30	
					Sept 22	ATM	60				60
					Sept 27	Groceries	25	25			
					Sept 28	Babysitter	30			30	
					Sept 30	Balance c/d	715				
		1,940	1,400	420			1,940	120	55	90	960
Oct 1	Balance b/d	715									

Graphic formats

It is said that a picture paints a thousand words. The same is often true of a thousand figures or even just a dozen. When people need to digest information quickly, figures can very often be better presented to them in a graphic rather than a tabular format.

Pie chart

Example 3: The Timmons family

The Timmons family's spending for the month of July was as follows:

Spending category	€
Groceries	895
Petrol	210
Medical expenses	340
Mortgage	650
Entertainment	190
Total	**2,285**

This table tells us a lot about how the Timmons family spent its money, but as we can see, a pie chart is much more effective:

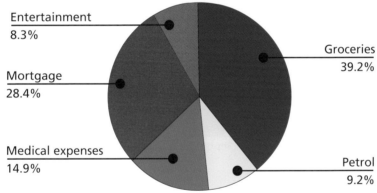

Entertainment 8.3%
Groceries 39.2%
Mortgage 28.4%
Medical expenses 14.9%
Petrol 9.2%

1 Find the percentage for each category:

$$\frac{\text{Category}}{\text{Total}} \times \frac{100}{1}$$

For example, the percentage spent on medical expenses:

$$\frac{340}{2,285} \times \frac{100}{1} = 14.9\%$$

2 Since there are 360 degrees in a circle, to calculate the angle:

$$360 \div 14.9 = 54 \text{ degrees}$$

exam focus

In your exam, if you are asked to draw a pie chart from a given set of figures, you would not be expected to draw the angles as precisely as perhaps you would be in a Maths exam, but you would be expected to label each section correctly.

Bar chart

Example 4: The Jones family

The Jones family's spending over the last six months of 2019 was as follows:

Month	Spending
July	€3,450
August	€2,345
September	€5,119
October	€2,678
November	€3,678
December	€5,312

The information can be more effectively presented in graphic format, this time as a bar chart:

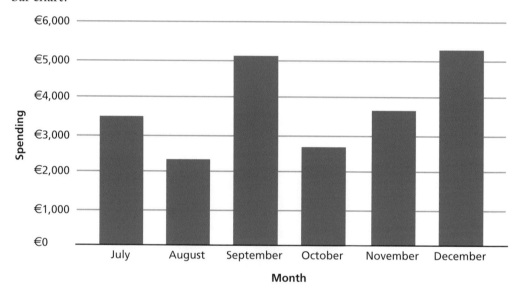

You will very likely collect statistics as part of either your CBA 1 or CBA 2 (see Chapter 37). Since the use of graphs is encouraged, it would therefore be a very good idea to be able to present your statistics in graphic format. YouTube has some very helpful videos on how to easily create a graph in either Microsoft Excel or Google Sheets.

Line graph

Example 5: The Boyce family

The Boyce family's income and expenditure for the first five months of 2020 was as follows:

Month	Income	Expenditure
January	€3,400	€3,200
February	€2,700	€3,700
March	€3,600	€3,100
April	€3,400	€4,200
May	€4,000	€3,300

Since this table displays both income and expenditure, we could choose to represent it graphically using a line graph:

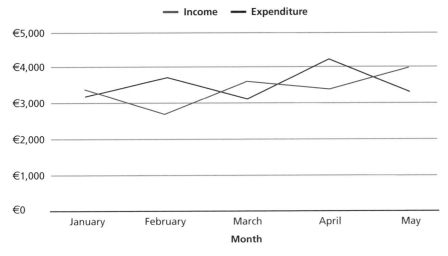

As we can see, the months in which the Boyce family spend more than they earn stand out more when seen on a graph.

Question 6, NCCA Sample Questions

Kate's parents are giving her an allowance of €150 per month towards her expenses. She has saved €3,600 from her summer job to help fund her first year in college from September until May.

(i) Calculate Kate's planned income per month.

Answer

- Allowance from parents: €150
- Savings: €3,600 / 9 months: €400
- Planned income per month: **€550**

(ii) As part of her plan, Kate is examining her planned monthly expenditure. Using an online spending calculator, her planned expenditure is detailed in the table below. Categorise Kate's expenditure per month.

Item	Frequency	Total per month	Category (Fixed, Irregular, Discretionary)
Going out	€55 per week	€220	Discretionary
Clothes/shoes		€100	Irregular
Coffee/snacks	€3 per day	€60	Fixed
Photocopying		€20	Irregular
Lunches	€7 per day	€140	Fixed
Phone credit		€70	Irregular
Cinema/shows		€5	Discretionary
Loan repayment		€260	Fixed

(iii) Draw a pie chart to illustrate Kate's expenditure per month using the three categories provided.

Answer

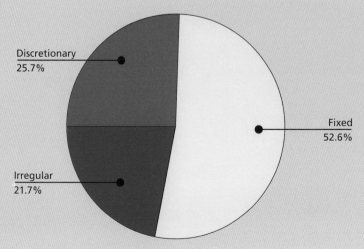

STRAND 2
Enterprise

Managing My Resources

Exploring Business

Using Skills for Business

Managing My Resources

14 Different Types of Enterprise

 Main Learning Outcome

2.1 Students should be able to identify different types of financial, cultural and social enterprise and appreciate the role each plays in society.

> **aims** By the end of this chapter you should:
> - understand the various kinds of financial, cultural and social enterprises that exist
> - be able to explain the role that each of these enterprises plays in society.

An enterprise is any organisation that is set up to undertake a purpose or a project, either for profit or for some other reason.

Types of enterprise

For-profit enterprise

Exists to sell goods and services in exchange for a profit for its shareholders, e.g. Smyths Toys.

- For-profit enterprises make a very valuable contribution to society, since they do not make a profit over the long run unless they consistently provide goods and services people want and need at attractive prices.
- They also employ many people and pay taxes to the government that fund vital public services.
- A **shareholder** is a part-owner of a company who hopes to earn a return on their investment in the form of a **dividend**, a share of the profits.

Not-for-profit enterprise

An organisation that has a goal other than making a profit, e.g. to help people in need, to promote a cause, etc.

- Their not-for-profit nature does not mean they can afford to lose money.
- The money raised by or donated to them is needed to achieve the organisation's objectives and to keep it in existence, e.g. the Society of St Vincent de Paul.

Financial enterprise

An organisation that provides financial services or advice to the public and to other organisations, e.g. banks, building societies, insurance companies, pension companies, credit unions.

Cultural enterprise

Any organisation that engages in artistic, cultural or sporting activity or promotion, e.g. theatres, art galleries, libraries, acting academies, music and film production companies. They can be either for-profit or not-for-profit.

Social enterprise

An organisation whose primary focus is the good of society, either on a local, national or international level. They apply commercial strategies to maximise improvements in financial, social and environmental well-being. They can be either for-profit or not-for-profit. Any profit made is reinvested in the social enterprise, e.g. Recycle IT, a neighbourhood, community and business collection service for all types of waste electrical and electronic equipment.

top tip

Make a list of all the financial, cultural and social enterprises in your area. You may find that it is very hard to imagine one without the other. We need both for-profit and not-for-profit organisations to make our economy – and, more importantly, our society – function.

Forms of business ownership

Sole trader

- A sole trader is a person who exclusively owns a business. They are entitled to keep all the profits, but are also liable for any losses.
- A sole trader has **unlimited liability**, meaning that personal assets, e.g. a house or car, can be taken and used to pay their creditors.
- The name of the business must be registered with the **Companies Registration Office (CRO)**.
- All health regulations must be obeyed if supplying food, and all safety at work regulations must be followed.
- It is necessary to register to collect and pay VAT if sales exceed a certain amount.
- If employing workers, all labour laws must be obeyed.

Benefits of being a sole trader

- There are few legal requirements. It is simple to set up and to close down.
- All profits go to the owner.

- It is not necessary to prepare financial statements.
- A sole trader can choose their own working hours and make all their own decisions.

Drawbacks of being a sole trader

- The owner is liable for all losses if the business fails. They bear all the risk.
- Banks prefer to lend to private limited companies.
- Success depends heavily on the sole trader's abilities. There is no partner to share the decision-making and responsibility.
- If the sole trader falls ill, the business may have to close.
- Stress and burnout can result from the long hours required to make the business a success.
- One owner means that there is little capital for expansion.
- Money earned is taxed at personal income tax rates, not at the lower corporate tax rate.

Partnership

- A partnership involves a minimum of two people conducting business with a view to making a profit.
- It must consist of at least two people and there is normally a maximum of 20.
- A partnership must have at least one general partner who is liable for all the debts and obligations of the firm.
- There must also be at least one limited partner.
- It is important to draw up a legal agreement to avoid disputes over the sharing of profits and losses.

Benefits of partnerships

- Limited partners enjoy **limited liability**, meaning that if the company goes bankrupt they cannot lose any more money than they invested. Their private assets are protected.
- More capital than a sole trader, because there are more investors.
- Better decision-making and shared responsibility due to greater number involved.
- Different skills and expertise are brought together.
- A partnership is relatively easy to set up.
- Accounts do not need to be audited. It would, however, be good business practice to have them audited anyway.

Drawbacks of partnerships

- Profits must be shared with other partners, unlike a sole trader.
- General partners are liable for all debts in the event of a collapse.
- Different points of view can lead to slower decision-making.
- The death or bankruptcy of a partner dissolves the partnership.
- Partnerships are more likely to be granted loans than sole traders, but less likely than private companies.

Private limited company

- A form of business ownership involving between one and 149 shareholders.
- A private limited company must have at least one director, responsible for managing the limited company on behalf of its shareholders, and at least one shareholder.
- A company with only one shareholder is called a single member private company.
- In order to set up a private limited company, a Form A1 and a Constitution, consisting of the articles of association, must be submitted to the Companies Registration Office (CRO). This can be done online.
- The company must decide on a company name, which must be unique and distinguishable against other names already registered with the CRO.
- It is necessary to set up a registered office address and a business address.
- The company is free to start trading once it receives a Certificate of Incorporation from the CRO.

Benefits of private limited companies

- Shareholders enjoy limited liability.
- It is a separate legal entity in the eyes of the law: it can sue and be sued.
- Access to more capital and borrowing than a sole trader.
- Greater expertise available due to larger number of shareholders.
- A private limited company survives the death of any shareholder.
- Profits are taxed at 12.5%.

Drawbacks of private limited companies

- The process of setting up a private limited company is longer and more expensive than for a sole trader.
- Unlike a sole trader, the manager is answerable to the shareholders and the Companies Registration Office.
- Bank loans may be subject to personal guarantees, making limited liability meaningless.
- In accordance with the Companies Act 2014, annual financial statements must be sent to the Companies Registration Office and to the Revenue Commissioners.

Franchise

- A franchise is a business that sells a product or service under licence in return for a fee.
- The firm making the franchise available is called the **franchiser**, while the firm accepting the agreement is the **franchisee**.
- The franchisee acquires the rights to use the name, logo, methods of operation, marketing strategy and product of the franchiser.
- In exchange, the franchiser provides building specifications and design, management and accounting support, and product specifications to ensure uniformity between outlets.

Benefits of franchises
- The franchiser can expand their business without the need for large investment.
- The franchisee can go into business without having to build up a brand name.
- The franchisee benefits from the franchiser's advertising campaign.
- The franchisee benefits from management training from the franchiser.
- Each outlet benefits from low-cost centralised purchasing of stock.

Drawbacks of franchises
- Little room for individual flair and freedom on the part of the franchiser.
- The fee paid to the franchiser can be high, depending on the level of brand recognition.
- Each outlet must achieve the standards set by the franchiser, forcing them to compete with each other.

Examples of franchises
- McDonalds
- Burger King
- Pizza Hut
- Subway

Co-operative
- A co-operative is an enterprise that is owned and controlled by its user members, and which operates for their benefit.
- Minimum of seven members; no maximum.

Benefits of co-operatives
- Co-operatives are democratic organisations controlled by their members, who actively participate in setting policies and making decisions.
- Members have only one vote regardless of their shareholding.
- Members enjoy limited liability.
- Members know each other or have a common bond.
- They provide an outlet for the produce of the farming and fishing sectors.

Drawbacks of co-operatives
- Members' influence falls as the size of the society grows.
- Due to the limited investment from individual shareholders, they often have to resort to borrowing, leading to an unhealthy debt–equity ratio.
- Due to the low volume of shares traded each year, members may find it difficult to value their shareholding.

Examples of co-operatives in Ireland
- Athenry Co-operative Livestock Mart
- Centenary Thurles Co-op Society Ltd
- Cloonsaran Group Water Scheme Co-operative Society Ltd

State-owned
A state-owned enterprise is a business set up and financed by the government. The taxpayer is essentially the entrepreneur in this type of business.

Benefits of state-owned enterprises
- Some provide vital national infrastructure or essential services, and hence a better standard of living for the citizens of the country.
- Many of the services they provide would not be provided by private firms because they are unprofitable.
- Various state bodies encourage industrial development, e.g. Enterprise Ireland.
- State-owned enterprises employ more than 50,000 people in Ireland.

> **top tip**
>
> Some of our most important pieces of infrastructure, such as Dublin Airport, the electricity network and Bord na Móna, were started by the government because no private business existed with the resources to do so.

Drawbacks of state-owned enterprises
- Many do not make a profit, requiring the taxpayer to provide financial support.
- Without competition, state-owned enterprises can become inefficient and uncompetitive.
- The directors are political appointees.
- Some state-owned enterprises have large debts.

Examples of state ownership in Ireland
- Raidió Teilifís Éireann (RTÉ)
- Bord na Móna
- Iarnrod Éireann (Irish Rail)

Business Type	Ownership	Liability	Control	Profits/Losses
Sole Trader	Single person	Unlimited	Owner has complete control	Owners keep all the profits and suffer all the losses
Private Limited Company	1–149 shareholders	Limited	One vote per shareholder	Owners keep all the profits and suffer all the losses
Partnership	2–20 partners	Unlimited liability	One vote per partner	Owners keep all the profits and suffer all the losses
Co-operative	7+ (no upper limit)	Limited	One vote per member	Owners keep all the profits and suffer all the losses

Question 7, Junior Cycle Examination 2019

Indicate whether the organisations listed below are a financial enterprise or a social enterprise:

Intel Ireland	*Financial*
Focus Ireland	*Social*
Bank of Ireland	*Financial*

Question 5, Junior Cycle Sample Paper (SEC)

'The government has announced grants of €56m to over 1,700 sporting projects under the Sports Capital Programme. This benefits sports teams, organisations and associations around the country.'

Adapted from: www.independent.ie/sport

(a) The GAA is one group that benefits from this programme. The GAA is a cultural enterprise. What is meant by cultural enterprise?

(b) GAA clubs may use the grant to purchase assets. State **one** example of an asset that a GAA club might purchase.

Answer

(a) A cultural enterprise is any for-profit or not-for-profit organisation that promotes some artistic, cultural or sporting activity in society, e.g. the GAA promotes Gaelic games.

(b) Floodlights, new dressing rooms, press facilities.

15 The Entrepreneur

Main Learning Outcome

2.2 Students should be able to describe the skills and characteristics of being enterprising and appreciate the role of an entrepreneur in an organisation, in society and to the economy.

> **aims** By the end of this chapter you should:
> - be able to explain the meaning of enterprise and the entrepreneur
> - understand the characteristics and skills an entrepreneur needs
> - be able to describe the various settings in which entrepreneurship is needed.

Introduction

- **Enterprise** can be defined as the human ability to be innovative and proactive, not just in business, but in any area of life. It involves being creative, coming up with ideas and turning opportunity into reality. It involves combining the other factors of production, land, labour and capital (see Chapter 27) into a business unit.

- An **entrepreneur** – a person who engages in enterprise – is willing to do something new and challenging with the possible risk of failure.

- An **intrapreneur** is a person who enterprises within an existing business, either by inventing a new product or service, improving an existing one, or discovering ways to produce it faster or more cheaply, e.g. using e-billing to reduce paper costs.

> **exam focus**
>
> Most large companies have dedicated Research and Development departments that make intrapreneurship their full-time job, e.g. IKEA, Lego, etc. They are a constant source of fresh product ideas.

- A **characteristic** is a special attribute or trait that distinguishes one person from another. We are born with our characteristics rather than learning them. It is important to recognise and value our characteristics and try to develop them over time.

- A **skill** is an ability people have gained through practice or knowledge. We are not born with them. We develop and improve our skills through education, practice and experience.

Characteristics of enterprising people

- **Creative:** Entrepreneurs imagine things differently and have a gift for coming up with new ideas.
- **Flexible:** Entrepreneurs can adapt to changing circumstances and are not afraid of uncertainty.
- **Risk-taking, but not reckless:** Entrepreneurs do not just hope for the best or go with their gut. They do take chances, but only after carefully weighing all options. They constantly try to minimise risks, e.g. by undertaking market research.
- **Optimistic, confident:** Enterprising people believe in a connection between hard work and success. They have faith in their abilities and believe they have what it takes.
- **Self-motivated, hard-working, resilient:** Being successful is more than just generating ideas; it's turning them into reality. This takes long hours, hard work, determination and sacrifice. It also requires recovering from and learning from failure. Good entrepreneurs keep going.
- **Ambitious:** Entrepreneurs don't want to settle for working for somebody else; they have a strong desire to make a name for themselves.
- **Analytical and decisive:** Enterprising people can quickly interpret information and decide on a course of action.

Skills of enterprising people

- **Inner control:** Enterprising people can take charge of a situation and impose their will on it. They don't wait for things to happen; they make them happen.
- **Planning:** Entrepreneurs know how to set short- and long-term goals, and how to develop ways of achieving them.
- **Human relations:** Enterprising people must develop an ability to interact with others. Far from being ruthless, enterprising people must be understanding, persuasive, and able to communicate ideas.
- **Leadership and delegation:** Entrepreneurs must be able to lead and inspire others, while also delegating the right tasks to the right people, in order to bring the best out in everybody and reduce the burden on themselves.
- **Reality perception:** Enterprising people must see things as they are and not as they wish them to be. They may love their own ideas, but it is the customer who will decide if it is going to succeed.

- **Self-organised:** Entrepreneurs must be good at multitasking and managing their time in order to keep stress to a minimum and achieve a good work–life balance.
- **Decision-making:** Entrepreneurs need to listen to different points of view, weigh the evidence carefully and have the courage to make a decision.

There has probably never been a single person who has possessed the perfect list of entrepreneurial characteristics and skills. In fact, one of the most important skills of a good entrepreneur is delegation; to turn to others for help with the abilities they themselves lack.

Enterprise in different settings

We may think of enterprise as confined only to business or that it has to involve making money, but this is not true.

- **For-profit organisations** are companies that were set up with the goal of making a profit, e.g. a hotel chain that stays in business if its revenues are greater than its costs, but eventually closes down if it makes a loss.
- **Not-for-profit organisations** include charities, lobby groups, sporting organisations or environmental groups whose goal is not to make a profit but to fulfil a need or solve a problem in society. They still must cover their costs via fundraising or government grants.
- **In the home:** People are enterprising at home when they learn to cook an exotic dish, grow their own food, buy and restore furniture from a charity shop, or rent out a room as an additional source of income.
- **In the community:** Many dedicated people make their local community a better place, by participating in Tidy Towns, helping to feed the homeless, getting elected to their local council, volunteering at weekends, or taking part in local sporting organisations.
- **In our personal lives:** As individuals, we are enterprising when we engage in charity or volunteer work, take on a second job to make more money, go back to college to get a degree, move house, take a year out to travel the world, or try to master a musical instrument or a new language.
- **In government:** Enterprise in government can involve subsidising electric cars, banning smoking in the workplace, raising taxes on sugary drinks, building a rail line to the airport, investing in rural broadband, or bringing the Special Olympics to Ireland.

- **At school:** Enterprise at school includes organising school trips abroad, doing a sleep-out for charity, setting up a film club or a homework club, fundraising for a new school hall, or amalgamating schools.
- **In business and the economy:** The entrepreneur takes the risk of setting up the business, comes up with new products and services that meet customer needs, invests their money, employs other people, sponsors sports teams and charities, generates tax revenue for the government, helps to grow the local, national and international economy, and inspires other people to become entrepreneurs.

Question 10, Junior Cycle Examination 2019
Enterprise is essential to the Irish economy. Identify one skill of an entrepreneur.

Answer
Entrepreneurs need to be good at planning. An entrepreneur needs to be able to set short-, medium- and long-term goals for their business and come up with strategies for achieving those goals.

Question 17, Junior Cycle Sample Paper (SEC)
In 2014 Karina Niland saw an advertisement for the sale of a small hotel in West Cork. She carried out some research and discovered that tourist numbers have increased significantly due to the Wild Atlantic Way. She decided to purchase the hotel. She refurbished the hotel, employed staff and opened in 2016 with the name 'Ocean Waves Hotel'.

State two skills that Karina needs as an entrepreneur.

Answer
- Karina needs the skill of inner control. It was up to her to take charge and impose her will on the situation to make her dream a reality. and she did. She didn't wait for things to happen, she put in the hard work and made them happen.
- Karina also needs the skill of human relations to interact with the many stakeholders in her business, including her staff, customers, suppliers, the local community and the government.

16 Work, Employment and Volunteerism

 Main Learning Outcome

2.3 Students should be able to differentiate between employment, work and volunteerism, identifying and describing features, benefits, rewards and careers within each.

> **aims** By the end of this chapter you should:
> - be able to differentiate between work, employment and volunteerism
> - understand the benefits and rewards of each
> - know the advantages and disadvantages of self-employment
> - be able to outline the various types of unemployment.

Introduction

Work

Any activity requiring mental or physical effort that is done in order to achieve a purpose or result, e.g. history homework, mowing the lawn, tidying your room.

> **top tip**
>
> Attending school and studying for exams is an example of work that is done partly so that it can lead to employment later on. Often, the rewards of what we do come later.

Features

- No payment is received.
- You have few, if any, legal, responsibilities.
- There is no contract of employment.
- You don't have a boss and you complete the task at your own pace.

Employment

Any work that is done in exchange for payment, e.g. a plumber, a software engineer, a professional rugby player.

Features

- You receive a wage or a salary.
- You have both legal rights and responsibilities.
- You are entitled to a contract of employment.
- A **job description** describes exactly what is expected of you.
- All employment is work, but not all work is employment.

Volunteerism

Giving your time and your skills for the benefit of other people and worthy causes, e.g. working in a charity shop, doing a charity cycle, packing bags in a supermarket to raise funds for a school sports hall.

Features

- No payment is received.
- You don't have an employer, but you may still be answerable to a supervisor.
- You have no contract of employment.

Benefits and rewards

Benefits and rewards of work

- A task that would have to be done eventually is now out of the way, e.g. that Geography project is over with.
- You get a sense of satisfaction when you complete a task, e.g. when you clean the kitchen.
- You form a better appreciation of where things come from, e.g. when you cook dinner for your family.
- People around you are grateful for what you have done, e.g. if you help to change a tyre.
- You learn skills that you can use again, e.g. how to make French toast.
- It builds your reputation and earns you goodwill, so that perhaps you can ask for something in exchange, e.g. to go into town at the weekend.
- You develop a work ethic, dedication and commitment that will stand to you when you later get a job.

> **exam focus**
>
> While there are many benefits and rewards of work, employment and volunteerism, in your exam you may only be asked for two or three.

Benefits and rewards of employment

- You earn money for yourself and for those that depend on you, e.g. your children have new shoes thanks to you.
- You can earn extra through overtime, increments, bonuses, commission and profit-sharing.
- You may receive benefits in kind, e.g. paid health insurance.
- You can start to save for a car, a nice jacket, a holiday, even a deposit for a house.

- You can begin paying into a pension to prepare for when you retire.
- If you work hard and do well, you may get promoted.
- A job gives you a purpose in life, increasing your self-worth and self-esteem.
- You gain valuable experience that improves your curriculum vitae.
- You gain skills and knowledge that you can also use in your personal life, e.g. computer skills.
- Employment brings a sense of security; you are less worried about the future when you know you have a steady income.
- You can meet like-minded people and gain strength from being around smart, hard-working people.

Benefits and rewards of volunteerism

- You gain satisfaction from having helped others, e.g. working with people with intellectual disabilities.
- Others thank you for the effort that you have made, e.g. helping out at a homeless shelter.
- Everyone is there because they want to be and not for money, so strong friendships often form between volunteers, e.g. organising a litter cleanup.
- You can see the difference you have made in your local community or in the world around you, e.g. environmental work.
- You gain knowledge and skills that can enhance your employment prospects, e.g. communication skills.
- It is also a chance for you to pass on your skills to others, e.g. computer skills.
- Prospective employers look for evidence on a CV of a rounded person; one who doesn't consider money to be the most important or the only reward, e.g. sailing around Ireland to raise funds for Syrian refugees.
- Since many successful people volunteer, it is a chance to make contacts. For many, their volunteer work becomes more important to them than their employment.

- High-profile people, such as celebrities, can raise money for good causes just by the publicity they bring to the cause.
- You become more humble and more grateful for what you have.
- Your local community, society in general and the environment may all gain from the volunteer work that you have done.

Self-employment

Benefits of self-employment

- You make all the decisions.
- You don't have a boss; you are the boss.
- You get to choose your own hours.
- You may get the chance to turn a hobby into a career.
- You may be able to work from home and avoid commuting.
- You keep all the profits, not earn them for somebody else.
- You can follow your passion and do what you love.
- You can choose who you work with.
- You gain a greater sense of satisfaction.

Disadvantages of self-employment

- You still have to answer to your clients.
- If you make a poor decision, you are responsible.
- Your income may be irregular; you never know how big the next pay cheque will be or when you will receive it.
- You have to shoulder any losses.
- You get no sick pay and no holiday pay.
- It is difficult to keep a boundary between your work and the rest of your life.
- You may have to work long hours in order to deliver on all your jobs and become successful.
- You may not like having to work alone a lot.
- You may have to hire people with skills that you lack.

top tip

Amid the uncertainty of our globalised world, e.g. the scarcity of permanent jobs and the rise in contract work, to a great degree we all have to think and act as though we are self-employed, even if somebody else officially pays us our wages (see Chapter 10).

Labour force, work force and unemployment

- The population can be divided into two categories:
  — those available for work, called the **labour force**
  — those not available for work, such as children and retirees; those unable to work due to a long-term illness or disability; those in full-time education; and anyone who doesn't need or want to work.
- The labour force can be further split into two groups:
  — those in employment, i.e. the **work force**, including those who are on holiday or sick leave
  — those who are **unemployed**, i.e. those without jobs but who are actively seeking employment.
- The **Live Register** includes everyone under 65 who gets Jobseeker's Benefit or Jobseeker's Allowance.
- Since it also includes part-time and casual workers and others, it is **not** a measure of unemployment, i.e. those without jobs who are actively seeking work.
- Unemployment is measured using the **Quarterly National Household Survey**.

Reasons for unemployment

- **Cyclical:** During recessions, firms sell less, and hence need fewer workers.
- **Seasonal:** Some industries need fewer workers at certain times of the year, e.g. retailers hire extra staff just for the Christmas season.
- **Frictional:**
  — People between jobs, usually for a short time.
  — People seeking work, but who don't have the skills for the jobs that are currently available.
- **Institutional:**
  — Obstacles to the mobility of labour, e.g. length of training.
  — A disincentive to work, e.g. wages that are not much higher than Jobseeker's Allowance.
- **Structural**:
  — **New technology** replaces workers, e.g. the increasing use of robotics in industry.
  — A **change in the pattern of demand** causes the decline of an industry, e.g. the effect of streaming and downloads on the music and movie industries.
- **Underemployment**: People who have work, but are not working at full capacity, e.g. people on a three-day week.

Question 18 (a), Junior Cycle Examination 2019

(i) Differentiate between volunteering and employment by answering true or false to each of the following statements. Place a tick (✓) in the correct box.

	True	False
An employee is entitled to a fair day's pay.	✓	
A volunteer gets paid.		✓
An employee has legal rights.	✓	
A volunteer must have a third level qualification.		✓

(ii) John volunteers in the local community. Outline the benefits of volunteering for John.

Answer

- John can take a huge feeling of satisfaction from having helped others. Volunteering is a chance to use your skills for the good of all, and see the results of your efforts with your own eyes.
- John can add his volunteering activities to his CV. Employers often look for people who do something different, who push themselves further and who care about more than just money.

Question 6, Junior Cycle Sample Paper (SEC)

Róisín Ó Brien, an entrepreneur, intends to set up a t-shirt printing company in Wexford called Trendy T-Shirts at the end of next year. In her spare time Róisín volunteers in her local sports centre helping to manage the accounts.

State **two** benefits for Róisín, as an entrepreneur, of volunteering in her local sports centre.

Answer

- Róisín can gain vital accounting experience. Every organisation has to be able to balance its books, and she can gain first-hand experience of how this is done.
- Róisín can also use the opportunity to create goodwill in the community before starting her business. The more people she meets and engages with, the more people will know and remember her.

Exploring Business

17 Employer and Employee Rights and Responsibilities

 Main Learning Outcome

2.4 Students should be able to distinguish between the rights and responsibilities of employer and employee from a legal, social, environmental and ethical perspective.

 By the end of this chapter you should:

- be able to differentiate between a right and a responsibility
- understand the importance of the legal, social, environmental and ethical perspective.
- be able to describe the rights and responsibilities of both employers and employees
- understand the causes and results of good and bad industrial relations
- be familiar with Irish employment legislation.

Introduction

As discussed in Chapter 7:

- a **right** is something you are legally entitled to
- a **responsibility** is something that you have a duty to deal with.

In this chapter, we will refer to your duties towards those for whom you work or who work for you. Rights and responsibilities of employees and employers fall into four categories:

- **Legal:** Things that you are entitled to or have a duty to do under Irish or EU law.
- **Social:** Things that you are entitled to or have a duty to do so that people are treated equally on the basis of gender, ethnicity and cultural background etc.
- **Environmental:** Things that you are entitled to or have a duty to do for reasons related to sustainability and the environment around us.
- **Ethical:** Things that you are entitled to or have a duty to do for reasons related to right and wrong.

 top tip

In defending unethical behaviour, sometimes people do so by saying what they did wasn't illegal. Sometimes this is true. However, it is possible for something to be legal but still unethical.

Rights of employees

Employees are entitled to:

Legal

- Receive a payslip and a contract of employment.
- Be paid the minimum wage or above it.
- Be given the correct number of days' holiday.
- Join a trade union.

Social

- Be treated equally regardless of gender, marital status, family status, sexual orientation, religion, age, disability, race or membership of the Traveller community.
- Be included and be treated with dignity and respect.
- Be protected from harassment in the workplace and be able to have complaints properly investigated.

Environmental

- Work in clean, safe and healthy surroundings.
- Be provided with appropriate training and protective clothing where necessary.

Ethical

- Be paid a fair day's wage for a fair day's work.
- Be informed about potential changes to conditions of employment.
- Not be pressured into engaging in illegal or unethical behaviour.

Responsibilities of employees

Employees have a responsibility to:

Legal

- Pay all taxes for which they are liable.
- Observe the terms of their contract of employment.
- Comply with all health and safety regulations.
- Obey all laws and regulations that apply to their employment, e.g. industrial relations laws, health and safety regulations, etc.
- Report illegal behaviour to the appropriate authorities.
- Abide by agreed procedures if taking industrial action.

Social

- Show respect towards their employer, fellow employees, customers and suppliers.
- Never engage in discrimination or harrassment.

Environmental

- Respect their employer's and fellow employees' property.
- Refrain from dumping or otherwise harming the environment in the course of their work, even if their employer doesn't discourage it.
- Report any breaches of environmental regulations.

Ethical

- Do a fair day's work for a fair day's pay, and to do their job to the best of their ability.
- Be punctual, reliable, honest and trustworthy.
- Respect the confidentiality of their employer's and clients' private information.

Rights of employers

Employers are entitled to:

Legal

- Expect that employees will carry out all legal and reasonable instructions in accordance with their contract of employment.
- Make employees redundant if there is a downturn in sales.
- Terminate a contract of employment in the event of misconduct.
- Make decisions about how they think their business should be run.

Social

- Demand that employees show respect and dignity toward them, their fellow employees, customers and suppliers.

Environmental

- Ask that employees respect their property and any equipment they are given in the course of their work.
- Expect employees to dispose of all waste in a responsible manner.

While all of the rights and responsibilities of employers and employees are explained here, an exam question may only ask for two or three.

Ethical

- Receive a fair day's work for a fair day's pay.
- Expect their employees to respect the confidentiality of private client and commercial information.
- Expect their employees to be honest and loyal at all times.

Responsibilities of employers

Employers have a responsibility to:

Legal

- Pay their employees at least the minimum wage.
- Give their employees payslips and a contract of employment, and to observe all their other legal requirements.
- Correctly deduct all taxes and forward them to the Revenue Commissioners.
- Be familiar with and obey all employment laws.

Social

- Refrain from any form of discrimination in the workplace and to protect their employees from discrimination by others.
- Promote inclusion and a sense of belonging among their employees.
- Try to involve their employees in decision-making, and to promote a culture of intrapreneurship.

Environmental

- Take all reasonable precautions to ensure that their employees are safe at all times, and to promote a healthy and pleasant workplace.
- Refrain from illegal dumping or otherwise harming the environment.
- Promote sustainable practices in the workplace, e.g. cycling to work, recycling of waste.

Ethical

- Pay their employees a fair day's pay for a fair day's work.
- Be honest and upfront about changes in working conditions, terms of employment, possible redundancies, etc.
- Refrain from misleading or exploiting their employees.
- Foster a positive industrial relations atmosphere.

Steps in hiring new staff

- Prepare a **job description** setting out the essential duties, skills and responsibilities of the job.
- Draft and publish an advertisement based on the job description.
- Invite suitable applicants to apply by **curriculum vitae (CV)** or application form, outlining their suitability for the job.
- Based on these, the employer can then invite some or all of the candidates for interview.
- After the interview process, the successful candidate or candidates are chosen and notified.
- If they accept the job, they are given a legal contract of employment.
- Before they take up their position, they receive initial training known as **induction**.

Industrial relations

Industrial relations refers to the way in which employers cooperate, communicate and consult with employees on a day-to-day basis in an effort to ensure a harmonious and productive workplace.

Causes of good industrial relations

- Mutual respect.
- Open communication.
- Commitments are kept.
- Good pay, working conditions and promotion prospects.

Results of good industrial relations

- High productivity, i.e. high output per worker.
- High levels of morale.
- Motivated workforce.
- More intrapreneurship.
- Disputes are resolved through discussion and compromise.
- Low labour turnover and lower training costs.
- Good public image and greater customer satisfaction and loyalty.
- Higher sales and profits.

Causes of poor industrial relations

- Management who don't listen to workers' concerns or suggestions.
- Lack of consultation and communication.
- Lack of conflict resolution procedures.
- Poor pay.

Results of poor industrial relations

- Low productivity, i.e. low output per worker.
- Absenteeism, i.e. workers staying home from work without good reason.
- High staff turnover, i.e. staff frequently leaving and having to be replaced.
- Frequent strikes and disputes.
- Loss of customer loyalty.
- Lower sales and profits.

Trade unions

A trade union is an organisation of workers designed to protect and promote their members' interests.

- Trade unions offer the security of belonging to a larger group and bring strength to bargaining that an employee trying to bargain alone does not have.
- Examples of unions in Ireland include the Irish Nurses and Midwives Organisation (INMO), the Teachers Union of Ireland (TUI) and the

> **top tip**
>
> The key to a trade union is solidarity. When people have the same interests, they are more likely to achieve their aims if they work together for the good of each other, not just for themselves as individuals.

National Bus and Rail Union (NBRU). The umbrella group for many Irish trade unions is the Irish Congress of Trade Unions (ICTU).
- A **shop steward** is a union member in a workplace who liaises between the workers and the employer. A shop steward:
  - recruits new union members
  - helps workers to resolve any disputes that arise with management
  - communicates with the union head office
  - holds management to any agreements made with the union.

Causes of industrial disputes

- Low wages or unsatisfactory working conditions.
- A general lack of trust between management and workers.
- The dismissal of a worker or workers.
- The size of redundancy payments to workers who are being let go.
- The threat of job losses.
- **Demarcation** disputes that arise when one worker is asked to do the job of another.
- The introduction of new technology, which can threaten job losses or change working conditions.
- The employer refuses to work with or 'recognise' the trade union.

Forms of industrial action

- **Work to rule:** Rules are followed to the letter of the law, making the smooth running of the business extremely difficult, if not impossible, e.g. workers decline to do overtime.
- **Go-slow:** Employees do their jobs, but at a very slow pace.
- **Token stoppage:** Employees demonstrate their seriousness to the management by staging a short but complete stoppage.
- **Strike:** A complete withdrawal of labour, designed to force management to agree to their demands. A strike can be either official or unofficial:
    - an **official** strike involves a secret ballot of workers and seven days' notice
    - an **unofficial/wildcat** strike happens when workers decide to strike without a secret ballot.

Irish employment legislation

Unfair Dismissals Acts 1977–2015

Workers cannot be dismissed due to:

- taking part in union activity
- pregnancy or any related issue
- religious or political views
- race, colour, age, sexual orientation or membership of the Travelling community
- taking legal action against their employer
- raising concerns about possible wrongdoing.

Workers can be dismissed due to:

- inability to do the job (incompetence)
- misconduct at work
- redundancy due to falling business
- unqualified for job.

If found to be dismissed unfairly, a worker can get their job back or be entitled to compensation.

Constructive dismissal occurs when an employer deliberately tries to make an employee resign. Every dismissal is assumed to be unfair and the burden of proof lies with the employer to show otherwise.

Employment Equality Acts 1998–2015

Discrimination (treating one person less favourably than another) is illegal on any of the following nine grounds:

- **gender**: man, woman or transsexual
- **civil status**: single, married, separated, divorced, widowed people, civil partners and former civil partners
- **family status**: this refers to the parent of a person under 18 or the resident primary carer or parent of a person with a disability
- **sexual orientation**: gay, lesbian, bisexual and heterosexual
- **religion**: religious beliefs, background and outlook, or none
- **age**: unless you are under 16
- **disability**: physical, intellectual, learning, cognitive or emotional disabilities and a range of medical conditions
- **race**: race, skin colour, nationality or ethnic origin
- **membership of the Traveller community**.

Workers must be paid the same wage for the same work unless:

- they have worked for the company for longer
- they have higher qualifications.

Protection of Young Persons (Employment) Act 1996

This law protects the health of young workers and ensures a young person's education is not put at risk during the school year.

- It establishes minimum age limits for employment.
- It defines a child as a person under the age of 16 and a young person as someone between the ages of 16 and 18.
- It sets out the records that employers must keep for workers under the age of 18.
- Employers must see a copy of the young person's birth certificate or other evidence of his or her age before employing them.
- If the young person is under 16, the employer must have the written permission of their parent/guardian.
- Young people aged under 18 are entitled to only 70% of the national minimum wage.
- It provides for rest intervals and working hours limits.
- It prohibits late-night employment for young persons under the age of 18.

Workplace Relations Commission (WRC)

The main functions of the WRC are to:

- promote good workplace relations and encourage compliance with relevant law
- provide guidance in relation to compliance with codes of practice
- conduct reviews of workplace relations
- conduct research and provide advice
- advise the government about implementing relevant laws
- provide information to the public in relation to employment law.
- offer a **conciliation service** that helps employers and employees to resolve disputes.

The Labour Court

The Labour Court will try to find a solution to a dispute that the WRC has not succeeded in resolving.

Question 18 (a), Junior Cycle Examination 2019

Mary enjoys her job with Ryanair but is concerned about industrial relations issues.

> Ryanair pilot strikes see hundreds of flights cancelled.
>
> The Irish Times, August 2018

Outline **two** rights and **two** responsibilities Ryanair has as an employer.

Answer

Rights as an employer

- An employer has a right to expect a fair day's work for a fair day's pay. When you agree to take up a job with Ryanair or anybody else either as a pilot or a flight attendant, you undertake to do it to the best of your ability.
- Ryanair has a right to expect that its employees will keep client information confidential, e.g. the names, addresses and bank details that Ryanair customers enter on their website on a daily basis.

Responsibilities as an employer

- To provide safe working conditions. Ryanair is obliged to do all in its power to ensure that Ryanair staff are not endangered in any way while they are at work, e.g. Ryanair must have rigorous flight safety checks.
- To prevent any form of discrimination in the workplace, whether on grounds of age, religion, race or any other such ground. All people are equal in human dignity and should be treated as such at all times.

18 How Organisations Impact the Community

Main Learning Outcome

2.5 Students should be able to investigate the positive and negative impacts on a community of an organisation from an economic, social and environmental perspective.

aims By the end of this chapter you should:
- be able to outline the positive and negative economic, social and environmental impacts an organisation can have on a community.

Economic impact

Positive

- Organisations create jobs in a community. When employees spend their wages, they contribute to the creation of spin-off jobs in local supermarkets, gyms, cinemas, etc.
- Organisations purchase raw materials from local suppliers, adding to the wealth, employment and opportunity in the community.
- Construction companies benefit from greater demand for local housing.

- The number and variety of local businesses grow, with restaurants of every kind and international chains opening outlets.
- Organisations pay taxes to the government, as do their employees. This revenue can be used to provide public services.

Negative

- Organisations, when they employ many people in an area, can drive up rents and house prices.
- Foreign transnationals sometimes send their profits back to their home countries and don't invest them in the Irish economy.

- Foreign transnationals are not as loyal to Ireland as Irish companies are. If they pull out and move their operations elsewhere, they can leave unemployment in their wake, particularly if an area has become overdependent on one company for investment and employment.
- Organisations sometimes evade tax or use unethical methods to avoid tax.

Social impact

Positive

- Organisations provide society with many valuable goods and services that feed and clothe us, solve our problems, keep us healthy, save us time and labour, educate and entertain us, and connect us with one another.

> **top tip**
>
> To bring this chapter to life, look no further than your local community. There are economic, social and environmental positives and negatives all around you. You and your classmates could make them the basis for a project, or even your CBA 1.

- When organisations employ people in an area, it means those people no longer have to emigrate or move away, except by choice.
- When more people are employed in an area, there will be a greater need for schools, hospitals and other public services, making it a more attractive place to live.
- There will also be a need for better lighting, transport and waste collection services, which all add to the quality of life in a community.
- In addition to the money that they generate, entrepreneurs act as an example to others, which brings a culture of hope and optimism to an area.
- An increase in local pride and prosperity can lead to a reduction in crime and vandalism.
- Organisations give much-needed sponsorship to local sporting and cultural events, as well as to local charitable organisations.

Negative

- Some products and services that are sold to us have harmful or addictive effects, e.g. gambling, alcohol, fatty foods, etc.
- The growth in employment can lead to traffic congestion, adding to commute times and lowering quality of life.
- Larger organisations can drive smaller competitors out of business.

- As towns and cities grow in size, there may be a loss of community spirit.
- New schools, parks and other facilities may not keep pace with the growth in population, putting pressure on existing infrastructure.

Environmental impact

Positive

- Greater wealth in an area can lead to the restoration of old buildings and investment in footpaths, parks and playgrounds.
- Organisations and entrepreneurs may invent new products and processes that help to solve the problem of climate change.
- Modern building and waste management methods are cleaner and more efficient than ever.
- More and more energy is generated from renewable sources, and conservation and recycling have increased.
- Many organisations encourage their employees to cycle or walk to work, and may even invest in bicycle lanes and bike rental schemes.
- Many organisations adopt the concept of **Corporate Social Responsibility (CSR)**, which means trying to always take into account the social and environmental consequences of what they do.

Negative

- Organisations generate waste and some may pollute the environment, e.g. chemicals in rivers.
- As more factories, houses and roads are built, there can be a negative visual impact on a community with the destruction of farmland and forestry.
- Development also leads to more noise and air pollution and more litter.

Question 17 (b), Junior Cycle Examination 2019

Food2Go Ltd is a fast food retailer which operates in ten locations in Dublin.

Food2Go Ltd has an impact on the local area in which it operates. Outline **two** contributions Food2Go Ltd makes to the area.

Answer
- Food2Go Ltd employs people in the local area. This raises their standard of living, enabling them to purchase goods and services they need and want, pay for their children's educations and save for the future.
- Food2Go Ltd pays taxes directly to the government in the form of corporation tax. In addition, its employees pay PAYE, PRSI and USC and its customers pay VAT on their purchases. This tax revenue helps the government to fund public services such as hospitals and schools.

19 Digital Technology and Organisations

→ **Main Learning Outcome**

2.6 Students should be able to discuss the impact of digital technologies on an organisation, debating the associated rewards and costs.

 By the end of this chapter you should:
- be familiar with important terms and concepts in relation to ICT
- be able to outline the benefits of digital technology for both business and consumers
- be aware of the challenges posed by digital technology.

Introduction

- In the broad sense, **technology** refers to all machinery and equipment developed from the application of scientific knowledge. It includes every tool we use, e.g. a pen, a washing machine, a digital camera.
- More specifically, **digital technology** is any technology that processes and uses digital information and computing power, e.g. laptops, smartphones, the internet. It can also be referred to as **information and communications technology (ICT).**
- Ever more products involve some element of digital technology and the vast majority of businesses make use of digital technology to deliver their products and services, and to manage their day-to-day operations.

Glossary of digital technology terms

- **3D printing:** A form of Computer Aided Manufacturing (CAM) in which three-dimensional objects can be transmitted electronically and printed layer by layer, e.g. replacement parts for machines.
- **App:** A software application designed to run on mobile devices, usually with a specific purpose, e.g. WhatsApp.
- **Artificial intelligence (AI):** The simulation of human intelligence processes by computer systems, so that technology can perform tasks that previously only humans could perform.
- **Augmented reality (AR):** A technology that superimposes a computer-generated image on a

> **exam focus**
>
> As artificial intelligence (AI) grows and develops and affects more areas of our lives, it is likely to be a very topical subject for exam questions.

user's view of the real world, giving a composite view that can assist with many tasks, e.g. to find nearby restaurants on a smartphone.

- **Automation**: When routine tasks can be carried out by machines without the need to be directly controlled by people, e.g. automated lawn mowers and vacuum cleaners.
- **Broadband:** A high-speed internet connection that enables a large number of messages to be communicated simultaneously and allows for the transmission of large files and high definition video.
- **Central processing unit (CPU):** The part of a computer system that performs the basic operations, such as processing data. The 'brain' of the computer.
- **Cloud computing:** When data is not stored locally on your own computer, but instead is spread out among a number of remote servers accessible through the internet, e.g. Google Drive, Instagram and Gmail. If you lose or damage your device, you can still access everything on any other device. Allows multiple users to collaborate on shared documents, e.g. sitcoms or animated movies created by writers and animators in multiple countries.
- **Computer-aided design (CAD):** Used by architects, engineers, drafters, artists and others to create two-dimensional (2D) drawings or three-dimensional (3D) models, e.g. to design a building.

- **Computer-aided manufacturing (CAM):** Using computer software and machinery to facilitate and automate manufacturing processes, e.g. an automated car assembly line. It can greatly speed up mass production of identical objects.
- **Database:** A collection of data organised by records and fields that can be easily stored, accessed, managed and updated, e.g. medical information on thousands of patients in a hospital.
- **Desktop publishing (DTP):** Software that enables companies to cheaply produce high-quality printed matter, e.g. advertisements and brochures, etc.
- **Digital currencies:** Electronic currencies that don't exist in paper form and have not been issued by governments or banks.
- **E-commerce:** Selling products or services online or through other electronic means, with an online mechanism for payment, e.g. Ryanair selling flights through its website.
- **Electronic point of sale (EPOS):** Self-contained, computerised equipment that performs all the tasks of a checkout counter, e.g. takes payment by bank or credit card, verifies transactions, provides sales reports and can be used to check stocks.
- **Encryption:** A way of securely storing and sending computer data, using mathematical formulae that only the intended recipient can decode, e.g. an online bank account that can only be accessed using a password.

- **Firewall:** A way of protecting a computer system from external security risks.
- **Global positioning system (GPS):** A radio navigation system that allows people to determine their exact location, speed and time 24 hours a day, anywhere in the world. Useful for making deliveries and for quickly accessing local services, e.g. finding an ATM.
- **Hard copy:** A printed version on paper of data held in a computer.
- **Hard drive:** Where data is physically stored on a device, e.g. a smartphone. It houses the hard disk, where the files and folders are physically located.
- **Hardware:** The machines, wiring, and other physical components of a computer, e.g. keyboard, monitor, etc.
- **Input devices:** The equipment used to get instructions and data into the CPU, e.g. touchscreen, microphone.

- **The internet of things (IoT):** A greater number of everyday devices are connected to the internet and can be remotely monitored and controlled, e.g. home heating and alarm systems.
- **Mail merge:** A tool for writing a personalised letter or email to many people at the same time by automatically importing and inserting names and addresses from a database, e.g. sending thousands of letters to customers telling them about a new product.
- **Malware:** Malicious software designed to interfere with the regular operation of a computer system, usually hidden inside other software to avoid user detection, e.g. spyware to steal passwords and other data.
- **Multimedia:** Using digital technology to present text, graphics, video, animation and or sound in an integrated way, e.g. a PowerPoint presentation.
- **Network:** A set of computers connected together for the purpose of sharing resources, e.g. so that customer data can be accessed by anyone in a company. The internet can also be considered a vast computer network.
- **Output devices:** The hardware that allows the CPU to give back the required data to the user, e.g. visual display unit.
- **Podcast:** An increasingly popular means of broadcasting involving audio files being made available on the internet for download and listening, e.g. an Irish history podcast.
- **Random access memory (RAM):** This is the memory of the CPU that is used for running the various programs. It can be changed, e.g. you can change the data contained in a Microsoft Excel spreadsheet.

- **Read only memory (ROM):** This is any memory built into a device that cannot be altered, e.g. Microsoft does not allow you to alter the code for Microsoft Excel.

- **Search engine:** An electronic tool for searching for and identifying items in a database that correspond to keywords or even photographs supplied by the user, e.g. Google can be used to rapidly search the entire internet.

- **Search engine optimisation (SEO):** When websites do what they can to ensure that they appear higher up in internet search results, e.g. getting into the top results when people search for 'Gel nails in Dublin'. SEO is a vital part of operating an online business.

- **Social network:** An online platform where you can build networks with other people who share similar personal or career interests, activities, backgrounds or real-life connections, e.g. Instagram, LinkedIn.

- **Soft copy:** An electronic copy of a document, that can be edited or shared on a computer, e.g. in Google Docs.

- **Software:** A set of instructions or programs instructing a computer to do specific tasks, e.g. the YouTube app.

- **Spreadsheet:** An electronic document in which data is arranged in rows and columns and can be easily searched and used in calculations, e.g. clients' contact information.

- **Virus:** A deliberately created piece of computer code that is capable of copying itself and spreading through a computer system, corrupting or destroying data.

- **Visual display unit (VDU):** The screen on which the output of a computer is displayed, e.g. the screen on your phone.

- **Web conferencing:** A way of holding meetings via the internet using audio or video, e.g. web seminars, webcasts, and web meetings. Can be conducted from conference rooms or even from smartphones anywhere in the world. It reduces the need for business travel.

- **Wi-Fi:** A facility allowing computers, smartphones, or other devices to connect to the internet or communicate with one another wirelessly within a particular area.

- **Wireless:** Transmitting signals without the need to plug in devices, e.g. Wi-Fi.

- **Word processing:** A computer program or device that provides for input, editing, formatting and output of text, e.g. Microsoft Word.

Benefits of digital technology

- **Greater precision in manufacturing**. Machines can do things that cannot be done by hand with the same consistency, if at all, e.g. manufacturing computer chips.

- **Repetitive tasks** can be better done by machines that don't get tired or bored, e.g. screwing mirrors onto cars on an assembly line.

- Robots can help to perform **dangerous tasks** such as mining, taking humans out of harm's way.

- **Output per worker increases**. A truck driver equipped with a Sat Nav can make deliveries faster than one studying a map.

- Technology **frees up employees** to perform other roles, e.g. self-service checkouts in supermarkets.

- Opportunities are created to assume new, potentially **higher-value roles** and responsibilities, e.g software engineers.

- **Communication** has been transformed, e.g. video conferencing. Communication on a national or global scale is **instant**, making location matter much less than it once did.

- **Delegation is facilitated**, as it is easier to monitor employees' work and give them the information they need to do their jobs.

- Cloud storage makes **information accessible from anywhere** and facilitates sharing by multiple people, allowing for better and quicker decision-making.

- People can **work from home**, reducing rental and transport costs. This may also facilitate regional development.

- **Collaboration is made easier**, as people can work together in real-time from different locations, even different countries, e.g. a team of architects working on a project or a team of animators working on a children's movie.

- Automation can produce **more goods in less time** with fewer materials, resulting in less waste, e.g. aluminium cans weigh a fifth of what they originally did.

- Digital technology can **reduce paperwork and storage costs**. Staff and customer records can be filed and accessed instantly from different locations.

- Software can be developed to complete **specialised tasks**, e.g. payroll, hotel booking, etc. More **complex forecasting models** can be developed.

- Training can be made more effective with the use of multimedia, and people can learn using their own devices. Digital technology can **transform education**, allowing teachers to bring more content into the classroom, reducing the need for textbooks, etc.

- Accounting software makes it easier to record transactions, manage accounts and perform accounting operations. Accounts can be accessed on any device, anywhere and anytime.
- Scheduling tools, such as Google Calendar, make it easier to **organise and keep track of your time**, and to share events and deadlines with others.
- Translation tools, such as Google Translate, **reduce language barriers** and may eliminate the need to learn foreign languages entirely with the advent of instant, accurate translation.
- **Online shopping:** Consumers can order online, inspect products remotely, read reviews, watch YouTube videos, etc.
- Companies can check stock levels and **reorder goods** with greater ease.
- **Marketing** and market research become **more precise**, as it becomes easier to collect information on consumer habits and preferences, and to respond to market changes more quickly, e.g. recommendations on Netflix.
- Companies and individuals can **interact with the government online**, e.g. organising tax credits, paying motor and property taxes, accessing citizens information, legislation and regulations online.

Drawbacks of digital technology

- The cost of installing new hardware or software and convincing and **training** people in how to use it. Technology is only as good as its users.
- Once a company is committed to a piece of technology, there are **additional costs** of maintenance and upgrade.
- It **does not offer an advantage over competitors for very long**, since every new technology is quickly available to all firms and to other people. Firms – and individuals – still need to develop a USP.
- As machines are developed that perform tasks previously only possible by hand, jobs will be lost and employees replaced. **Mass production replaces job production.**
  — **Valuable skills may decline** or be lost entirely. Technology cannot replace customer service or the human touch.
  — **Less skilled workers are most at risk**, e.g. driverless cars may put truck and taxi drivers out of work.
  — There is a **cost associated with redeploying workers** to other roles whose jobs have been replaced by technology.
  — There is also the cost of **severance payments** if people are laid off.
  — If fewer people are working, there will be **reduced income tax receipts** and higher social protection payments for greater numbers of unemployed people.
  — **Greater insecurity**, if your job can be replaced by technology, leads to greater uncertainty, e.g. what to study in college, where to buy a house.

- **Relentless pressure** for both companies and individuals **to upskill** and stay abreast of the latest technological developments. Just as you have mastered one technology, another one comes along to replace it. This can cause **tech fatigue**.
- **Demand for energy** to run machines consumes additional resources and produces more **environmental pollution**.
- The risk and cost of **obsolescence**, i.e. when a costly technology is no longer needed shortly after – or even before – it comes into use.
- Risk of **overdependence** in the event of power outage or cyber attack/hacking/data theft, increasing the cost of systems failure.
- Digital technology can cause illnesses such as **eyestrain or repetitive strain injury** (RSI). This can result in costly damage claims.
- Employees can be contactable even when they don't want to be, i.e. via email outside of normal working hours. This can interfere with their **work–life balance**.
- Digital technology can create **increased barriers to entry** into an industry due to the higher need for capital investment and training, e.g. the computerisation of banking.
- Local communities may suffer if traditional skills are lost due to machine-made products replacing handmade goods.
- Digital technology can worsen **wealth inequality** if huge profits flow to the small minority who develop it.
- Digital technology can be **addictive** and can **shorten people's attention spans**. Access to the internet can result in time-wasting and **procrastination**.
- Parents are not always able to **monitor or control what their children access online**. The internet is difficult, if not impossible, to police.
- **News can become less reliable**, due to the ability of bots to spread falsehoods, software that can mimic any human voice perfectly, etc.

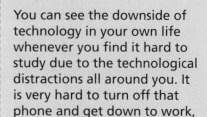

top tip

You can see the downside of technology in your own life whenever you find it hard to study due to the technological distractions all around you. It is very hard to turn off that phone and get down to work, but it still has to be done.

- **Digital technology can make life seem 'too easy'**. If people know they can Google something, they don't need to remember anything. If they don't need to master second languages, many will not. Avoiding effort and challenge is not always a good thing.
- Digital technology makes it possible for companies to **monitor and perhaps manipulate consumers** more easily, e.g. stealing of data, possible end to privacy.

Question 16 (a), Junior Cycle Examination 2019

(v) Investing in Information and Communication Technology (ICT) can bring many benefits to a local business. Illustrate how a business could use technology to its advantage.

Answer

- ICT can make tasks such as payroll and stock-taking cheaper, more accurate and more efficient, requiring less time and human effort than was previously the case.
- ICT can enable a business to market its products and services to a wider potential market, not just the relatively small Irish market.

(vi) Outline **two** possible costs associated with investing in ICT.

Answer

- ICT makes a company vulnerable to malware, viruses and cyberattacks. If an attack takes down a company's site for even a few hours, it can lose substantial amounts of money in lost revenue.
- Investing in ICT imposes added training costs on businesses. Management and staff alike have to keep up to speed with ever-changing technology.

Question 16 (c), Junior Cycle Examination 2019

There has been a large increase in consumers using contactless transactions to pay for goods and services. Outline one advantage and one disadvantage to the consumer of using contactless payments.

Answer

- **Advantage**: Contactless payment makes payment quicker, with no need to enter the card in a machine or enter a PIN, meaning that queues at tills move quicker.
- **Disadvantage**: Contactless payment makes it easier for thieves to use your card if it is stolen. For this reason, it is vital to cancel your card as soon as you notice it is missing.

Using Skills for Business

20 Marketing and Conducting Market Research

 Main Learning Outcome

2.7 Students should be able to conduct market research in order to investigate an entrepreneurial opportunity and analyse, interpret and communicate the research findings using relevant terminology and representations.

 By the end of this chapter you should:
- be able to define key marketing terms
- be able to differentiate between desk and field research
- be familiar with methods of market research
- know the steps involved in conducting market research
- be able to outline the benefits of market research.

Key marketing terms

- **Marketing** is the process of identifying, anticipating, and satisfying the needs of customers profitably. It should be the concern of everyone in the firm, not just the marketing department. It continues over the lifetime of the business, not just at its creation.

  > *exam focus* This chapter will be of central importance to you in your Classroom-Based Assessments, when you will be expected to support your findings with research and evidence.

- A **market** exists wherever, whenever and however sellers and buyers come together to trade. It can be a physical place such as a supermarket or, more frequently, it is online.

- A **target market** is the segment of the market to which a business sells its goods or services. There are very few products that everyone buys, and it would be a waste of time and money for a business to promote a product to everyone, e.g. many people buy milk, but fewer people buy almond milk. A business should know its target market.

- **Niche marketing** means that a firm finds a particular market which no one else is yet serving or whose needs are very specific. Niche markets tend to be quite small, e.g. a shop that just sells umbrellas.

- **Mass marketing/undifferentiated marketing** means that the market is treated as one segment, so only one strategy is used, e.g. laundry detergent, paper towels.

- **Market research** includes the collection, recording and detailed examination of all the data concerned with the transfer of goods or services from the producer to the consumer.

Varieties of market research

- **Desk research** (or **secondary research**) means finding relevant information that has already been collected, e.g. census figures, income statistics, government reports, newspapers, websites, etc. It need not involve sitting behind an actual desk, though it often does.
- **Field research** (or **primary research**) involves the collection of original or new information by means of direct contact with the public, e.g. a house-to-house survey.

Methods of desk research

- **Online:** The internet provides a vast store of free information on every imaginable subject. It is now the starting point for all research.
- **Government publications:** Government bodies such as the Central Statistics Office (CSO) and the Central Bank regularly conduct research into the state of the economy and make it available free of charge.
- **Media:** Newspapers, magazines, television and social media offer a great insight into people's preferences and attitudes.
- **Market research agencies**: Market researchers collect general 'off-the-peg' research about particular markets, which they sell to companies wishing to enter those markets.

Methods of field research

- **Direct observation:** This involves watching how people or consumers behave in their natural setting, e.g. how they move around a shop, which section they go to first, etc. It tells you what people do, but not why.
- **Test marketing:** Rather than release its product to the entire market in one go, a company can test it on a small section first, e.g. the trial of a new juice flavour in just one city. Feedback can then be used to make changes before it is launched to the entire market.
- **Focus groups/consumer panels:** This is a group of consumers carefully chosen to be representative of a larger target market. They are asked to provide input and opinion on a company's new products and services.
- **Surveys and questionnaires:**
  — A **survey** involves asking members of the public a series of questions and taking note of the answers. It can be conducted over the phone, on the street or door-to-door.
  — A **questionnaire** is a written set of questions that people are asked to complete and return themselves, either by post or online.

Steps involved in conducting market research

- **Conduct desk research first:** It is quicker, cheaper and will signal what field research is then required.
- **Decide on a field research method:** This will depend on your budget, what you are trying to find out, and the best way of doing so, e.g. researching children's favourite toys should be done by direct observation rather than detailed questioning.
- **Sampling:** It's too expensive to ask everybody, and you don't need to. A representative sample can give a sufficiently accurate measure of the attitudes of a larger group.
  - **Cluster sampling** asks people in one place, e.g. coming out of a shop. This should be avoided.
  - **Quota sampling**, which aims to have the same breakdown of age, gender, income, as the larger group, is more accurate.

How to conduct a survey or questionnaire

- **Clarity:** Avoid confusing questions. Use clear language. Ask one question at a time.
- **Ask different types of questions:**
  - closed questions, i.e. with 'yes' or 'no' answers
  - open questions, e.g. 'What do you think of . . .?'
  - multiple choice questions.
- **Avoid leading questions:** These are questions that may suggest a particular reply, e.g. 'Do you agree that this brand of shampoo is very good?' A better question would be, 'What is your opinion of this brand of shampoo?'
- **Use control questions:** This means asking similar questions in different parts of the test. If the respondent gives different answers, it means they are not taking the survey seriously.

Sample questionnaire

1 How likely are you to recommend us to family, friends, or colleagues?
   (a) Extremely unlikely ☐   (d) Somewhat likely ☐
   (b) Somewhat unlikely ☐   (e) Extremely likely ☐
   (c) Neutral ☐

2 Who did you purchase these products for?
   (a) Yourself ☐   (d) Colleague ☐
   (b) Family member ☐   (e) On behalf of a business ☐
   (c) Friend ☐   (f) Other ☐

3 Have you shopped for a new phone in the last three months?
   (a) Yes ☐   (b) No ☐

4 Describe what you like about the product:
_____

Benefits of market research

- **Size of the market:** Market research indicates the potential numbers willing to buy the product or service, e.g. how many people go to the cinema on a weekly, monthly or yearly basis. This can assist in estimating potential sales and revenues, which in turn indicates if it is worth launching the product at all, and if so, the likely production and advertising budgets.

- **Consumer preferences:** Market research reveals the goods and services people want, the prices they are willing to pay and the features they want, e.g. favourite pizza toppings, ice-cream flavours, etc. If sales start to fall, market research can also help to tell what needs to change in order to win customers back.

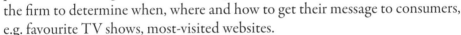

- **Competitors:** Extensive research should be done into each competitor, what they offer, the prices they charge, and what makes them different.

- **Advertising and promotion:** Market research looks into the preferences and pastimes of the target market, allowing the firm to determine when, where and how to get their message to consumers, e.g. favourite TV shows, most-visited websites.

- **Pricing policy:** Market research can help to answer the crucial question of what price to charge. This will be determined by income levels, competitors' prices, quality of the product, etc.

- **Desk research identifies field research needs:** Desk research should be conducted first. Any gaps that remain can then be filled using field research, e.g. census figures will tell you the number of 13- to 19-year-olds there are; field research is needed to identify their favourite singers.

- **Desk research is inexpensive:** It often does not have to be paid for, e.g. free information on a government website.

- **Desk research has already been collected:** It is available to you now, so you don't have to wait for the results.

- **Reduces the risk of failure:** Market research is ultimately aimed at reducing the chances that a product or service is launched that will not sell.

top tip

Market research is aimed at taking all reasonable steps to reduce risk. However, it cannot ever reduce it to zero. Even with extensive research, a new product or service may still fail.

Drawbacks of market research

- **Desk research may not be specific enough:** It may have been carried out by people asking different questions than yours, and therefore may not give the information you need. Field research may be required.
- **Field research can be expensive:** You may need to hire a market research agency to carry out surveys.
- **Limitations of questionnaires:** Most people do not like answering questions, do not always give truthful answers, and many do not return questionnaires at all.
- **Out of date:** In a fast-changing world, what was true last year may not be any longer, e.g. if incomes rise or fall.
- **No substitute for selling:** Market research can never fully answer the ultimate question: will your product sell? To really know, you have to offer it for sale and see if consumers buy it. Market research reduces risk, but does not eliminate it.

Question 12, Junior Cycle Sample Paper (SEC)
Use a tick (✓) to identify whether each of the following is an example of field research or desk research.

	Field Research	Desk Research
Websites		✓
Conducting interviews	✓	

Question 18 (a), Junior Cycle Sample Paper (SEC)
The Pure Confectionery Company has conducted market research for its new protein bar.
(i)   Explain why the Pure Confectionery Company would conduct market research.
(ii) Explain the term target market.
(iii) Identify a suitable target market for the protein bar.

Answer
(i)   To reduce the risk of business failure. The more information the Pure Confectionery Company has about its competitors and its potential market, the more likely it is to satisfy its customers and make a profit.
(ii) A target market is a section of the population, defined by age or income or some other characteristic, at which a company aims its product in order to maximise its sales.
(iii) Young, urban, affluent, educated, health-conscious customers.

Main Learning Outcome

2.8 Students should be able to devise and apply a marketing mix in order to promote a new or existing product or service.

> **aims** By the end of this chapter you should:
> - be able to explain the elements of the marketing mix
> - know how to draw and explain the product lifecycle
> - be able to outline the steps involved in new product development.

Introduction

The **marketing mix** is the particular blend of marketing tactics that is used to position a product or service in the market. It has four ingredients or elements, called the **4 Ps** of marketing:

- Product
- Price
- Promotion
- Place.

Like four members of a band or four pieces of a jigsaw, the 4 Ps must be in sync with or fit with each other. When one changes, the others are also affected.

Example: BMW

- **Product:** A luxury, high-performance car.
- **Price:** A premium price, in line with the product.
- **Promotion:** Television, internet and magazine ads that focus on the high quality and luxury of BMW.
- **Place:** BMW dealerships that reflect the quality and calibre of the product.

 top tip

You could quickly research the 4 Ps of a number of companies by forming a group of four classmates, assigning each member a company to study, and then sharing the results when you have finished.

Product

A product or service is whatever the business offers consumers in order to satisfy a particular need or want. A good product should have several characteristics:

- It must achieve customer acceptability. It must do what the customer expects it to do, e.g. a microwave should cook food.
- It must have an attractive design, be straightforward to assemble and operate, and, if appropriate, easy to transport and store, e.g. an Apple iPhone.
- It should not pose a danger to consumers and should comply with health and safety laws.

Unique selling point (USP)

The product needs to have a unique selling point (USP). A USP is something about a product which is:

- unique to that product
- of benefit to the consumer
- something that the competition cannot or do not offer.
- Products made by firms such as Coca-Cola, Amazon and Disney are considered to have very strong USPs. Without a USP, you're not offering the consumer anything they cannot get elsewhere.
- If the firm has invented an entirely new product, they can obtain a **patent** that prevents other firms from copying their design.

Brand name

A good or service should be sold under a distinctive brand name that can be registered to protect the owner. A brand name has many advantages:

- It differentiates the product from similar rivals and makes it easier to identify, e.g. Tommy Hilfiger.
- It creates customer loyalty, since consumers often prefer familiarity, e.g. Supermacs.
- It should give the brand a distinctive personality, e.g. 'Brown Thomas' reminds people of luxury and exclusivity.
- **Own-brand goods** involve large retailers selling goods under their own name rather than that of the manufacturer, thus generating increased loyalty, e.g. Tesco own-brand cornflakes.

Successful brand names:
— are often short and easy to pronounce, e.g. Nike, Opel, Inglot
— should be distinctive and easily remembered, e.g. Abercrombie & Fitch
— often give some idea of the characteristics of the product, e.g. YouTube, KittenSoft, Fitbit
— must be capable of being protected by copyright.

Packaging

The packaging of a product should:

- keep it safe and preserve its quality
- provide details about the contents
- advertise and market the product, remind existing customers about it and also bring it to new markets
- clearly display the firm's logo or trademark, helping to generate loyalty, recognition and sales.

> **exam focus**
>
> Packaging has become a significant ethical and sustainability issue due to the volume of plastic waste in our landfills and in our oceans (see Chapter 9).

Price

The price of a good or service has a number of functions. It:

- affects the level of demand
- determines the revenue that will be earned
- persuades people to buy
- helps to develop the product's image.

Factors that affect pricing

Prices are set according to a number of factors, usually more than one at the same time:

- **Cost-plus pricing:** Calculating total cost and adding on a percentage profit. Research and development costs must be included in this calculation.
- **Premium pricing:** Charging a higher price based on higher quality.
- **Competitive pricing:** Charging less than or equal to competitors' pricing.
- **Market pricing:** The more disposable income the customer is thought to have, the more the seller will try to charge.
- **Penetration pricing:** When trying to establish a product and rapidly gain market share, a company will often lower its price at first.

Price may change in response to:

- A change in consumer incomes. As consumers grow wealthier, firms can charge them higher prices. If a recession occurs and people's incomes fall, firms must lower their prices.
- An increase in the cost of production, such as labour or rent.
- A reduction in competitor's prices or the entry of a new firm into the market.

Promotion

Promotion refers to all the ways in which a firm communicates with the public about its product or services in order to increase sales. Promotion can include:

- advertising
- sales promotion
- personal selling
- direct marketing
- merchandising
- public relations (PR)
- guerrilla marketing
- sponsorship
- product placement.

The mix of promotional methods used will depend on:

- The type of product or service being offered.
- The stage in the product lifecycle, i.e. is the product new or established?
- The sort of consumer the product or service is intended for.
- The budget that the firm has available.

Advertising

Advertising, the most common form of promotion, involves the communication of information about a product or service in order to initiate, maintain or increase sales. It uses media rather than people to carry its message.

Types of advertising

- **Informative advertising** gives factual information about the product, e.g. the processor speed of a tablet.
- **Persuasive advertising** is designed to convince people that they should buy the product.
- **Competitive advertising** aims to convince the consumer that the product is better than its rivals.
- **Generic advertising** promotes a product type, not just a particular brand, e.g. eat more fruit and vegetables.
- **Reminder advertising** is designed to keep the public aware of a product.

Functions of advertising

- Introduces products and makes people aware of them for the first time.
- Gives consumers information about a product.
- Attempts to increase sales.
- Persuades people to choose a product over competing brands.
- Reminds consumers about a product.
- Can be used to target particular market segments.
- Distinguishes the product from its competitors and emphasises its uniqueness.

Advertising media

- television
- radio
- newspapers
- magazines
- cinema
- direct mail and text messages
- internet, particularly social media
- commuter advertisements, e.g. buses, subways, billboards

Other forms of promotion

- **Sales promotion**: The promotion of a product using a variety of techniques other than direct advertising or personal selling, e.g. free samples, special offers, coupons, discounts and competitions. It is often used in combination with an advertising campaign.
- **Personal selling:** Sales representatives try to convince customers of the merits of their particular good or service, most commonly through face-to-face contact or by phone.
- **Direct marketing:** A firm contacts potential customers directly by mail or telephone to market goods or services, e.g. fast food fliers in your letterbox.
- **Merchandising:** Displaying goods at or near points of sale in retail outlets so as to increase sales, e.g. make-up displays in department stores.
- **Public relations (PR):** Establishing and maintaining a good public image for a firm and its products and to build confidence and goodwill, e.g. soccer players giving interviews after matches, actors appearing at movie premieres.

- **Guerrilla marketing:** A company uses the element of surprise to promote its products and services, e.g. creating viral videos.
- **Sponsorship:** Paying to be associated with, e.g. a sports team, a charitable or sporting event, or with a sports stadium or other venue such as the Emirates Stadium or the 3Arena. It means that your logo gains high visibility and your company name is mentioned regularly in media coverage.
- **Product placement:** A firm's product is featured prominently in a television show or music video, e.g. Calvin Klein clothing in a Justin Bieber video.

Place

Place is about how a business distributes its product to its customers. It is necessary to have the right product in the right place at the right time and in the right quantity. This means choosing the best **channel of distribution**. The channel of distribution is the path the product takes on its way from the producer to the consumer.

The channel of distribution

Manufacturer ↓ Consumer	Manufacturer ↓ Retailer ↓ Consumer	Manufacturer ↓ Wholesaler ↓ Retailer ↓ Consumer	Manufacturer ↓ Internet ↓ Consumer
Examples: Tailored suits, wedding cakes, fitted kitchens	**Examples:** Most goods sold by large multiples, e.g. SuperValu	**Examples:** Most goods sold by smaller retailers, e.g. Spar	**Examples:** Flights, ebooks, hotel rooms

Both wholesalers and retailers are intermediaries who demand a share of the profits in exchange for the service they provide, e.g. a range of locations or an established distribution network.

- **Wholesalers** are firms that buy products in bulk from manufacturers and resell them in smaller quantities to retailers, e.g. Musgraves.
- **Retailers** are firms that break the bulk they buy down into individual units for sale to consumers, e.g. Centra.

Factors affecting the choice of distribution channel

- Potential sales through that channel.
- Transport, marketing and other costs.
- Profit margins demanded by intermediaries, e.g. a retailer may demand a large share of the profits in exchange for stocking a firm's product in their store.
- The demands of the customer, e.g. if aftersales service is important, it may be necessary to deal directly with consumers.
- Selling online gives a firm access to a wider market.

Factors affecting the choice of transport method

- Costs, including fuel, insurance and pilferage (theft).
- The perishability of goods and how quickly they need to be moved. Air transport should be used for more urgent delivery.
- The distance over which the good must be transported.

The product lifecycle

The product lifecycle explains the stages a product goes through over its lifetime. There are five stages:

- **Introduction**: The product is launched. The firm aims to build public awareness and expand the market for the product.
- **Growth**: Sales are rising at their fastest rate. The firm aims to increase market share.
- **Maturity**: Sales continue to increase, but at a slower rate. New competitors may enter the market.
- **Saturation**: Sales are near their peak and the rate of growth slows down. Price must be cut to increase consumption.
- **Decline**: Sales decline. The firm may engage in **product harvesting** (reducing the price to make the most of any remaining profit available) or discontinue the product altogether.

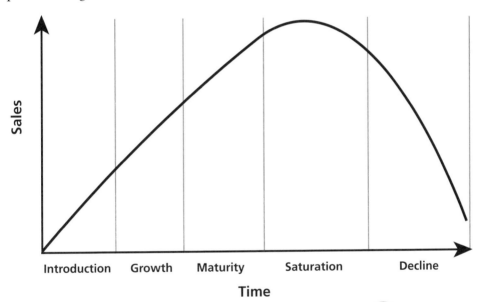

A firm can **extend a product's lifecycle** by:

- lowering its price
- launching a fresh advertising campaign
- targeting a new market segment by finding a new market for a declining product, e.g. vinyl records as a collectors' item.

Don't forget to label the axes whenever you are drawing a graph.

New product development

As their older products reach their saturation and decline stages, firms need to constantly generate new products so that they can survive and expand into the future. This process of new product development involves six main stages:

1. **Idea generation:** Ideas can come from inside and outside the firm, e.g. customer complaints, research and development (R&D), feedback from sales representatives.

2. **Product screening:** Firms select particular products or service ideas for further development. This must be carefully done so potential winners are not weeded out.

3. **Concept development:** The firm identifies the particular customer needs its new product is intended to satisfy. It should have a unique selling point (USP).

4. **Feasibility study:** This examines in detail the ability of the firm to actually produce the new good or service at a reasonable cost and in a profitable manner.

5. **Prototype development:** A prototype is an early sample or model of a product, built to prove that the product actually works and to identify any problems before it goes into mass production, e.g. to see if a tent keeps out rain. Many products go through dozens of prototypes before developers are satisfied.

6. **Product testing:** Finally, the product must be tested thoroughly in a variety of situations, e.g. an airplane is flown in different weather conditions.

If the product makes it through the six stages – and very few do – a decision is then taken as to whether it should be released onto the market.

Question 6, Junior Cycle Examination 2019

Explain two factors that a business should consider when deciding on the selling price for a product.

Answer

- The cost of production. The company cannot make a profit unless its selling price is high enough to cover all of its costs.
- Prices charged by competitors. The company must try either to sell a better product for the same price as its competitors or a similar product at a lower price. It cannot ignore its competitors' prices.

Question 12, Junior Cycle Sample Paper (SEC)

On the diagram below complete the remaining three elements of the marketing mix.

1. Product	2. Price
3. Promotion	4. Place

22 Developing a Business Plan

 Main Learning Outcome

2.9 Students should be able to develop a simple business plan for a new or existing product or service.

> **aims** By the end of this chapter you should:
> - understand the reasons for preparing a business plan
> - know how to conduct a SWOT analysis of a business
> - be familiar with the main elements of a business plan and how to draft one.

Introduction

Whenever we form a plan, we must answer three questions:

- Where am I right now?
- Where do I want to go?
- How am I going to get there?

Example 1

- Tara has only €23 in her bank account.
- She wants to go to a concert in the Aviva next month that will cost her €200, between tickets, travel and accommodation.
- She decides to cut lawns in her neighbourhood until she has earned the money she needs.

A business plan is a document that attempts to answer the same three questions for a business:

- It describes the current status of the business.
- It sets out the business's future objectives.
- It outlines the strategies for achieving those objectives.

Purpose of a business plan

- Give a clear description of how the business started and developed.
- Establish the goals of the business.
- Provide details about its key personnel.
- Identify its strengths and weaknesses.
- Set out its short-, medium- and long-term plans.
- Specify how it will achieve its objectives and the resources required to do so.
- Give a timescale for the achievement of its objectives.
- Describe the products and services it intends to produce.
- Outline how it intends to market its products and services to the public.
- Enable its performance to be measured against its goals.
- Help to anticipate problems and devise solutions.
- Explain how it is intended to be financed.
- Provide vital information to banks and investors to help them decide whether to lend the business money.

SWOT analysis

A SWOT analysis looks at the strengths and weaknesses of a business and the opportunities and threats that it faces.

Strengths

Strengths are internal positive factors.

- Well-known brand name, e.g. Tommy Hilfiger.
- High-quality product, e.g. Fitbit watch.
- Reputation for great customer service.
- Dominant market position or high market share, e.g. Apple.
- Strong unique selling point (see Chapter 21).
- Extensive branch network, e.g. Costa Coffee.
- Loyal, dedicated workforce, e.g. Facebook.
- Good industrial relations.
- Great aftersales service.
- Wide product range, e.g. Tesco.
- Capable and dedicated management.
- Culture of intrapreneurship and innovation.
- Low costs, e.g. cheap raw materials.
- Low debt.

Weaknesses

Weaknesses are internal negative factors.

- Poor quality product, e.g. poor customer reviews.
- Low market share.
- Unhappy workforce, high labour turnover.
- Poor industrial relations, e.g. regular strikes and industrial disputes.
- High costs, e.g. expensive raw materials.
- High debt.

Opportunities

Opportunities are external positive factors.

- Rising incomes and, therefore, more demand in emerging markets, e.g. China.
- Favourable legal changes, e.g. a lowering of the minimum wage.
- Cost decreases, e.g. a fall in the price of oil, the availability of cheaper raw materials.
- General improvement in the economy, e.g. a rise in average incomes.

Threats

Threats are external negative factors.

- New firms entering the industry such as a new competitor in the mobile phone market
- Unfavourable legal changes, e.g. restrictions to the maximum size of a retail outlet
- Cost increases, e.g. electricity prices, wage increases, interest rate increases
- Downturn in the performance of the economy, e.g. inflation, rising unemployment
- Online shopping, e.g. consumers buying cheaper alternatives on a Chinese website.

top tip

When doing a SWOT analysis, don't confuse a strength with an opportunity, or a weakness with a threat. Strengths and weaknesses are **inside** the company; opportunities and threats are in the **outside world**.

Example: SWOT analysis of the fashion retailer Zara

Strengths	Weaknesses
● Global brand	● Only sells through its own stores
● 10,000 stores worldwide	● Low advertising budget
● Distinctive look	
● Extensive range	
● Competitive prices	

Opportunities	Threats
● Online sales	● Fierce competition
● Expansion into emerging markets	● Economic downturn
	● Rent increases

Elements of a business plan

Description of the business

- Name and address of the business.
- Its mission statement, i.e. its long-term aims.
- Brief history of the business.
- Information about the management team, their experience and qualifications, and the roles they play.
- Details of its legal status, e.g. sole trader, private limited company, etc.

> **exam focus**
>
> If you and your group follow the Enterprise Option for your CBA 1, you will need to draw up a business plan as part of your project.

Market opportunity

- The size of the market and how much it is worth.
- Details about the firm's competitors.
- The unique selling point (USP) of the company's product or service.
- Projected sales, market share and growth estimates.

Marketing plan

- A description of the target market.
- Details about the marketing mix:
  — the product and its packaging
  — the pricing strategy
  — the promotional methods to be used.
  — how it will be distributed (Place).

Staffing and operations

- Current and planned staffing levels and skills required.
- How the product or service will be produced.
- What production facilities the firm requires.

Financial analysis

- Total amount of finance required to launch the product or service.
- Amount of finance available.
- Value of the loan required.

Appendices

- Details of market research conducted.
- Cash-flow forecast.
- Projected income statements and statements of financial position.

Example of a business plan

Arán Glas Bread Company Ltd

Description of the business

- Arán Glas Bread Company Ltd, Tinvoher Industrial Estate, Tallaght, Dublin 24.
- Mission Statement: 'To serve the people of Dublin with the best organic, vegan, and gluten-free baked goods in the country.'
- Arán Glas was set up in Walkinstown in 2013 by Catherine and Tony Collins and now employs 14 people at its bakery in Tallaght.

Management team

- Managing Director: Catherine Collins, Bachelor of Business Studies: Managing Director of Arán Glas since 2013; 12 years' previous management experience with Bachelor Breads Ltd.
- Marketing Manager: Tony Collins, Degree in Marketing and Sales, 13 years' experience in advertising.
- Arán Glas Ltd is a private limited company. Catherine and Tony Collins are its only shareholders.

Market opportunity

- The market for organic, vegan, and gluten-free baked goods in Dublin is estimated to be worth €76m annually.
- Arán Glas's main competitors are the Briscoe Bakery and the Better Bread Bakery, who together control 90% of the market.
- The Unique Selling Point (USP) of Arán Glas's product is its freshness and superior flavour. Arán Glas is also the only organic bakery in Dublin that is 100% Irish-owned.
- Arán Glas hopes to control 20% of the organic bread market within five years, translating into annual sales of €15m.

Marketing plan

- The target market is affluent, health-conscious and environmentally aware consumers of bread in the greater Dublin area.
- Details about the marketing mix:
  — **Product:** Arán Glas sells organic, vegan, and gluten-free baked goods in its distinctive blue and green packaging.
  — **Price:** Arán Glas's products are priced just below those of competitors.
  — **Promotion:** Arán Glas is promoted on local Dublin radio, on bus shelters and billboards.
  — **Place:** Arán Glas primarily targets health food stores, but is also available in all major supermarket chains.

Staffing and operations

- Arán Glas currently employs 14 people but, as part of its expansion plan, it needs to hire four new bakers and eight new drivers over the next 18 months.
- All its breads are produced at the company's bakery in the Tinvoher Industrial Estate in Tallaght.
- In order to expand its operations, Arán Glas needs four new ovens and eight new delivery vans.

Financial analysis

- Arán Glas requires a total capital employed of €560,000.
- At present, €230,000 is invested in owners' capital and there is an additional €120,000 long-term loan.
- Therefore, Arán Glas needs to borrow an additional €210,000 in order to expand so that it can achieve its goal of 20% market share.

Appendices

- Appendix 1: Details of market research conducted.
- Appendix 2: Cash-flow forecast.
- Appendix 3: Projected income statements and statements of financial position.

Question 11, Junior Cycle Examination 2019
State **two** reasons why a business should prepare a business plan.

Answer

- A business plan sets out the overall goals of a business and its reason for existing. This helps the business to focus its energy on achieving its goals.
- A business plan is a vital document for convincing banks and investors to put their money into the business.

Main Learning Outcome

2.10 Students should be able to complete and interpret key business documents that an organisation uses to manage its transactions for accountability purposes.

> **aims** By the end of this chapter you should:
> - understand the importance of keeping a record of every business transaction
> - know the purpose and layout of each of the main business documents
> - be familiar with the procedure for processing each of the business documents.

Keeping a record of business transactions

- There are two sides to every transaction. You give something (usually money) and you receive something else (usually goods) in return.
- When running a business, a record must be kept of every transaction – every purchase, every sale, every delivery, every return, every payment.
- Until relatively recently, this was done on paper, but today it can largely be done electronically with the help of specialist software, which reduces stationery, filing and postage costs, while also being kind to the environment.

Records are kept for several reasons

- There are so many buyers and sellers and products and services that it would be impossible to run a business any other way.
- Firms are required by law to submit returns to the Revenue Commissioners.
- Disputes may arise between buyers and sellers, and they are far more likely to be resolved quickly and amicably if there are accurate records.

- As with a student attending school or people playing sports, it is not enough to do something; it is also vital to measure how well you have done it. We measure learning by means of exam results; we measure performance in sport by counting goals, points, tries, etc. Similarly, managers have to be able to reconstruct a firm's transactions so that they can calculate the profit earned and establish the current value of their business (see Chapters 25 and 26).

- Business transactions are recorded by means of business documents. It is vital at every stage for both buyers and sellers to check all documents for accuracy, to check all calculations, to reply promptly, and to file all documents carefully.
- The typical documents that pass between buyers and sellers are as follows:

Buyer sends		Seller sends
1. Enquiry	➡	
	⬅	2. Quotation
3. Order	➡	
	⬅	4. Delivery Docket
	⬅	5. Invoice
	⬅	6. Credit Note
	⬅	7. Debit Note
	⬅	8. Statement of Account
9. Payment	➡	
	⬅	10. Receipt

Selling on credit

- When selling to the public, businesses usually only sell for cash – sell now, get paid now. When selling to other businesses however, they frequently sell **on credit** – sell now, get paid later (see Chapter 24).
- Before selling on credit, a business should first investigate the **creditworthiness** of the potential customer, i.e. the likelihood that they will be able to pay for the goods when it is time to do so.
- This is in order to minimise **bad debts** (see Chapter 26), which occur when a customer is unable to pay you.
- There are several ways of checking the creditworthiness of a customer:
  — Ask for a **trade reference**, a letter from other firms who have sold to them on credit and are satisfied with their history of paying their bills.
  — Request a **bank reference**, a similar letter from a bank stating that the customer has a track record of repaying their loans.
  — Examine the **customer's accounts**, information about which can often be found online or purchased for a fee.
  — Check **Stubbs Gazette** to see if they have ever been declared bankrupt.
  — Request a copy of their credit report from a **credit rating agency**, such as the Irish Credit Bureau, which will give details of their record of repaying loans.

The business documents

1. Enquiry (buyer to seller)

- The first step in a business transaction involves the potential customer making an enquiry either by letter, telephone, email or by browsing the websites of potential suppliers.
- Just as individuals and households shop around, it is wise for businesses to do likewise. This is called **effective purchasing.**

Example

ENQUIRY

Foxborough Ltd, Parteen, Co. Clare

061-04081982   admin@foxborough.ie   VAT Reg. No. 412116978 G

Date: 11/11/2019

Mr Ryan Cooper
Sales Manager
Wondemall Ltd
Maynooth
Co. Kildare
AY7 5F42

RE: Request for Price Quotation

Dear Mr Cooper,

Please send me a quotation for the supply of the following:
- 50 × red Lisaf picture frames
- 60 × white Pila mirrors
- 30 × Ebun coaster sets
- 70 × Malbork placemat sets

Yours sincerely,
Sheila Mellows,
Purchasing Manager

---

2. Quotation (seller to buyer)

- In reply – and not before checking that the goods enquired about are actually in stock – the seller should promptly send a quotation and a catalogue of their product range.
- A **quotation** normally includes:
  - The model/product number and unit price of the items the potential customer enquired about.
  - The **terms of sale**, i.e. the rate of VAT to be charged, any discount available, the cost of delivery, etc.

Example

QUOTATION
Wondemall Ltd, Maynooth, Co. Kildare
01-21101975   sales@Wondemall.ie   VAT Reg. No. 274330868 S

Quotation No. 31
Date: 14/11/2019

Ms Sheila Mellows
Purchasing Manager
Foxborough Ltd
Parteen
Co. Clare
HY9 9E41

Dear Ms Mellows,

Thank you for your enquiry of November 11th last. Please see below the quotation you requested.

Description	Product No.	Unit Price €
Lisaf picture frame, red	BP18386	13
Pila mirror, white	RJP12880	26
Ebun coaster set	SJ191989	11
Malbork placemat set	MB30379	9

Yours sincerely,
Ryan Cooper,
Sales Manager

Terms of Sale:
VAT 23%, trade discount 10% for 7 days, carriage paid.
E&OE

Explanation

- The **trade discount** is the discount the seller is prepared to offer the potential customer if they pay for the goods within seven days of ordering them. This is to encourage prompt payment.
- **Carriage paid** means that in this case, Wondemall will pay the cost of delivery.
- **E&OE** (Errors and Omissions Excepted) means that the sender of the document will not be bound by any errors contained in it, e.g. if they mistakenly charged a lower price than intended.

3. Order (buyer to seller)

- The potential customer must then decide which, if any, of the quotations they are prepared to choose from.
- Once they have done so, they send an order to the supplier of their choice.
- This will not necessarily be the one that provided the cheapest quote, since price – although important – is not the only factor involved in making a decision. Quality, aftersales service, delivery options and terms of sale will also be taken into account.

Example

ORDER

Foxborough Ltd, Parteen, Co. Clare

061-04081982   admin@foxborough.ie   VAT Reg. No. 412116978 G

Order No. 127
Date: 16/11/2019
Your Quotation No.: 31

Mr Ryan Cooper
Sales Manager
Wondemall Ltd
Maynooth
Co. Kildare
AY7 5F42

Dear Mr Cooper,

Thank you for your quotation of November 14th last. Please supply the following goods:

Quantity	Description	Product No.	Unit Price €
40	Lisaf picture frame, red	BP18386	13
60	Pila mirror, white	RJP12880	26
30	Ebun coaster set	SJ191989	11
70	Malbork placemat set	MB30379	15

Yours sincerely,
Sheila Mellows,
Purchasing Manager
E&OE

4. Delivery docket (seller to buyer)

- The delivery docket accompanies the goods.
- It does not list the prices, but simply the quantities and descriptions.
- It is signed by the buyer as proof that the goods were delivered.
- The buyer should endeavour to check that the correct goods were delivered and that they were in good condition.
- This is rarely possible in practice, due to the volume of deliveries, the quantities of goods in each one, and the delivery driver's need to rush to their next delivery.
- The buyer is given a copy of the delivery docket for their records.

A common mistake in the documents question is to confuse the buyer and the seller. Check this carefully when composing your answer.

Example

DELIVERY DOCKET
Wondemall Ltd, Maynooth, Co. Kildare

01-21101975   sales@Wondemall.ie   VAT Reg. No. 274330868 S

Delivery Docket No. 164
Date: 24/11/2019
Your Order No.: 127

Ms Sheila Mellows
Purchasing Manager
Foxborough Ltd
Parteen
Co. Clare
HY9 9E41

Quantity	Description	Product No.
50	Lisaf picture frame, red	BP18386
60	Pila mirror, white	RJP12880
30	Ebun coaster set	SJ191989
70	Malbork placemat set	MB30379

Received by: Anthony Stevens, Purchasing Department
E&OE

5. Invoice (seller to buyer)

- Next the seller sends the buyer an invoice. This is a request for payment, i.e. a bill.
- It shows the calculation of the total cost and re-states the terms of sale.
- It usually accompanies the goods along with the delivery docket, but it may be sent separately.

Example

INVOICE
Wondemall Ltd, Maynooth, Co. Kildare
01-21101975   sales@Wondemall.ie   VAT Reg. No. 274330868 S

Invoice No. 148
Date: 25/11/2019
Your Order No.: 127

Ms Sheila Mellows
Purchasing Manager
Foxborough Ltd
Parteen
Co. Clare
HY9 9E41

Quantity	Description	Product No.	Unit Price €	Total €
50	Lisaf picture frame, red	BP18386	13	650.00
60	Pila mirror, white	RJP12880	26	1,560.00
30	Ebun coaster set	SJ191989	11	330.00
70	Malbork placemat set	MB30379	9	630.00
		Total (excluding VAT)		3,170.00
		Trade discount (10%)		317.00
		Subtotal		2,853.00
		VAT (23%)		656.19
		Total (including VAT)		**3,509.19**

Terms: Carriage paid, 10% trade discount for 7 days.
E&OE

6. Credit note (seller to buyer)

A credit note reverses or partially reverses an invoice by reducing the amount owed. This may need to happen for any of the following reasons:

- The goods supplied were faulty, in which case, it would be wise to check if other customers were also sent faulty produce.
- The buyer was accidentally sent goods they did not order at all.
- The buyer was supplied with too many of an item or items.
- The buyer was charged too much for the goods.
- The goods did not arrive by the agreed time.
- The buyer was supplied with goods, but not the ones they ordered.

Example

- Compare the delivery docket and invoice sent by Wondemall Ltd with the order submitted by Foxborough Ltd. You can see that a mistake has been made: Foxborough Ltd ordered only 40 Lisaf picture frames, not the 50 that were supplied and invoiced.
- When Sheila Mellows brings this to Ryan Cooper's attention, he issues a credit note and the 10 unordered picture frames are returned to Wondemall Ltd.

CREDIT NOTE
Wondemall Ltd, Maynooth, Co. Kildare
01-21101975   sales@Wondemall.ie   VAT Reg. No. 274330868 S

Credit Note No. 48
Date: 27/11/2019
Your Order No.: 127

Ms Sheila Mellows
Purchasing Manager
Foxborough Ltd
Parteen
Co. Clare
HY9 9E41

Quantity	Description	Product No.	Unit Price €	Total €
10	Lisaf picture frame, red	BP18386	13	130.00
Comment: 10 too many Lisaf picture frames supplied		Total (excluding VAT)		130.00
		Trade discount (10%)		13.00
		Subtotal		117.00
		VAT (23%)		26.91
		Total (including VAT)		**143.91**

E&OE

7. Debit note (seller to buyer)

A debit note has the opposite effect of a credit note and can be issued in the event that the buyer was undercharged on the original invoice.

top tip

Rather than send a debit note, many firms prefer to send a credit note to cancel the original order and then a fresh invoice for the correct amount.

Example

- While reviewing the invoice sent to Foxborough Ltd, Ryan Cooper notices that Foxborough Ltd was incorrectly charged €9 for the Malbork placemat sets instead of the quoted price of €15.
- Wondemall Ltd therefore sends Foxborough Ltd a debit note for the shortfall of €6 per item.

DEBIT NOTE
Wondemall Ltd, Maynooth, Co. Kildare
01-21101975   sales@Wondemall.ie   VAT Reg. No. 274330868 S

Debit Note No. 4
Date: 29/11/2019
Your Order No.: 127

Ms Sheila Mellows
Purchasing Manager
Foxborough Ltd
Parteen
Co. Clare
HY9 9E41

Quantity	Description	Product No.	Unit Price €	Total €
70	Malbork placemat set	MB30379	6	420.00
		Total (excluding VAT)		420.00
		Trade discount (10%)		42.00
		Subtotal		378.00
		VAT (23%)		86.94
		Total (including VAT)		**464.94**

E&OE

8. Statement of account (seller to buyer)

This document is sent at the end of the month, listing all the transactions during the month and the amount still outstanding.

- Transactions that increase the amount owed, such as invoices or debit notes, are listed in the debit column.
- Transactions that decrease the amount owed, such as credit notes or payments received, are listed in the credit column.
- The statement of account restates the discounts on offer for early payment.

Example

STATEMENT OF ACCOUNT
Wondemall Ltd, Maynooth, Co. Kildare

01-21101975   sales@Wondemall.ie   VAT Reg. No. 274330868 S

Statement No. 352
Date: 30/11/2019
Your Order No.: 127

Accounts Department
Foxborough Ltd
Parteen
Co. Clare
HY9 9E41

Date	Details	Debit	Credit	Balance
25/11/19	Invoice No. 148	3,509.19		3,509.19
27/11/19	Credit Note No. 48		143.91	3,365.28
29/11/19	Debit Note No. 4	464.94		**3,830.22**

Terms: 10% trade discount for 7 days.
E&OE

9. Payment (buyer to seller)

- Payment can be made using a variety of methods including debit card, credit card or credit transfer.
- Many suppliers offer the facility to pay through their website.

Example

Foxborough Ltd pays Wondemall Ltd by debit card on December 2nd, 2019.

10. Receipt (seller to buyer)

Once payment has been received, a receipt is sent to the buyer as proof of purchase.

Example

RECEIPT
Wondemall Ltd, Maynooth, Co. Kildare
01-21101975   sales@Wondemall.ie   VAT Reg. No. 274330868 S

Receipt No. 604
Date: 3/12/2019
Your Order No.: 127

Received with thanks from: Foxborough Ltd, Parteen, Co. Clare

Three thousand, eight hundred and thirty-euro and twenty-two cent only	€3,830.22

Signed:
Tina Mellows, Accounts Dept.

Question 5, Junior Cycle Examination 2019
Using the information given on the invoice extract below, complete the blank boxes.

	€
Total (excluding VAT)	25,000
Trade discount (12%)	3,000
Subtotal	22,000
VAT (23%)	5,060
Total (including VAT)	27,060

Question 4, Junior Cycle Sample Paper (SEC)
Using the information given on the invoice extract below complete the three blank spaces.

	€
Total (excluding VAT)	27,000
Trade discount (12%)	2,700
Subtotal	24,300
VAT (23%)	5,589
Total (including VAT)	29,889

24 Cash Flow and Business Finance

> **Main Learning Outcome**

2.11 Students should be able to assess the importance of planning an organisation's cash flow, propose suitable sources of finance to manage expenditure and prepare a budget.

> By the end of this chapter you should:
> * understand why a business prepares a cash-flow statement
> * be able to prepare a cash-flow statement for a business
> * be able to describe the various sources of finance available to a business.

Cash-flow statement

Similar to a household budget (see Chapter 12), a cash-flow statement (or cash budget or cash-flow forecast) is an estimate of the receipts and payments of a business for a set period of time in the future.

Why a business should prepare a cash-flow statement

* So the business knows how much money will be flowing into and out of the business and when.
* To identify months in which it will have a deficit and will need to put finance in place, e.g. a bank overdraft.
* To identify months in which it will have a surplus so that it can put this money to good use, e.g. invest it in machinery, pay off debt, etc.
* To make sure there is sufficient cash to implement its plans.
* A cash-flow forecast would also be required as part of a loan or a grant application.
* Not-for-profit organisations also need to prepare cash-flow statements in order to manage their finances effectively.

Example 1: Dromina Ltd

Cash-flow Statement for Dromina Ltd					
	Sept.	Oct.	Nov.	Dec.	Total Sept.-Dec.
Receipts	€	€	€	€	€
Sales	56,000	51,000	57,000	46,000	210,000
Government grant	30,000				30,000
Loan		50,000			50,000
Total receipts	86,000	101,000	57,000	46,000	290,000
Payments					
Purchases	30,000	28,000	31,000	24,000	113,000
Electricity	600		750		1,350
Wages	2,500	2,700	2,500	2,900	10,600
Purchase of equipment			60,000		60,000
Telephone and internet	400	400	400	400	1,600
Rent	3,000	3,000	3,000	3,000	12,000
Total payments	36,500	34,100	97,650	30,300	198,550
Net cash	49,500	66,900	(40,650)	15,700	91,450
Opening cash	15,500	65,000	131,900	91,250	15,500
Closing cash	65,000	131,900	91,250	106,950	106,950

Explanation

- Dromina Ltd will start September with opening cash of €15,500. As with a household budget, this will also be the opening cash in the total column.
- Correspondingly, the closing cash in the total column will be the closing cash for December.
- As can be seen, payments in a cash-flow statement are not divided into fixed, irregular and discretionary as in a household budget. Nevertheless, costs can still be broken down into:
  - **Fixed costs** remain the same each month, e.g. rent, loan repayments.
  - **Variable costs** vary from month to month, e.g. raw materials, electricity, wages, light and heat, etc.

Example 2: Farthingville Ltd

From the following information, prepare a cash-flow statement for Farthingville Ltd for the months January to April. The company has opening cash of €13,000.

Receipts

- Sales: January €13,000, February €11,000, March €14,000, April €17,000.
- The company will receive a grant from the Department of Enterprise of €16,000 in February.

Payments

- Raw materials: January €7,000; February €8,000; March €10,000; April €12,000.
- Wages will be €1,500 per month.
- Electricity bills are estimated to be €320 in February and €240 in April.
- Buildings insurance of €800 is due in March.
- Farthingville Ltd will purchase machinery in February at a cost of €13,000.
- Advertising costs will be €295 per month.

Cash-flow Statement for Farthingville Ltd					
	Jan.	Feb.	Mar.	Apr.	Total Jan.–Apr.
Receipts	€	€	€	€	€
Sales	13,000	11,000	14,000	17,000	55,000
Grant		16,000			16,000
Total receipts	13,000	27,000	14,000	17,000	71,000
Payments					
Raw materials	7,000	8,000	10,000	12,000	37,000
Wages	1,500	1,500	1,500	1,500	6,000
Electricity		320		240	560
Buildings insurance			800		800
Purchase of equipment		13,000			13,000
Advertising	295	295	295	295	1180
Total payments	8,795	23,115	12,595	14,035	58,540
Net cash	4,205	3,885	1,405	2,965	12,460
Opening cash	13,000	17,205	21,090	22,495	13,000
Closing cash	17,205	21,090	22,495	25,460	25,460

Explanation

- As we can see, Farthingville Ltd expects to have a net cash surplus every month.
- However, they are highly dependent on the grant of €16,000. Without it, their final net cash figure would be in deficit.

Dealing with persistent deficits

If a company repeatedly finds itself spending more than it is taking in, there are several steps it can take:

Increase sales revenue

- Drop its prices to attract more customers, e.g. reduced pricing to undercut competitors.
- Offer discounts to encourage prompt payment, e.g. 10% off if you pay within seven days.
- Raise the price if existing customers are willing to pay more, e.g. a designer brand.
- Find new market segments for the product, e.g. older people.
- Find new export markets for the product, e.g. China.

Cut costs

- Lay off non-essential workers.
- Move to a cheaper premises, e.g. away from the city centre.
- Shop around for cheaper materials and suppliers, e.g. from southeast Asia.
- Reduce waste, e.g. electricity.
- Negotiate a wage cut with your staff.

> **top tip**
>
> Attempting to lay off workers or introduce cuts in wages that can lead to more industrial relations problems (see Chapter 17), if not handled skilfully.

Sources of business finance

In Chapter 5, we examined ways in which households finance themselves. In this chapter, we do the same but from a business perspective. There will be many similarities but also some differences between the two chapters.

Similarities between household and business finance

- They need to earn enough to cover their needs.
- Both need to make the best use of their money.
- They plan using a cash-flow forecast or a budget.
- Both regularly review their finances as circumstances change.
- They both borrow money if necessary, mindful of the need to be able to repay it.

Differences between household and business finance

- Households are motivated to improve their standard of living, while businesses are motivated by profit.
- Businesses usually have more money flowing through them.
- Households need to spend less time on their finances.
- Businesses are required to keep more detailed records.
- Most households need to borrow less money than businesses do.
- Businesses must provide more detail when opening accounts or applying for loans.

Short term (less than one year)

Bank overdraft

You have permission from your bank to withdraw more money from your account than is in it, e.g. to pay short-term expenses such as wages, electricity bills, etc.

- It is a flexible form of finance.
- No collateral/security is needed.
- The size of the overdraft is usually relatively small.
- Interest is only charged on the amount overdrawn, even if you are allowed to overdraw more.
- It must be cleared for at least thirty days in the year.
- Your bank can recall the overdraft at any time.
- Making regular use of an overdraft is a sign that your finances are not under control.

Credit card

Provides a convenient cashless method of paying for short-term business expenses, e.g. petrol.

- The card is presented at the time of purchase, and a receipt is given.
- The holder receives a statement at the end of the month and has 25 days to pay part or all of the balance.
- A high rate of interest is charged on the amount outstanding.

Trade credit

When businesses buy goods now and pay for them later.

- There is no interest to be paid and no need for security.
- Overuse of this source of finance is called 'leaning on the trade' and a firm's credit rating may suffer as a result.
- Discounts available for fast payment may be lost, e.g. 10% within seven days.
- **Accrued expenses** (or **expenses due**) involves paying your expenses in arrears, e.g. phone and electricity bills, VAT returns.

top tip

Until you pay a bill, you are essentially 'borrowing' the money you owe for free, since no interest is applied.

Medium term (up to five years)

Medium-term loan

- A loan given to a business for up to five years. Its features include:
  - — an agreed period of time
  - — an agreed amount
  - — repayment by instalments agreed in advance.
- The interest rate can vary over the life of the loan.
- A term loan should be used to pay for assets that last one to five years, such as delivery vans or computers.

Hire purchase (HP)

A form of credit that allows you the immediate use of an item while paying for it over an agreed period of time in instalments.

- Payment consists of an initial deposit and an agreed number of instalments.
- Ownership is only transferred after the last instalment.
- It carries a high rate of interest.
- It should be used for medium-term assets such as computers or office furniture.

Leasing

This is another name for renting an asset.

- The customer never owns the item.
- A deposit is paid, followed by a number of instalments, usually monthly.
- At the end of the agreement, the item is returned and the deposit is returned to the customer on condition that the item is in good condition.
- No security is required, and no capital is tied up in the asset.
- Many businesses lease premises, vans, machinery, etc.

Long term (longer than five years)

Ordinary share capital

This is also called **equity capital/finance.** It is money invested in a business by its owners.

- The owners receive shares in the business and are called **shareholders**.
- Shareholders invest in the hope of earning a share of the profit called a **dividend**, and that the value of their shares will rise over time if the company is successful.
- Payment of dividends can vary according to the profit made or if the company decides to use the profits for expansion.
- Equity capital is not a loan. It does not have to be repaid unless the company is wound up (disbanded).
- If applying for a loan from a bank, equity finance is a demonstration of the owner's commitment to the business.

- Each ordinary share gives its owner one vote at the Annual General Meetings (AGMs) of the company.
- If the company is successful, it becomes easier to sell more shares and thus raise more finance.

Retained earnings

Also called **reserves**, these are profits reinvested or 'ploughed back' into the business instead of being paid as dividends.

> *exam focus*
>
> If shareholders are patient enough to allow their profits to be reinvested rather than paid as dividends, their shares can rise significantly over time.

- No interest has to be paid, making it a free form of long-term finance.
- Some shareholders may be unhappy not to receive dividends.

Long-term loan

These are loans with a maturity of longer than five years that are used by businesses to buy property and other long-term assets.

- If the rate of interest is fixed, the loan is called a **debenture**.
- When a business is applying for a loan, the bank will seek to examine its accounts.
- By monitoring the cash flow, the ability of the business to repay the loan can be assessed.
- The deeds to the property are used as collateral/security.
- Failure to repay means that the asset may be repossessed.

Sale and leaseback

This involves selling a fixed asset, such as a premises, on condition that you can rent it back from the new owner over the long term.

- It releases cash tied up in an asset that can be invested in the business instead.
- The company can continue to use the asset as before, for as long as the agreement with the new owner is in place.
- However, rent must now be paid, and this can increase after the agreement ends.
- If the asset rises in value after it is sold, the company misses out since they don't own it anymore.

Grants

A form of finance provided either by Irish government or EU agencies for a variety of purposes, e.g. training of workers.

- They are often subject to conditions such as performance targets.
- If these conditions and targets are not met, the grant may have to be repaid.

Matching sources with uses

As with household finance, sources of business finance need to match their use:

- day-to-day expenditure should be financed by short-term methods
- medium-term finance is used for items that last up to five years
- long-term finance is best for longer-term spending.

Example 3

- A delivery van is a medium-term asset, usually lasting one to five years.
- If you buy a van using short-term finance, you will be repaying the loan before you have earned the money to do so.
- If you buy it using a long-term method, you pay more interest than you need to because the longer you borrow for, the more it costs.
- The best form of finance for a van would be hire purchase or a term loan, since the payments match the lifetime of the asset.

Matching Sources With Uses					
Short Term		Medium Term		Long Term	
Sources	Uses	Sources	Uses	Sources	Uses
Bank overdraft	Purchase of stock for resale	Term loan	Machinery	Share capital	Premises
Credit card		Hire purchase	Equipment	Retained earnings	Buildings
Trade credit	Utility bills	Leasing	Computers		Land
Accrued expenses	Wages		Office furniture	Long term loan	Buying other companies
	Rent		Fixtures and fittings	Sale and leaseback	
			Vehicles	Grant	

Question 13, NCCA Sample Questions

Maria decided to set up her own business called 'Knits & Names'. The business sells personalised hats, scarves, gloves, babygros and blankets for children.

(a) Explain the importance of managing the cash flow of a business.

Answer

It is important to properly manage the cash flow of a business to ensure that at all times, there is sufficient money flowing into the business to cover the money that is flowing out, and to help to anticipate periods when extra sources of finance, such as a loan, may need to be put in place.

With reference to the Table (below), complete the cash budget (cash-flow forecast) for Maria.

Cash Budget (Cash-Flow Forecast)					
	Sept.	Oct.	Nov.	Dec.	Total
Receipts					
Cash sales	4,025	2,700	4,500	5,750	16,975
Capital		2,000			2,000
Grant	1,000	1,000	1,000	1,000	4,000
Total Receipts	5,025	5,700	5,500	6,750	22,975
Payments					
Rent of stall	250	250	250	250	1,000
New equipment		1,750			1,750
Purchases	1,100	3,500	2,800	1,200	8,600
Wages and overheads	1,000	1,000	1,000	1,500	4,500
Administration costs	800	500	500	500	2,300
Total Payments	3,150	7,000	4,550	3,450	18,150
Net Cash Flow	1,875	(1,300)	950	3,300	4,825
Opening Cash	2,000	3,875	2,575	3,525	2,000
Closing Cash	3,875	2,575	3,525	6,825	6,825

(b) Based on Maria's cash budget (cash-flow forecast)
- Explain one aspect in which the cash flow of her business is doing well
- Recommend one aspect in which the cash flow of her business could be improved.

Answer

Maria's cash flow is doing well in the following aspect:

Maria has generated a net cash over the four months of €4,825, and has a closing cash of €6,825. Apart from October, her sales also grew month-on-month.

Maria's cash flow could improve in the following aspect:

Maria had a deficit in the month of October, largely due to the purchase of new equipment. She could have used a term loan or hire purchase to spread the payment for the equipment over a longer period of time.

25 Analysed Cash Book, Ledgers and Trial Balance

 Main Learning Outcome

2.12 Students should be able to prepare a cash account to monitor income received and payments made by an organisation, evaluate its financial position and recommend a course of action; post figures to relevant ledgers and extract a trial balance.

 By the end of this chapter you should:

- understand the logic behind double-entry bookkeeping.
- be able to enter a series of transactions in the ledgers and analysed cash book of a business, balance the accounts and extract a trial balance.

In Chapter 13, we learned how to compile an analysed cash book for a household. In this chapter, we will do the same for a business. More importantly, we will also learn how to record transactions using a system that is at least a thousand years old, called double-entry bookkeeping.

Double-entry bookkeeping

We know from Chapter 23 that there are two sides to every transaction:

- We *receive* something – usually goods.
- We *give* something – usually money – in return.

Therefore, in double-entry bookkeeping we record every transaction in two places:

- first, on the debit side of the 'receiving' account
- then, on the credit side of the 'giving' account.

 top tip

Double-entry does not mean double-counting. The same money is being entered twice, but on opposite sides.

Example 1: R&J Sportswear Ltd

- On February 1st, R&J Sportswear Ltd purchased €1,000 worth of jerseys for resale.
- R&J spent €1,000 (money out), and much like in Chapter 13, this will appear on the credit side of its Bank account.
- However, since R&J now has €1,000 worth of jerseys to sell, €1,000 will also go on the debit side of its Purchases account.

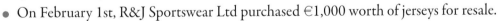

DR			Bank A/C		CR
			1/2/2019	Purchases	1,000
DR			Purchases A/C		CR
1/2/2019	Bank	1,000			

- R&J then sold the jerseys for €2,000.
- Since we know that this goes on the debit side of the Bank account (money in), it must therefore go on the credit side of some other account – the Sales account.

DR		Bank A/C				CR
5/2/2019	Sales	2,000				
DR		**Sales A/C**				**CR**
			5/2/2019	Bank		2,000

- However, we also need to be able to record purchases and sales that include VAT. This is a little more complicated.
- If the jerseys R&J purchased carried VAT at a rate of 20%, then R&J did not just pay €1,000 for them, they paid €1,200. Therefore, €1,200 goes on the credit side of the Bank account (money out).
- This means that €1,200 must go on the credit somewhere else. Where?
- The answer is that €1,000 still goes on the debit side of the purchases account, because €1,000 is the value of what was purchased. The VAT of €200 goes on the debit side of the VAT account, to make a total of €1,200 on the debit.

DR		Bank A/C				CR
			1/2/2019	Purchases		1,200
DR		**Purchases A/C**				**CR**
1/2/2019	Bank	1,000				
DR		**VAT A/C**				**CR**
1/2/2019	Bank	200				

- Similarly, if VAT of 20% is also applied to the sales of €2,000, then we must debit the Bank account with €2,400 (money in), credit the Sales account with the value of what was actually sold (€2,000) and credit the VAT account with €400, to make a total of €2,400 on the credit.

DR		Bank A/C				CR
5/2/2019	Sales	2,400				
DR		**Sales A/C**				**CR**
			5/2/2019	Bank		2,000
DR		**VAT A/C**				**CR**
			5/2/2019	Bank		400

- We can also use double-entry bookkeeping to record day-to-day expenses such as the payment of wages.
- If R&J pays its staff €500, this will go on the credit side of the Bank account (money out), and also on the debit side of the Wages account.

DR				Bank A/C			CR
				8/2/2019	Purchases		500
DR			Wages A/C				**CR**
8/2/2019	Bank		500				

- Similarly, if it pays an electricity bill of €200, it will go on the credit side of the Bank account (money out) and on the debit side of the Electricity account.

DR				Bank A/C			CR
				13/2/2019	Purchases		200
DR			Electricity A/C				**CR**
13/2/2019	Bank		200				

- In fact, regardless of the expense, it is recorded by crediting the Bank account and debiting the expense account.
- Sometimes, the owners of a business wish to invest more money. In exchange, they are given more shares in the business.
- Therefore, we debit the Bank account (money in) with €5,000, and we credit the Share Capital account with €5,000.

DR				Bank A/C			CR
17/2/2019	Share Capital		5,000				
DR			Share Capital A/C				**CR**
				17/2/2019	Bank		5,000

In summary

- As you can see, at all times, for every euro entered on the debit side, we must find a place on the credit side to enter it also.
- When money goes into our Bank account, we debit it and we credit the account(s) on the other side of the same transaction with the same amount.
- When money leaves our Bank account, we credit it and we debit the account(s) on the other side of the same transaction with the same amount.

Debit the receiving account.
Credit the giving account.

- We then balance each of the accounts, including the analysed cash book (see the following page).

Analysed cash book

Analysed Cash Book of R&J Sportswear Ltd

DR | | | | | | CR | | | | | |

Date	Details	Total	Sales	VAT	Share Capital	Date	Details	Total	Purchases	VAT	Wages	Electricity
2019		€	€	€	€	2019		€	€	€	€	€
Feb 5th	Sales	2,400	2,000	400		Feb 1	Purchases	1,200	1,000	200		
Feb 17th	Share capital	5,000			5,000	Feb 8	Wages	500			500	
						Feb 13	Electricity	200				200
						Feb 28	Balance c/d	5,500				
		7,400	2,000	400	5,000			7,400	1,000	200	500	200
Mar 1st	Balance b/d	5,500										

Balance the ledger account

Remember from Chapter 13 that an analysed cash book is the same as a Bank account except that the entries are broken down by category: sales, VAT, share capital, etc.

DR		Purchases A/C				CR
1/2/2019	Bank	1,000	28/2/2019	Balance c/d		1,000
		1,000				1,000
1/3/2019	Balance b/d	1,000				

DR		Sales A/C				CR
28/2/2019	Balance c/d	2,000	5/2/2019	Bank		2,000
		2,000				2,000
			1/3/2019	Balance b/d		2,000

DR		VAT A/C				CR
1/2/2019	Bank	200	5/2/2019	Bank		400
28/2/2019	Balance c/d	200				
		400				400
			1/3/2019	Balance b/d		200

- We can use the same VAT account for purchases and for sales.

DR		Wages A/C				CR
8/2/2019	Bank	500	28/2/2019	Balance c/d		500
		500				500
1/3/2019	Balance b/d	500				

DR		Electricity A/C				CR
13/2/2019	Bank	200	28/2/2019	Balance c/d		200
		200				200
1/3/2019	Balance b/d	200				

DR		Share Capital A/C				CR
28/2/2019	Balance c/d	5,000	17/2/2019	Bank		5,000
		5,000				5,000
			1/3/2019	Balance b/d		5,000

Trial balance

Finally, we compare the total of the debit balances b/d with the total of the credit balances b/d in a trial balance:

Trial balance of R&J Sportswear Ltd 28 February 2019	Dr	Cr
Bank (analysed cash book)	5,500	
Purchases	1,000	
Sales		2,000
VAT		200
Wages	500	
Electricity	200	
Share capital		5,000
	7,200	7,200

- The purpose of the trial balance is to check that we have correctly entered everything on both sides. If you debit an account, but neglect to credit another account, the trial balance will not balance.
- In Chapter 26, we will then use the trial balance to draw up the final accounts of the business.

Other possible transactions

top tip

Transactions like these used to be manually entered on paper in a book called a ledger. Today, thanks to specialist accounting software, much of the process is automatic, but it is still important to understand how double-entry works.

To purchase an asset

- For example, a company bought a van for €20,000.
- We credit the bank account (money out) and debit the van account with €20,000.

DR			Bank A/C			CR
			1/6/2019	Van		20,000
DR			Van A/C			CR
1/6/2019	Bank	20,000				

To sell an asset

- For example, a company sold equipment for €10,000.
- We debit the bank account (money in) and credit the equipment account with €20,000.

DR			Bank A/C			CR
1/6/2019	Van	10,000				
DR			Equipment A/C			CR
			1/6/2019	Bank		10,000

Example 2: Question 17, Junior Cycle Sample Paper (SEC)

Post all totals and balances from the analysed cash book of Waves restaurant to the relevant ledger accounts below.

DR   Analysed Cash Book of Waves restaurant   **CR**

Date	Details	Total	Sales	VAT	Capital	Date	Details	Total	Purchases	VAT	Light and Heat	Wages
		€	€	€	€			€	€	€	€	€
July						July						
1	Capital	15,000			15,000	4	Purchases	2,943	2,700	243		
7	Sales	3,052	2,800	252		15	Light and Heat	2,620			2,620	
19	Sales	2,180	2,000	180		21	Wages	1,750				1,750
						30	Purchases	1,962	1,800	162		
						31	Balance c/d	10,957				
		20,232	4,800	432	15,000			20,232	4,500	405	2,620	1,750
Aug												
1	Balance b/d	10,957										

Answer

DR	Light and Heat A/C				CR
15/07/18	Bank	2,620	31/7/18	Balance c/d	2,620
		2,620			2,620
1/8/18	Balance b/d	2,620			

DR	Wages A/C				CR
15/7/18	Bank	1,750	31/7/18	Balance c/d	1,750
		1,750			1,750
1/8/18	Balance b/d	1,750			

DR	Capital A/C				CR
31/7/18	Balance c/d	15,000	1/7/18	Bank	15,000
		15,000			15,000
			1/8/18	Balance b/d	15,000

DR	Sales A/C				CR
31/7/18	Balance c/d	4,800	7/7/18	Bank	2,800
			19/7/18	Bank	2,000
		4,800			4,800
			1/8/18	Balance b/d	4,800

DR	VAT A/C				CR
4/7/18	Bank	243	7/7/18	Bank	252
30/7/18	Bank	162	19/7/18	Bank	180
31/7/18	Balance c/d	27			
		432			432
			1/8/18	Balance b/d	27

DR	Purchases A/C				CR
4/7/18	Bank	2,700	31/7/18	Balance c/d	4,500
30/7/18	Bank	1,800			
		4,500			4,500
1/8/18	Balance b/d	4,500			

Using the previous ledger balances complete the trial balance below for
Waves restaurant.

Trial balance of Waves restaurant 31 July 2018		
	Dr	Cr
Bank	10,957	
Light and heat	2,620	
Wages	1,750	
Capital		15,000
Sales		4,800
VAT		27
Purchases	4,500	
	19,827	19,827

Question 17 (a), Junior Cycle Examination 2019

Food2Go Ltd is a fast food retailer which operates in 10 locations in Dublin.

Complete the Analysed Cash Book of Food2Go Ltd for the month of May from the information provided below and balance the account.

Post all totals and balances from the analysed cash book of Food2Go Ltd to the relevant ledger accounts below.

Date	Transaction	Amount
		€
01/04/2019	Shareholders invest in company	21,500
04/05/2019	Sold goods	12,000 + VAT @ 13.5%
06/05/2019	Paid wages	3,000
15/05/2019	Purchased goods for resale	5,600 + VAT @ 13.5%
23/05/2019	Paid electricity	670
27/05/2019	Paid wages	2,850

Answer

Analysed Cash Book of Food2Go Ltd

DR

Date	Details	Total	Sales	VAT	Capital
2019		€	€	€	€
01/04/2019	Share capital	21,500			21,500
04/05/2019	Sales	13,620	12,000	1,620	
		35,120	12,000	1,620	21,500
1/5/2019	Balance b/d	22,244			

CR

Date	Details	Total	Purchases	VAT	Wages	Electricty
2019		€	€	€	€	€
06/05/2019	Wages	3,000			3,000	
15/05/2019	Purchases	6,356	5,600	756		
23/05/2019	Electricity	670				670
27/05/2019	Wages	2,850			2,850	
30/4/2019	Balance c/d	22,244				
		35,120	5,600	756	5,850	670

Answer

DR		Share Capital A/C				CR
30/4/2019	Balance c/d	21,500	01/04/2019	Bank		21,500
		21,500				21,500
			1/5/2019	Balance b/d		21,500

DR		Sales A/C				CR
30/4/2019	Balance c/d	12,000	04/05/2019	Bank		12,000
		12,000				12,000
			1/5/2019	Balance b/d		12,000

DR		VAT A/C				CR
15/05/2019	Bank	756	04/05/2019	Bank		1,620
30/4/2019	Balance c/d	864				
		1,620				1,620
			1/5/2019	Balance b/d		864

DR		Wages A/C				CR
06/05/2019	Bank	3,000	30/4/2019	Balance c/d		5,850
27/05/2019	Bank	2,850				
		5,850				5,850
1/5/2019	Balance c/d	5,850				

DR		Purchases A/C				CR
15/05/2019	Bank	5,600	30/4/2019	Balance c/d		5,600
		5,600				5,600
1/5/2019	Balance b/d	5,600				

DR		Electricity A/C				CR
23/05/2019	Bank	670	30/4/2019	Balance c/d		670
		670				670
1/5/2019	Balance b/d	670				

26 Preparing and Analysing Final Accounts

Main Learning Outcome

2.13 Students should be able to prepare final accounts to assess the financial performance of an organisation at the end of a trading period, analyse and evaluate its financial position and recommend a course of action.

aims By the end of this chapter you should:

- understand the relevance of the various sections of the final accounts of a business
- be able to prepare the final accounts of a business from the trial balance
- know how to use ratios to analyse the performance of a business based on its final accounts.

In preparing the final accounts of a business, we need to prepare two financial documents:

- The **income statement**, which tells us the profit the business made during the year.
- The **statement of financial position** (or **balance sheet**), which tells us how much the business is worth at the end of the year.
- They are compiled from the information in the trial balance (see Chapter 25).

The final accounts are organised as follows:

Final Accounts	
Income Statement	**Statement of Financial Position**
Trading Account	Total Net Assets =
Profit and Loss Account	Fixed Assets + (Current Assets – Current Liabilities)
Profit and Loss Appropriation Account	
	Capital Employed

A good rule of thumb is that everything in the trial balance goes into the final accounts only once, while each item of additional information goes in twice.

Example 1: Maneycon Ltd

From the following information, prepare an income statement for Maneycon Ltd for the year ended 31/12/2019 and a statement of financial position as on that date. Maneycon Ltd has an authorised share capital of 300,000 €1 ordinary shares.

Trial Balance of Maneycon Ltd for the year ended 31/12/2019		
Details	Debit €	Credit €
Sales		130,000
Sales returns	20,000	
Opening stock	10,000	
Purchases	60,000	
Purchases returns		5,000
Import duty	2,000	
Rent receivable		7,000
Wages	12,000	
Electricity	1,000	
Light and heat	1,500	
Bad debts	500	
Rent	6,000	
Reserves (profit and loss balance)		47,000
Premises	500,000	
Equipment	150,000	
Cash	2,000	
Bank	5,000	
Debtors	20,000	
Creditors		17,000
Bank overdraft		4,000
Issued share capital		250,000
30-year loan		350,000
Dividend paid	20,000	
	810,000	810,000

Additional information as at 31 December 2019

- Closing stock: €15,000
- Depreciation of equipment: 10%

Trading account

The purpose of the trading account is to calculate the **gross profit**, the profit the firm made before expenses are deducted.

Step 1

Trading Account of Maneycon Ltd			
	€	€	€
Sales		130,000	
Less sales returns		20,000	110,000
Less cost of sales			
Opening stock		10,000	
Add purchases	60,000		
Less purchases returns	5,000	55,000	
Import duty		2,000	
Cost of goods available for sale		67,000	
Less closing stock		15,000	
Cost of goods sold			52,000
Gross profit			58,000

Explanation

- **Sales (or turnover)** is the value of every item the company sold added together.
- **Sales returns** is the value of all the items sold but later returned, usually because they were faulty. This figure is taken from sales because it is the same as if it was never sold at all. Sales returns are not found in all income statements.
- **Net sales** is sales minus sales returns. In the above example, it is the unlabelled €110,000 figure in the third column. When there are no sales returns, the sales and the net sales are the same, so the figures go straight into the third column.
- **Less cost of sales** is a heading, hence there is no figure next to it. Below it, the cost of the goods sold will be calculated. Some items will be added, others subtracted:
  - **Opening stock** is the cost price of the goods the company had in stock on its shelves and in its warehouses at the beginning of the year. Opening stock always appears in the middle column. Since it was bought with the intention of selling it, it is part of the cost of sales.

— **Purchases for resale** (or **purchases**, for short) is the value of everything the company bought during the year for the purposes of reselling. It is also part of the cost of sales.

— **Purchases returns** is the value of all goods the company bought for resale but later returned, again usually because they were faulty. This figure is subtracted from purchases because it is the same as if it was never bought at all, and therefore is not part of the cost of sales. Purchases returns do not appear in every income statement.

— **Net purchases** is purchases minus purchases returns. In the example above it is the €55,000 figure in the middle column.

— **Possible additions to net purchases.** These are items which may appear in a trading account. They are added to net purchases. While they are not part of the purchase price, the goods could not have been bought without paying them. They are part of the cost of sales. Only import duty appears in this example, but you can get the others in other questions.

　o **Import duty** is a tariff on certain imported goods.

　o **Customs duty** (see Chapter 4) is a tax paid on some imports from outside the EU.

　o **Carriage in** is the cost of transporting purchases from your supplier to you.

　o **Manufacturing wages** are any wages that can be directly linked to the manufacturing process, and therefore to the cost of sales, e.g. the cost of assembling furniture before sale.

— **Closing stock** is the cost price of all the goods the company had in stock on its shelves and in its warehouses at the end of the year. Since it wasn't sold, it is subtracted from the cost of sales.

Closing stock appears in the final accounts twice. Once in the trading account, and again in the current assets.

● The **cost of goods sold** is the same as cost of sales. After the net sales, it should always be the next figure to appear in the third column.

● The cost of goods sold is taken from the net sales to give us the **gross profit**.

Profit and loss account

The purpose of the profit and loss account is to calculate the **net profit**, the profit the firm made after expenses are deducted.

Step 2

Profit and Loss Account of Maneycon Ltd			
Add gains:			
Rent receivable			7,000
			65,000
Less expenses:			
Wages		12,000	
Electricity		1,000	
Light and heat		1,500	
Bad debts		500	
Depreciation of equipment (10%)		15,000	
Rent		6,000	36,000
Net profit			29,000

Explanation

- **Gains** refers to income the company made other than from sales. Gains are added to the gross profit. They will always have the word 'received' or 'receivable' after them. They can include:
  - **Commission receivable**: a payment received from a supplier as a reward for goods sold.
  - **Dividends receivable:** a share of the profits in another firm in which the company owns shares.
  - **Interest receivable**: interest on any money the firm has in its bank account.
  - **Rent receivable**: rent earned from a property the firm owns or is renting but does not currently need for its own use, e.g. unused office space.
- **Expenses** are costs the firm incurs in the day-to-day running of the business in its effort to generate sales. They do not include capital spending, e.g. buying new machinery.
- The total expenses, in this case €36,000, are taken from the net profit plus gains to give us the net profit, in this case €29,000.

exam focus

> Depreciation appears in the final accounts twice. Once in the expenses, and again when it is subtracted from the fixed assets.

Expenses will vary from question to question. They include:

Administration costs	Advertising	Auditor's fees
General expenses	Insurance	Internet
Light and heat	Director's fees	Electricity
Fuel	Office expenses	Packaging
Postage	Rates	Repairs
Rent	Stationary	Sundry expenses
Telephone	Wages and salaries	
Bad debts: when a debtor is unable to pay you.	Carriage out: the cost of transporting your sales from you to your customer.	
Depreciation: a fall in the value of a fixed asset.	Interest on bank overdraft/bank loans	

Profit and loss appropriation account

The profit and loss appropriation account shows how much of the net profit is appropriated (distributed) between the shareholders as dividends, and how much is reinvested in the business as reserves/retained earnings.

Step 3

Profit and Loss Appropriation Account of Maneycon Ltd			
Net profit			9,000
Dividend paid			20,000
Reserves/Retained earnings			9,000
Add opening reserves			47,000
Reserves 31/12/2019			56,000

Explanation

- The **dividend paid** is the amount of the profits that the company has decided to pay out to its shareholders as a dividend. It is deducted from the net profit.

- The remaining profit of €9,000 is **reserves** (also called retained earnings) that will be reinvested/'ploughed back' into the business (see Chapter 24).

exam focus

If you are asked for 'dividend declared', you work it out as a percentage of the Issued Share Capital. It is then entered in two places:

- in the appropriation account, just like dividend paid
- in the current liabilities in the statement of financial position, because it has only been declared rather than paid, so therefore it is still owed.

- The **opening reserves** are retained earnings from the previous year's profits. This figure is the **profit and loss balance** you can see on the credit side of the trial balance.
- The reserves/retained earnings and the opening reserves are added to give an updated reserves figure of €56,000. This will appear in the 'financed by' section of the statement of financial position.

The **statement of financial position** is compiled in order to calculate how much a business is worth. This is done in two ways, both of which must give the same answer:

- by calculating the **total net assets**
- by calculating the **capital employed.**

Total net assets

The total net assets are equal to the fixed assets plus the difference between the current assets and liabilities.

Step 4

Total Net Assets of Maneycon Ltd			
Fixed assets	**Cost** €	**Depreciation** €	**Net Book Value** €
Premises	500,000		500,000
Equipment	150,000	15,000	135,000
	650,000	15,000	635,000
Current assets			
Cash	2,000		
Bank	5,000		
Debtors	20,000		
Closing stock	15,000	42,000	
Current liabilities			
Creditors	17,000		
Bank overdraft	4,000	21,000	
Working capital			21,000
Total net assets			656,000

Explanation

- An **asset** is anything a company owns or is owed. It is worth something.
- **Fixed assets** are assets that you would expect to own for longer than a year. As they age, fixed assets depreciate in value. They will vary from question to question, but can include:

Buildings	Equipment
Premises	Vehicles
Land	Motor vans
Machinery	Fixtures and Fittings

- When the depreciation is subtracted from the cost of the fixed asset, we get the **Net Book Value (NBV).** In the case of Maneycon Ltd, equipment was depreciated by 10% to give a net book value of €135,000. The cost plays no further role in the calculation of total net assets.
- **Current assets** are assets that you would expect to last less than a year or to change within a year. They include:
  - cash (also called 'cash on hand')
  - bank (also called 'cash at bank')
  - **debtors:** customers to whom you have sold on credit and who have not yet paid you. If they are unable to pay you, this becomes a bad debt (see above).
  - closing stock, also found in the trading account
- A **liability** is anything that a company owes.
- **Current liabilities** are what you owe and must pay within a year. They include:
  - **creditors:** suppliers from whom you have bought on credit and whom you have not yet paid. They are the opposite of debtors
  - bank overdraft.
- **Working capital** (also called circulating capital) is equal to current assets minus current liabilities. It should be entered in the third column.
- The **total net assets** is equal to fixed assets plus working capital. This is a measure of how much the business is worth. It must equal the capital employed (see following page).

Financed by

The financed by section of the statement of financial position is where the long-term sources of finance of the business are added together to give the capital employed.

Step 5

Capital Employed of Maneycon Ltd			
Financed by			
Share capital	**Authorised**	**Issued**	
€1 ordinary shares	300,000	250,000	
Reserves 31/12/2019		56,000	
Long-term liabilities			
30-year loan		350,000	
Capital employed			656,000

Explanation

- **Authorised share capital** is the maximum amount of share capital that the company is authorised to issue to its shareholders by its own constitution. By law, it must be listed in the statement of financial position, but it does not form part of the calculations.
- **Ordinary share capital** (see Chapter 24) is money invested in a business by its owners. It is the value of any shares the company has actually sold. It can be less than or equal to, but not greater than, the authorised share capital.
- The **reserves** are taken from the appropriation account and are made up of the opening reserves of €47,000 from previous years and the retained earnings of €9,000 from 2019.
- **Long-term liabilities** are loans with a maturity of longer than five years that are used to finance long-term assets. In this case, Maneycon has a thirty-year loan of €350,000.
- **Capital employed** is the sum of the ordinary share capital, the retained earnings and the long-term loans. It must equal the total net assets.

Example 2: Clooniron Ltd

From the following information, prepare an Income Statement for Clooniron Ltd for the year ended 31/12/2020 and a Statement of Financial Position as on that date. Clooniron Ltd has an authorised share capital of 300,000 €1 ordinary shares.

Trial Balance of Clooniron Ltd for the year ended 31/12/2020		
Details	Debit €	Credit €
Sales		140,000
Sales returns	24,000	
Opening stock	12,000	
Purchases	52,000	
Purchases returns		9,000
Carriage in	3,500	
Rent receivable		4,600
Wages	10,500	
Repairs	1,300	
Advertising	3,400	
Carriage out	900	
Interest on loan	4,000	
Rent and rates	5,100	
Reserves (profit and loss balance)		36,000
Buildings	400,000	
Vehicles	100,000	
Cash on hand	12,000	
Cash at bank	7,500	
Debtors	16,000	
Creditors		30,300
Bank overdraft		5,300
Issued share capital		240,000
25-year loan		200,000
Dividend paid	13,000	
	665,200	665,200

Additional information as at December 31st 2020
- Closing stock: €11,000.
- Depreciation of vehicles: 15%.

Solution

Income Statement of Clooniron Ltd for the year ended 31/12/2020			
	€	€	€
Sales		140,000	
Less sales returns		24,000	116,000
Less cost of sales			
Opening stock		12,000	
Add purchases	52,000		
Less purchases returns	9,000	43,000	
Carriage in		3,500	
Cost of goods available for sale		58,500	
Less closing stock		11,000	
Cost of goods sold			47,500
Gross profit			68,500
Add gains:			
Dividend receivable			4,600
			73,100
Less expenses			
Wages		10,500	
Repairs		1,300	
Advertising		3,400	
Carriage out		900	
Depreciation of vehicles (15%)		20,000	
Interest on loan		4,000	
Rent and rates		5,100	45,200
Net profit			27,900
Dividend paid			13,000
Reserves/Retained earnings			14,900
Add opening reserves			36,000
Reserves 31/12/2019			50,900

Statement of Financial Position of Clooniron Ltd as at 31/12/2020			
Fixed assets	**Cost**	**Depreciation**	**Net Book Value**
Buildings	400,000		400,000
Vehicles	100,000	20,000	80,000
	500,000	20,000	480,000
Current assets			
Cash on hand	12,000		
Cash at bank	7,500		
Debtors	16,000		
Closing stock	11,000	46,500	
Current liabilities			
Creditors	30,300		
Bank overdraft	5,300	35,600	
Working capital			10,900
Total net assets			490,900
Financed by			
Share capital	**Authorised**	**Issued**	
€1 ordinary shares	300,000	240,000	
Reserves 31/12/2019		50,900	
Long-term liabilities			
25-year loan		200,000	
Capital employed			490,900

Stock control

- Stock should be kept at the optimum level:
  - too little stock means the firm will lose business, and may be paying rent for warehouse space it is not using
  - too much stock means that cash is tied up in stock, with a knock-on increase in storage and insurance costs and the risk of obsolescence and pilferage.
- Having a good stock control system involves:
  - setting the right maximum and minimum stock levels
  - ordering goods at the right time, taking account for delivery times
  - keeping accurate stock records.

Monitoring the performance of the business

- The final accounts can tell us a lot more about a company than just the profit it made and what it is worth.
- We can also use a series of business ratios to examine the business under a number of headings.

People who might wish to analyse the performance of the business

- **Management** who will want to know if their management strategies are working and if the company is doing better than in previous years.
- **Potential lenders**, such as banks, who want to be sure that the business is profitable enough to be able to repay its loans with interest.
- **Prospective shareholders** who want to be confident of a return on their investment.
- **Suppliers** who sell on credit will want to reassure themselves that the company has the finances to pay its bills as they fall due.
- **Employees** who are concerned about the security of their employment.
- The **Revenue Commissioners** will wish to know if the company is accurately reporting its profits and paying its due taxes.

Business ratios

Profitability

Return on capital employed

The return on capital employed tells us how much of a return the money invested in the business made in the year. The higher the percentage, the better.

$$\frac{\text{Net Profit}}{\text{Capital Employed}} \times \frac{100}{1}$$

Example 1: Maneycon Ltd	Example 2: Clooniron Ltd
$\frac{29,000}{656,000} \times \frac{100}{1} = $ **4.4%**	$\frac{27,900}{490,900} \times \frac{100}{1} = $ **5.7%**

- This means that for every €100 invested, Maneycon Ltd generated a return of €4.40, while Clooniron Ltd yielded €5.70.
- Not only can we compare these two companies, but their return can also be compared with the interest in banks and the return on other investments.

Gross profit margin

The gross profit margin tells us the percentage gross profit made on sales, i.e. the percentage of sales revenue that is available to pay expenses. The higher the percentage, the better.

$$\frac{\text{Gross Profit}}{\text{Net Sales}} \times \frac{100}{1}$$

Example 1: Maneycon Ltd	Example 2: Clooniron Ltd
$\frac{58{,}000}{110{,}000} \times \frac{100}{1} = $ **52.7%**	$\frac{68{,}500}{116{,}000} \times \frac{100}{1} = $ **59.1%**

- This means that for every €100 of sales, Maneycon Ltd has €52.70 to spend on expenses and still not make a net loss, while Clooniron Ltd has done slightly better at €59.10.
- You can compare the figure, not just with other companies, but with your own company in previous years.
- A falling gross profit margin could mean:
  - the company cut its price, but its costs remained the same
  - the cost of materials has risen but the sale price has not
  - customs duty, carriage in, etc. have risen but the sale price has not.

Net profit margin

The net profit margin tells us the percentage net profit made on sales. The higher the percentage, the better. Due to expenses, the answer will always be lower than the gross profit margin.

$$\frac{\text{Net Profit}}{\text{Sales}} \times \frac{100}{1}$$

Example 1: Maneycon Ltd	Example 2: Clooniron Ltd
$\frac{29{,}000}{110{,}000} \times \frac{100}{1} = $ **26.4%**	$\frac{27{,}900}{116{,}000} \times \frac{100}{1} = $ **24.1%**

- This means that for every €100 of sales, Maneycon Ltd has made a net profit of €26.40, while Clooniron Ltd has €24.10.
- Both get to keep roughly a quarter of the value of what they sold.
- They can pay this money out as a dividend to their shareholders or reinvest it as reserves/retained earnings.
- This can be compared with the performance of other companies or with your own performance in previous years.
- A falling net profit margin can mean:
  - expenses have risen but the sale price has not
  - the company has dropped its prices while expenses have remained the same.

Liquidity

Current asset ratio

Current Assets : Current Liabilities

- The current asset ratio is a comparison of a firm's current assets (cash, bank, debtors, closing stock) with its current liabilities (creditors, bank overdraft).
- Ideally, the ratio should be 2:1.
- If it is less than 2:1, it means you run the risk of being able to pay your creditors on time.
- If it is much greater than 2:1, it means that too much of your money is lying idle in the bank, or tied up in stock, when it might better be used to buy more assets, thus earning a greater return.

Example 1: Maneycon Ltd	Example 2: Clooniron Ltd
42,000 : 21,000	45,600 : 36,500
2 : 1	1.25 : 1

Maneycon Ltd has a healthy ratio, but Clooniron Ltd has a ratio significantly below what it should be.

Acid test ratio

Current Assets – Closing Stock : Current Liabilities

- The acid test ratio also compares the firm's current assets and current liabilities, but it applies a tougher test.
- It excludes closing stock because it's not very liquid, i.e. not very easy to turn into cash that can be used to pay creditors.
- Ideally, the acid test ratio is 1:1.

Example 1: Maneycon Ltd	Example 2: Clooniron Ltd
42,000 – 15,000 : 21,000	45,600 – 11,000 : 36,500
27,000 : 21,000	35,600 : 36,500
1.29 :	0.98 : 1

- Both Maneycon Ltd and Clooniron Ltd have healthy acid test ratios, although Maneycon's is slightly higher than it needs to be.

Gearing

Debt to equity ratio

$$\frac{\text{Debt Capital}}{\text{Equity Capital}} \times \frac{100}{1}$$

- The debt to equity ratio breaks down a company's capital employed into debt capital (money it has borrowed) and equity capital (money its shareholders have invested).
- A company should not borrow too much, since profits end up being paid as interest on loans rather than being reinvested to expand the business.
- On the other hand, a company that is perhaps too careful and doesn't borrow at all runs the risk of missing out on the chance to expand.
- If debt is greater than equity, the company is said to be highly geared. If equity is greater than debt, it is said to be lowly geared.

Example 1: Maneycon Ltd		
Issued share capital + Reserves	:	Long-term liabilities
250,000 + 56,000	:	350,000
306,000	:	350,000
0.87	:	1

Example 2: Clooniron Ltd		
Issued share capital + Reserves	:	Long-term liabilities
240,000 + 50,900	:	200,000
290,900	:	200,000
1.45	:	1

- This means that while the shareholders of Clooniron Ltd have invested €1.45 for every €1 the company has borrowed, the shareholders of Maneycon have only invested 87c for every €1 it has borrowed.
- Maneycon Ltd is lowly geared, while Clooniron Ltd is highly geared.
- Clooniron is paying a larger percentage of its profits as interest on its bank loan and may find it difficult to raise finance in the future.

Solvency

- Solvency compares the value of total assets with the value of external debts.

Total Assets	:	External Liabilities

- It assesses the ability of the firm to pay all its debts as they fall due.
- If its total assets are greater than its external debts, the company is **solvent**.
- If external debts exceed total assets, it is **insolvent**.

Example 1: Maneycon Ltd

Fixed and current assets : Long-term loans and current liabilities

635,000 + 42,000 : 350,000 + 21,000

677,000 > 371,000

Example 2: Clooniron Ltd

Fixed and current assets : Long-term loans and current liabilities

480,000 + 46,500 : 200,000 + 35,600

526,500 > 235,600

Both Maneycon Ltd and Clooniron Ltd are comfortably solvent. They both would have more than enough assets to pay off their external liabilities if they needed to.

Question 14, Junior Cycle Examination 2019

Complete the trading account of Blake Ltd for the year ended 31/12/2018:

Trading Account of Blake Ltd for the year ended 31/12/2018		
	€	€
Sales		850,000
Less cost of sales		
Opening stock	75,000	
Purchases	450,000	
	525,000	
Less closing stock	115,000	
Cost of sales		410,000
Gross profit		440,000

Question 8, Junior Cycle Sample Paper (SEC)

Complete the following extract of the balance sheet (statement of financial position) of O'Gorman Ltd as at 31/12/2018.

- Depreciation on buildings is 2% of cost.
- Depreciation on vehicles is 15 % of cost.

Fixed Assets	Cost	Depreciation	Net Book Value
	€	€	€
Buildings	500,000	10,000	490,000
Vehicles	65,000	9,750	55,250

STRAND 3
Economics

Managing My Resources

Exploring Business

Using Skills For Business

Managing My Resources

 Main Learning Outcome

3.1 Students should be able to explain how scarcity of economic resources results in individuals having to make choices; predict possible consequences of these choices.

 By the end of this chapter you should:
- understand the meaning of economics, and the importance of the concepts of scarcity, choice and opportunity cost
- be able to outline the four factors of production
- be able to differentiate between macroeconomics and microeconomics.

Scarcity, choice and cost

top tip

- **Economics:**
  - is the study of the production, distribution and consumption of goods and services by society
  - examines **how** we use our scarce resources, which have alternative uses, to attempt to satisfy our infinite needs and wants.

- While our resources (see Chapter 1) are limited or finite, the needs and wants of society are unlimited or infinite.
  - A **need** is something that cannot be done without, e.g. food, shelter or clothing. Our needs are finite.
  - A **want** is anything else we might wish to consume once our needs have been satisfied, e.g. a holiday in Portugal. Wants tend to be unlimited or infinite.

'Scarcity' does not have to mean that there is hardly any of something. In Economics it means that while there may be lots of it, the demand is greater still, e.g. millions of barrels of oil are produced every day, yet the demand for it is greater still.

- The concept of **scarcity** is therefore central to Economics. If our needs and wants are greater than our resources, then our resources are scarce – even if we have a lot of resources. This is the fundamental problem that economics tries to solve.
- When there is scarcity, there are **choices** to be made between alternatives. Economics studies how society – individuals, businesses and the government – makes these choices.
  - **Short-term choices** are ones that affect us over less than a year, e.g. which car insurance policy to buy.
  - **Long-term choices** affect us over a period longer than a year, e.g. which house to buy.

Choices are not always easy to make. A number of factors can impact on our decisions:

Financial cost

Neither individuals, nor businesses nor the government can spend money they do not have or cannot afford to borrow.

- Individuals may have to earn extra money through overtime or else cut back on spending, e.g. eating out.
- Businesses may need to generate extra sales revenue or cut down on spending, e.g. travel costs.
- Governments must find sources of tax revenue, e.g. carbon taxes.

Opportunity cost

The alternatives that must be done without in order to have an item. Just like scarcity, opportunity cost is central to Economics.

- Maeve has enough money to purchase either a tablet or a concert ticket, but not both. If she buys the tablet, the concert ticket is the opportunity cost.
- If a medical devices company has €100m, it can build a factory in Westport or in Copenhagen, but not in both.
- If the Irish government has €1bn, it can build a motorway or hire more Gardaí, but not both.

Additional costs

- Individuals need to include additional costs for their choices, e.g. buying a car means paying for insurance, tax, fuel, parking.
- Firms need to consider additional costs, e.g. buying expensive machinery means training or hiring staff to operate and maintain it.
- Governments face additional costs, e.g. a motorway requires constant maintenance and repair.

Priority

- Individuals must pay for their needs before buying what they want, e.g. Lisa shouldn't go on a trip to Las Vegas unless she has first paid her mortgage.
- Businesses must be able to pay their rent, wages, electricity bills, etc. before redecorating their offices.
- Governments should pay the wages of nurses and look after social welfare recipients before announcing tax cuts.

Potential benefits

- It might be better for an individual in the long run to invest in further education, rather than spend their money on travel and entertainment.
- It could be wiser for a firm in the long run to invest in research and development of new products rather than hand out bonuses.
- It may be better for society in the long run for the government to invest in rural broadband or education, rather than hand the money out in tax cuts.

Impact on society

- Individuals should think about how their choices affect others and the environment, e.g. pollution, packaging, their carbon footprint.
- Businesses need to consider how their activities affect the local and global community in terms of noise pollution, waste, traffic disruption, etc.

top tip

As you can see, Economics can be brought to life by looking at everyday examples of products and services that you or your family have bought or plan to buy.

- Governments need to be aware of how their decisions can help society and protect the environment, e.g. lower taxes for fuel-efficient cars, grants to install solar panels, investment in cycle paths, etc.

Four factors of production

When we speak about resources, we are talking about the four factors of production:

- **Land** is anything we get from nature that is used in the production of goods and services, e.g. agricultural land, water, minerals taken from the earth, even the weather. Virtually all production requires at least some land. The return earned by land is **rent**.
- **Labour** is any human effort used in the production of goods and services, e.g. a miner, a shop assistant, a psychologist. The return earned by labour is **wages**.
- **Capital** is anything made by humans which is used in the production of goods and services, e.g. machinery, buildings or stock. All capital is ultimately made from land. The return earned by capital is **interest**.
- **Enterprise** (see Chapter 15) is the factor that organises the other three factors into a business unit. **Entrepreneurs** anticipate consumer demand and invent products and services to satisfy that demand. They take risks in starting and running a business. Entrepreneurs can be sole traders, partnerships, co-operatives, private limited companies, public limited companies, joint ventures or even the government. The return earned by enterprise is **profit.**

Labour and enterprise are **human resources**, land and capital are **non-human resources**.

We must remember that while our resources are limited, they are not fixed. Over time, if we grow our **wealth**, we can increase the amount of resources that we have, and therefore decrease the number of choices we are forced to make:

- If Lisa works hard and gets promoted, she can pay her mortgage and afford the trip to Las Vegas.
- If a business sells more products, it can pay its wages and also upgrade its offices.
- If the government invests in the education system and transport infrastructure of the country, it can generate the tax revenue to offer tax cuts, which can, in turn, generate further growth.

Macroeconomics and microeconomics

Economics is divided into two parts:

- **Macroeconomics** (macro means 'large') studies the decision-making process of government as it relates to such topics as income, employment, inflation, the balance of payments, international trade, growth, etc.
  - It is concerned with broad aggregates, the big picture.
  - It doesn't deal with the behaviour of individuals.
- **Microeconomics** (micro means 'small') studies the decision-making process of individual units in the economy, at the level of the individual consumer, supplier, and producer.
  - It is concerned with how supply and demand determine the quantity of individual goods that will be produced and at what price.

Question 10, Junior Cycle Examination 2019
Fill in the missing factors of production below:

1. *Land*	2. *Labour*
3. *Capital*	4. Enterprise

Question 15, Junior Cycle Examination 2019
The following items were identified as the main areas of expenditure for Irish consumers in 2018. Classify each item of expenditure as a need or a want.

Items of expenditure	Need/Want
Food	*Need*
Holidays	*Want*
Clothing and Footwear	*Need*

Question 3, Junior Cycle Sample Paper (SEC)
'A living wage provides for needs not wants.'

www.livingwage.ie

Explain the difference between needs and wants. Give an example in **each** case.

Answer
A need is anything you need in order to survive, it is essential. A want is something you desire but can still do without.

- Example of need: *Food, shelter, clothing.*
- Example of want: *A Giorgio Armani watch.*

28 How the Economy Operates

 Main Learning Outcome

3.2 Students should be able to explain how individuals, organisations (for-profit and not-for-profit) and the government work together to distribute economic resources used to produce goods and services

 By the end of this chapter you should:

- be able to differentiate between the public sector and the private sector
- be able to outline the advantages and disadvantages of free market, centrally planned and mixed economies
- know how to illustrate and explain the circular flow of income.

In the last chapter, we learned about how the government makes decisions about how economic resources are distributed that can have major effects on society, on businesses, on individuals, and on the environment. However, some governments are more involved in how resources are distributed than other governments are.

Private sector

The private sector is the part of the economy that is not owned or operated by the government.

- It includes **for-profit** private companies such as Supermacs or Facebook, whose goal is to make a profit for their shareholders.
- Larger companies often benefit from **economies of scale**, i.e. as output increases, the average cost of producing each unit falls. If you produce a thousand cars, each might cost €30,000 to make, but if you produce ten thousand cars, each might only cost €20,000. These cost savings are passed on to consumers in the form of lower prices.
- The private sector also includes **not-for-profit** entities whose purpose is not to make a profit, but to play a positive role in society or solve a problem that the government and for-profit businesses are neglecting, e.g. charities, sporting organisations. They are often funded by the government in the form of grants.

Public sector

The public sector is the part of the economy under the control of the government. It provides services that are considered to be vital, but which the private sector is unwilling to provide since they do not return a profit.

- It includes the various government departments, such as the Department of Education and Skills, the Department of Justice and the Department of Health, which provide us with schools, Garda stations and hospitals.
- It includes local government, made up of city and county councils around the country. They provide vital services in local areas, such as council housing, street lighting and street cleaning, public libraries, parks, etc.
- It also includes many **semi-state companies**, such as RTÉ, Iarnród Éireann and Electric Ireland, which provide public service radio and television, rail transport and electricity, etc.

Public–private partnerships (PPPs)

These partnerships involve the public and private sectors working together, e.g. on transport, telecommunications or energy projects. In exchange for providing part of the funding, a private company is allowed to earn some of the profit, e.g. via a toll gate on a motorway.

Privatisation

This means selling a previously public sector company to the private sector, e.g. Aer Lingus.

The way economic resources are distributed within an economy, and the balance that is struck between public and private sectors, determines the type of **economic system**. The three main types are:

- free market economy / free enterprise economy
- centrally planned economy / command economy
- mixed economy.

> **top tip**
>
> The opposite of privatisation, i.e. when the government takes over a previously privately owned company, is called **nationalisation**.

Free market economy/Free enterprise economy

A free enterprise economy has very little, if any, government involvement, meaning that it has a large private sector and a small public sector. The factors of production are privately owned, prices are decided by the interaction of supply and demand, and producers are motivated by self-interest and profit. The government only exists to defend the country and to resolve disputes between citizens. Free enterprise does not exist in its pure form, but countries such as the United States are often described as free market.

Advantages

- The freedom and choice it gives to consumers. Since anyone who wants to can attempt to enter any industry, there is often more variety and competition.
- Allows people to keep the rewards of their own efforts. If you work hard to provide products and services that people need and want, you earn more money than other people do.
- Rewards efficiency and innovation. Firms must compete in order to survive, meaning that they must devise better products at cheaper prices.
- Since the government plays less of a role, it collects less tax, allowing people to keep and spend more of their own money as they choose, rather than the government telling them how to spend it.
- The growth of the private sector can result from **deregulation** of areas previously controlled by the government, which allows more efficient private companies to enter and operate in the market, e.g. the mobile phone market.

Disadvantages

- Inequality between rich and poor. Those who are better at anticipating and satisfying consumer demand make more money than those who are not. There is very little, if any, redistribution of wealth.
- Success and failure in life is often judged by what you own or earn. Greed may be rewarded, or even admired.
- Vital services will not be provided if they are unprofitable, e.g. primary and secondary education, public parks.
- A lack of government regulation may leave consumers vulnerable to dishonest practices or dangerous products.
- The emergence of large multinational companies that can squeeze out smaller local suppliers.
- A cycle of booms and recessions rather than steady, predictable growth.
- Markets are not always as competitive as they should be; they are sometimes dominated by just one or two large firms.

Centrally planned economy/Command economy

A centrally planned economy is defined by government control of the factors of production, meaning that it has a large public sector and a small private sector. The government decides what is produced, how much, and at what price. The benefits are allocated according to need, not ability. North Korea is an example of a centrally planned economy.

Advantages

- Vital services are provided, even if they do not make a profit.
- Wealth is more evenly distributed. There are not the extremes of wealth and poverty often found in free market economies.
- People are less prone to comparing what they have with what others have, and they make what they have last longer.
- Duplication is reduced because the government is the only producer.

Disadvantages

- Absence of a profit motive leads to inefficiency and a lack of innovation. People tend not to work as hard if they know the rewards will be confiscated and given to everyone else.
- As a result, there is often an equality of poverty rather than of wealth.
- There is no reason why a government should be better at deciding what to produce than producers and consumers themselves. When your income depends on getting things right and avoiding mistakes, you tend to produce better goods than if you get paid anyway.
- There is less variety, and frequent shortages of even basic necessities.
- Central planning has often been associated with dictatorship and a lack of individual freedom, e.g. in Cuba.

Mixed economy

A mixed economy tries to incorporate the best of both free enterprise and central planning, meaning that both the private and public sectors play an important role in the economy. Ireland, France and the UK are all examples of mixed economies. Some mixed economies are much closer to free markets, others are closer to centrally planned economies.

Advantages of a mixed economy

- Most of the advantages of a free market system: efficiency is still rewarded, people are allowed to keep most of what they earn, there is a wide variety of goods and services. The private sector is allowed and encouraged to do what it does best.
- Vital services are provided by the government if it is unprofitable for private companies to provide them, e.g. schools, hospitals, public parks.
- Government regulation prevents private companies from selling unsafe products or misleading consumers, e.g. the Sale of Goods and Supply of Services Act 1980.
- Many things the government provide actually assist private enterprise, e.g. policing, good roads and public transport.

Disadvantages of a mixed economy

- Sometimes too many government regulations make it harder to set up and run businesses profitably. Such rules are known as 'red tape'. Sometimes the government tries to make decisions that are better left to private individuals and businesses to make for themselves.
- Higher taxes are required in order to fund government services. These reduce the incentive to set up businesses and to innovate.

top tip

No system of government is perfect. There will always be debate about what is the best degree of government involvement in the economy, and people change opinions many times over their lifetimes or depending on the issue at stake.

Circular flow of income

This is a way of explaining how an economy works by showing how money circulates around between individuals, firms and the government.

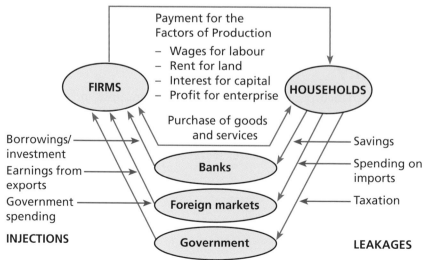

Circular flow of income

- Imagine an economy made up of only households and firms. Households sell the four factors of production (mostly labour) to firms, and in return they receive income in the form of wages, rent, interest and profit. They then spend this income on the goods and services produced by the firms. The firms use the income from the sale of those goods and services to buy more of the four factors. Again and again, the same money goes around and around in a **circular flow**.
- Households may choose not to spend all of their income on goods and services, but to save some of it instead. So now we need to add a **banking sector**.
  - Savings represent a **leakage**, since they're being taken out of the circular flow.
  - On the other hand, others can then borrow that money from the banks and either invest it or spend it. That represents an **injection** into the circular flow.
  - If savings exceed borrowings, there's a reduction in economic activity: GNP falls. If borrowings exceed savings, there's an increase in economic activity: GNP rises.
- Up until now, this was a **closed economy**, i.e. no trade with the outside world. Let's now make it an **open economy**.
  - When we spend money on imported goods and services, this is a **leakage** from the circular flow of income.
  - When Irish goods or services are sold abroad, we experience an **injection** into the circular flow.
  - If imports exceed exports, there's a reduction in economic activity: GNP falls. If exports exceed imports, there's an increase in economic activity: GNP rises.
- Finally, let's give our imaginary country a **government**.
  - When governments collect taxes, that leaves less to be spent on goods and services, and hence it's a **leakage**.
  - But governments also spend money in the economy, and that spending represents an **injection**.
  - If taxation exceeds government spending, there's a reduction in economic activity: GNP falls. If government spending exceeds taxation, there's an increase in economic activity: GNP rises.

Sample Question 1
Indicate in each case whether the characteristic is associated with a free market or a centrally planned economy. Tick (✓) the correct box below.

	Free Market	Centrally Planned
Privately owned businesses	✓	
Little competiton		✓
Inequality	✓	
Even distribution of wealth		✓

Sample Question 2
Explain the term 'mixed economy'.

Answer
A mixed economy is one that has elements of both free market and centrally planned economies. Most goods and services are provided by private companies, whose goal is to make a profit. However, the government tries to ensure that public services are provided to all and that everyone has a certain minimum level of income. Ireland is an example of a mixed economy.

Main Learning Outcome

3.3 Students should be able to evaluate how changes in the supply and demand of goods and services in different markets can affect prices.

By the end of this chapter you should:

- be able to outline the assumptions economists make about consumers
- understand the law of demand and the factors that influence demand
- understand the law of supply and the factors that influence supply
- be able to describe how the interaction of supply and demand results in equilibrium.

Assumptions about consumers

A consumer (see Chapter 7) is anybody who buys goods and services for their own use. In Economics, certain assumptions are made about how consumers behave:

- Demand depends on **income**. Even people on high incomes want more than they can buy. Our needs may be finite, but our wants are infinite.
- Therefore, we must **choose** between those wants and needs we can satisfy and those that must wait. We face **opportunity costs**.
- Consumers are assumed to be **rational** in how they spend their limited incomes, i.e. they follow their own self-interest and seek value for money.
- The **law of diminishing marginal utility** is assumed to operate. As you consume more units of a good, the satisfaction or benefit gained from each extra unit will eventually begin to be less than for the previous unit, e.g. if I have lasagne for dinner on Monday and Tuesday, I'm ready for a change by Wednesday.

As we saw in Chapter 20, a **market** exists wherever, whenever and however buyers and sellers come together to trade:

- **Factor markets:** Land, labour, and capital are purchased by entrepreneurs to be combined into a business unit, e.g. a flour mill buys wheat from a farmer.

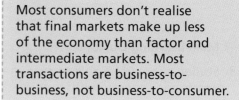

top tip

Most consumers don't realise that final markets make up less of the economy than factor and intermediate markets. Most transactions are business-to-business, not business-to-consumer.

- **Intermediate markets:** Raw materials and partially finished goods are purchased for use in making other goods, e.g. flour is bought by a bakery to bake bread.

- **Final markets:** Finished goods are purchased by the final consumer, e.g. a shopper buys a loaf of bread.

All markets share one thing: they involve the interaction of supply and demand. When supply and demand interact, they determine the price.

Demand

Demand refers to the quantity of a good that consumers are willing to buy at any given market price over a period of time.

- A **demand schedule** is a list of prices and, alongside it, a list of the quantities a consumer is prepared to buy at each of those prices.
  - Example: Below is a list of possible prices Agata is charged for coffee, and beside it a list of the number of cups of coffee she is prepared to buy each year at each of those prices.

top tip

There are a number of strange exceptions to the Law of Demand, e.g. 'snob goods' – when the price of an item such as a designer watch goes up, some people are more likely to buy it because it is now more exclusive.

Price	Quantity
€1.00	350
€1.50	320
€2.00	300
€2.50	270
€3.00	240
€3.50	200

- The higher the price charged by the seller, the less coffee Agata understandably wishes to buy. This relationship is called the **law of demand**:
  - as the price charged rises, quantity demanded falls
  - as the price charged falls, quantity demanded rises.

- This can be graphed as a **demand curve**. A demand curve is usually downward sloping, since it obeys the law of demand:

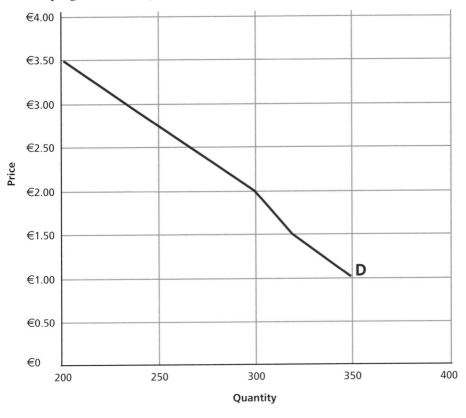

Factors that can change demand

Apart from a change in the price charged for a good, the following factors can also affect its demand:

- The price of **substitute goods**, i.e. competing products that do the same thing. If another coffee shop across the street charged a lower price, Agata could go there instead.
- The price of **complementary goods**, i.e. products that are consumed along with the original good. If Agata likes a Danish pastry with her coffee, and the price of a Danish pastry rises, her demand for them will go down – and so will her demand for coffee.
- The **income** of the consumer:
  - A **normal good** is any good you buy more of as your income rises, e.g. foreign holidays.
  - An **inferior good** is any good you buy less of as your income rises, e.g. baked beans.
- The consumer's tastes, which can be influenced by a successful advertising campaign, e.g. a new superhero movie.

- The consumer's **expectations**:
  - If you expect the price of the good to fall in the future, you'd rather wait, so you demand less now.
  - If you expect the price of the good to rise in the future, you'll want to buy it before it does, so you demand more now.
- The availability of **credit**. Our ability to buy some items depends on our ability to borrow, e.g. a new car.
- **Unplanned/unexpected** events can suddenly alter demand, e.g. losing your job.
- **Government policy**: a tax change or a new law can cause demand to change, e.g. a tax on soft drinks.

Effect on demand curve

- If any of these factors cause more to be demanded at the same price, the demand curve shifts to the right.
- If any of these factors cause less to be demanded at the same price, the demand curve shifts to the left.

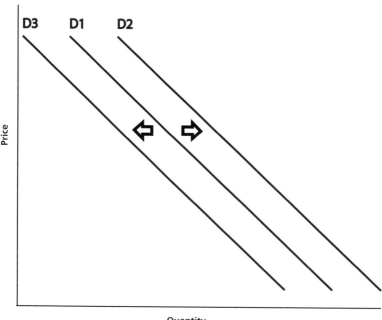

Supply

Supply means the quantity of a good that producers are willing to sell at any given market price over a period of time.

- A **supply schedule** is a list of prices and, alongside it, a list of the quantities a supplier is prepared to sell at each of those prices.
  - Example: This is a list of possible prices Stephen is offered for coffee, and beside it a list of the number of cups of coffee he is prepared to sell each year at each of those prices.

Price	Quantity
€1.00	230
€1.50	260
€2.00	300
€2.50	310
€3.00	330
€3.50	360

- The higher the price offered by the buyer, the more coffee Stephen understandably wishes to supply. This relationship is called the **law of supply**:
  - as the price offered rises, quantity supplied rises
  - as the price offered falls, quantity supplied falls.
- This can be graphed as a **supply curve**. A supply curve is usually upward sloping, since it obeys the law of supply:

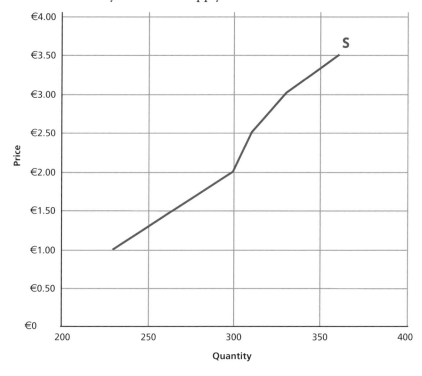

Factors that can change supply

Apart from a change in the price offered for a good, the following factors can also affect its supply:

- The price of **related** goods, other goods that the producer can offer instead of the original good, e.g. if smoothies became more popular, Stephen could sell more smoothies and reduce his supply of coffee.
- If the **cost of production** falls, a firm can supply more, e.g. due to a fall in electricity prices.
- An improvement in **technology** can make it possible to produce more of a good, e.g. a better coffee machine.
- **Unplanned/unexpected events** can have either a positive or negative effect on supply, e.g. closure due to water damage from a leak.
- Availability of **credit:** a firm cannot expand unless it can borrow money, e.g. to open a new outlet.
- The **government** can offer incentives to promote the supply of desirable products e.g. lower taxes on electric cars.

Effect on supply curve

- If any of these factors cause more to be supplied at the same price, the supply curve shifts to the right.
- If any of these factors cause less to be supplied at the same price, the supply curve shifts to the left.

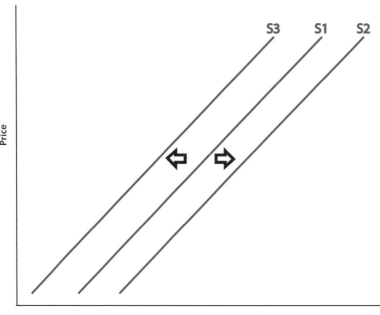

Equilibrium

Equilibrium is the point at which the quantity demanded is equal to the quantity supplied, i.e. where the demand and supply curves intersect.

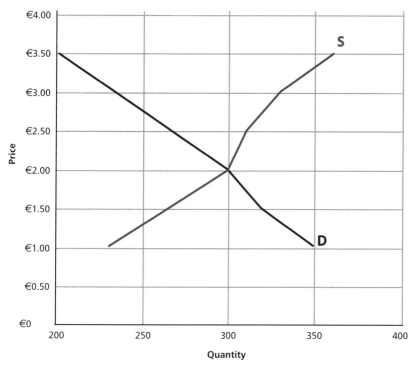

- Above €2, Stephen is prepared to sell more coffee than Agata is prepared to buy, so he must lower the price he charges to encourage her to buy as much as he's prepared to sell. When supply is greater than demand, the market price will be forced down until it reaches an equilibrium.
- Below €2, Agata is prepared to buy more coffee than Stephen is prepared to sell, so she must offer a higher price to encourage him to sell as much as she wants to buy. When demand is greater than supply, the market price will be forced up until it reaches an equilibrium.
- In this example, equilibrium occurs when 300 cups of coffee are sold at €2 each. There is neither excess demand or excess supply.

Question 16, Junior Cycle Examination 2019

New Chapter is an award-winning traditional bookshop located in Tinahely, Co Wicklow. The demand and supply curves for one of its books *The Great Irish Weather Book* are shown in the diagram below.

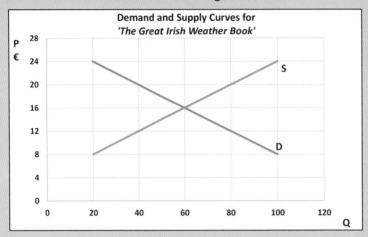

Use the above diagram to answer each of the following questions.

(i) Indicate the quantity supplied of *The Great Irish Weather Book* at €20.	*80 copies*
(ii) Indicate the quantity demanded of *The Great Irish Weather Book* at €8.	*100 copies*
(iii) Indicate the equilibrium price of *The Great Irish Weather Book*.	*€16*

(iv) What impact would the following have on the demand for books in New Chapter?

	Increased demand for books in New Chapter	Decreased demand for books in New Chapter
A reduction in the price of books	✓	
An increase in taxes (VAT)		✓
Roll out of broadband to all areas in Wicklow		✓
An Eason's store opening in the town		✓

Question 18 (b), Junior Cycle Sample Paper (SEC)

The demand and supply curves for the Pure Confectionery Company's protein bars are shown in the diagram below.

(i) On the diagram below show the equilibrium price and quantity of the protein bars.

Write your answers in the spaces provided below.

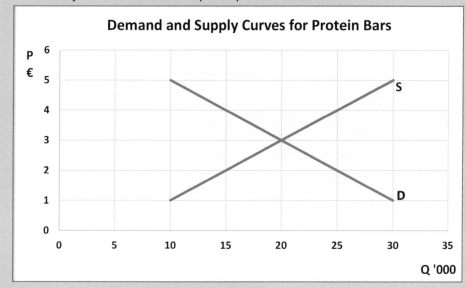

Demand and Supply Curves for Protein Bars

Answer

Equilibrium price:	€3	Equilibrium quantity:	20,000

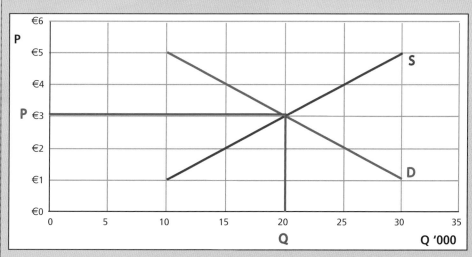

(ii) Use the above diagram to identify the price at which the Pure Confectionery Company would be prepared to supply 25,000 protein bars.

Answer

Price: €4

30 Government Revenue and Expenditure

 Main Learning Outcome

3.4 Students should be able to differentiate between different sources of government revenue and government expenditure.

> **aims** By the end of this chapter you should:
> - be able to outline the main sources of government revenue and the main areas of government expenditure
> - understand how to draft a national budget, and how to deal with both budget surpluses and deficits.

The government spends billions of euro in the economy every year on public services such as health and education; on paying the wages of nurses, doctors and teachers; and on infrastructure projects such as motorways, airports and hospitals. It has to get this money from somewhere, mostly in the form of taxation from Irish citizens. The collection of this money is called **government revenue**.

- **Current revenue** means day-to-day revenue that the government collects, e.g. from taxation.
- **Capital revenue** refers to one-off sources of revenue, e.g. the sale of a state asset such as Aer Lingus.

Sources of government revenue

Taxation
(See also Chapter 4.)

- **Pay as You Earn (PAYE):** Also called Income Tax. Charged on wages earned by employees.
- **Pay Related Social Insurance (PRSI):** An additional, smaller deduction from wages that helps to fund social protection payments.
- **Universal Social Charge (USC):** Payable on all income, not just wages.

- **Value Added Tax (VAT):** Charged on the purchase of goods and services.
- **Corporation Tax:** Charged on the profits of companies.
- **Deposit Interest Retention Tax (DIRT):** Charged on interest earned on deposit accounts.
- **Stamp duty:** A tax on documents transferring ownership of property or shares.
- **Local Property Tax (LPT):** Charged on the market value of residential properties.
- **Capital Gains Tax (CGT):** Charged on profits earned from the sale of assets.
- **Capital Acquisitions Tax (CAT):** Charged on gifts or inheritances.
- **Customs duty:** Charged on certain goods imported from outside the EU.
- **Excise duty:** Payable on alcohol, tobacco and other products.
- **Motor tax:** A tax on cars and other vehicles.
- **Vehicle Registration Tax (VRT):** A separate tax you must pay when you first register a motor vehicle.
- **Sugar Sweetened Drinks Tax (SSDT):** Charged on drinks containing added sugar.
- **Carbon tax:** Charged on electricity, natural gas and solid fuel.

top tip

You can find out more about Ireland's tax system at www.citizensinformation.ie or at www.revenue.ie.

The **tax base** is the total amount of assets or income that the government can tax. A narrow tax base means that the government has few sources of taxation. To **broaden the tax base** means to introduce new taxes that did not previously exist, e.g. local property tax.

Non-tax income

- **Sale of semi-state assets**, such as Aer Lingus or Bord Gáis Energy
- **Profits of semi-state companies**, such as Bórd na Mona
- **EU grants**, including funds paid to Ireland for infrastructure projects or for the farming sector
- **Fees** for sitting state exams and for planning permission, etc
- **Licences**, such as gun, TV and dog licences
- **Passport** and **citizenship** fees
- **Carbon allowance auctioning**
- **Central bank surpluses**.

Main areas of government expenditure

Current expenditure

Day-to-day expenditure, including:

- Social welfare payments such as Jobseeker's Allowance, Carer's Allowance and pensions.
- Wages of more than 300,000 government employees, such as:
  — Gardaí
  — prison officers
  — primary and secondary teachers
  — special needs assistants
  — college lecturers
  — civil servants
  — Army, Air Corps and Naval Service personnel
  — nurses
  — doctors
  — consultants.
- General running costs of government departments such as electricity, rent, etc.
- **Debt servicing**, the interest that must be paid on the national debt.

Capital expenditure

Or one-off expenditure on long-term projects, including:

- Providing infrastructure such as motorways, airports, hospitals and schools.
- Repaying part of the national debt. This is different to debt servicing, which is merely paying the interest.
- Investing in and replacing machinery, such as ambulances for hospitals, helicopters for the Air Corps, computers for schools.
- Grants paid to households and businesses, farmers, students and others.

The national budget

Even though it has many billions of euro at its disposal, the government's revenue is still limited since the cost of what it would like to provide exceeds the funds available. Therefore, it is necessary to formulate a detailed plan of the government's revenue and expenditure for the year ahead, called the **national budget**. It is prepared as follows:

- Each government department submits an estimate of its expenditure needs to the Department of Finance and to the Department of Public Expenditure and Reform.
- The Departments of Finance and of Public Expenditure and Reform then examine the estimates and decide how much money to allocate to each department.
- The ministers then announce their decisions to the Dáil on Budget Day.

Budget surplus

A budget surplus occurs when revenue is greater than expenditure. It enables the government to do some or all of the following:

top tip

- Reduce taxes, thereby putting more money into the economy, creating more jobs and increasing the standard of living.
- Increase government spending, improving or expanding government services.
- Pay back some of the national debt, hence reducing future interest payments.

When it has a surplus, the government is very often tempted to do with it whatever is most likely to win them the next election. So even though paying off the national debt might be the wiser option, if cutting taxes attracts more votes, the government will cut taxes.

Budget deficit

A budget deficit is when expenditure exceeds revenue. It requires the government to do some or all of the following:

- Reduce government spending, causing a reduction of government services.
- Increase taxes, taking money out of the economy, reducing employment and economic activity, and thus lowering the standard of living.
- Borrow, thereby adding to the national debt and to the interest that must be paid on it.
- Sell some or all of a semi-state company.

While occasional budget deficits are not harmful, and may even be beneficial if they inject money into the economy, repeated government deficits are a sign that the government is overspending.

A **balanced budget** happens when revenue and expenditure are approximately equal.

Example of a national budget

Revenue

Customs	€1.4Bn
Excise duty	€7.7Bn
Capital gains tax	€1.2Bn
Capital acquisitions tax	€0.7Bn
Stamp duty	€2.4Bn
Income tax	€27.4Bn
Corporation tax	€8.8Bn
VAT	€13.7Bn
Motor tax	€0.8Bn
Central bank surplus	€1.3Bn
Dividends	€0.2Bn
Other	€0.4Bn
Total Revenue	€66.0Bn

Expenditure

Social protection	€15.6Bn
Health	€14.1Bn
Education	€11.7Bn
Justice	€2.1Bn
Agriculture	€1.8Bn
Debt servicing	€6.2Bn
Transport	€3.4Bn
Other	€10.6Bn
Total Expenditure	€65.5Bn
BUDGET SURPLUS	€0.5Bn

Question 13, Junior Cycle Examination 2019

Gardaí to recruit 800 new officers with €60 million funding increase.
The Journal, October 2018

The Government will spend €60 million in the Department of Justice and Equality to recruit additional Gardaí in 2019. State one example of expenditure in the Government Departments below:

Government Department:	Example of expenditure:
1. Health	*Nurses' and doctors' pay*
2. Education and Skills	*Hiring new Special Needs Assistants (SNAs)*
3. Transport, Tourism and Sport	*Advertising abroad to attract tourists to Ireland*

Question 7, Junior Cycle Sample Paper (SEC)

The graphic below shows Irish Government spending by category for 2018.

2018 Total Expenditure: €72.5 billion			
Justice	Health	Education	Social Protection
€2.6 billion	€15.3 billion	€10.1 billion	€20.0 billion
Agriculture	Debt Servicing, EU Payments	Transport	Other
€1.5 billion	€10.8 billion	€2.0 billion	€10.2 billion

(a) In which category does the Government spend most?

(b) State one capital and one current expenditure under the health category.

Answer

(a) *Social Protection.*

(b) • **Capital:** *The National Children's Hospital.*

   • **Current:** *Wages of anaesthetists, porters, administrators.*

Exploring Business

31 The Purpose of Taxation

 Main Learning Outcome

3.5 Students should be able to examine the purpose of taxation from a financial, social, legal and ethical perspective

 By the end of this chapter you should:
- be able to describe the various reasons why the government collects tax.

The government collects tax for multiple reasons.

Financial

- Without taxation, the government would not be able to provide the services that the country and its people need:

  — Social protection payments such as Jobseeker's Allowance.
  — Infrastructure such as roads, bridges and airports.
  — The wages of public sector workers such as teachers and prison officers.
  — The pensions of retired people.
  — Public amenities such as parks, public lighting and litter bins.
- The tax system acts as a built-in **stabiliser**:
  — When the economy grows, tax revenues rise and social protection payments fall.
  — When the economy slows, taxes fall and social protection payments rise.
  — Ireland's low corporation tax rate of 12.5% has encouraged investment, particularly from foreign transnational companies.

Social

- The taxation system is used to close the gap between high and low earners by deducting higher rates of tax from the better-off and lower rates from those who are less well off.
  - A **progressive tax** takes a greater percentage of your income as your income rises, e.g. PAYE.
  - A **regressive tax** takes a greater percentage of your income as your income falls, e.g. a TV licence fee of €160 takes a greater percentage of a poor person's income than a rich person's.

top tip

Most people understand the need for the government to collect tax. However, we are very good at nominating other people to pay it instead of ourselves.

- The government has made certain income free of tax, e.g. charitable donations, inheritance from a spouse, artists' incomes.
- The tax system is often used to incentivise socially desirable behaviour, e.g. to encourage people to switch to cleaner cars.
- It can likewise be used to disincentivise socially undesirable behaviour, e.g. to punish those who smoke in the hope that they will stop.

Legal

- Taxes are imposed by law and any changes to them require legal changes in the budget when it is announced each year.
- The **Office of the Revenue Commissioners** (see Chapter 4) is the state agency empowered to collect tax in Ireland on behalf of the government.
- **Tax evasion** is the illegal non-payment or underpayment of tax. It can result in fines, penalties or even imprisonment.
- **Tax avoidance** means legally reducing your tax bill, e.g. by forming a private limited company to take advantage of corporation tax rates.

- The **black market** refers to the trading of a good or service without any tax being paid to the government, e.g. illegally smuggled cigarettes.
- Employers and retailers are required to act as free tax collectors for the government. Employers are legally obliged to deduct PAYE, PRSI and USC from their employees' wages. Retailers are legally required to collect VAT on their sales.
- High tax rates may encourage tax evasion and the black economy.

Ethical

- The tax system is intended to be fair to all citizens, regardless of income.
- Most of us accept that those on higher incomes should be asked to pay more than those on lower incomes so that everyone can receive a minimum standard of living.
- In this way, ability to pay is taken into account.
- However, it is also important that high taxes not discourage those who start businesses, employ workers and generate wealth. Without them, we would have nothing to redistribute.
- The cost to the government of collecting a tax should be a small fraction of what is collected.
- People should know in advance what the tax rates will be, allowing them to plan their spending and investment.
- The tax system can be used to achieve environmental objectives as well as economic ones:
  - The plastic bag tax has helped to reduce the use of plastic bags and resultant litter.
  - The Bike to Work scheme provides tax-free bikes for cycling to work, helping to take cars off the roads.
  - Carbon taxes have been imposed on fossil fuels such as oil, petrol, diesel, gas, coal and peat in order to encourage the shift to renewable energy.

top tip

The reason it is important to know the tax rates in advance is that uncertainty is the enemy of economic activity. When consumers – and investors – don't know the tax rate, they tend to wait and see. If everyone does this, it reduces the amount of economic activity.

Question 17 (b), Junior Cycle Examination 2019

(ii) Food2Go Ltd pays VAT at the new rate of 13.5% following the increase in VAT rates announced in Budget 2019 for the hospitality sector. Complete the blanks below:

| VAT stands for *Value Added Tax.* |
| VAT is charged on *goods* and *services.* |
| VAT is a source of income for *the government.* |

(iii) Food2Go Ltd pays corporation tax (a tax on company profits). Ireland has a low rate of corporation tax at 12.5%. Explain one benefit to Ireland of having a low corporation tax rate.

Answer

Our low corporation tax rate helps to attract foreign multinational companies to locate in Ireland, where they employ over 200,000 people directly, and possibly the same number again indirectly. This raises the standard of living of our people and contributes billions of euro to the exchequer that can be spent on public services.

Question 16 (c), Junior Cycle Examination 2019

'A proposed "latte levy" could reduce disposable coffee cups by 250,000 a day.'

The Government has proposed a new 15 cent levy on disposable coffee cups.

The Irish Times, March 2018

Outline **two** benefits of the proposed 'latte levy'.

Answer

- It would reduce waste by reducing the number of single-use coffee cups discarded every day.
- The tax revenue received by the government would provide more money for street-cleaning, litter wardens. etc.

Question 17 (b), Junior Cycle Sample Paper (SEC)

Karina operates a small restaurant called Waves. The government has announced that the current 9% VAT rate for the hospitality sector will be increased to 13.5% in January 2019.

State **one** effect, for restaurant owners like Karina, of this increased VAT rate.

Answer

The VAT rate forces Karina and restaurant owners like her to increase their prices, thus making their restaurants less attractive to the public. This will reduce sales and profits and may force restaurants to lay off workers.

32 Economic Growth and Sustainable Development

 Main Learning Outcome

3.6 Students should be able to explain how economic growth can impact positively and negatively on society and the environment and justify the promotion of sustainable development.

 By the end of this chapter you should:

- understand how the economic performance of the country is measured and how economic growth is calculated
- be able to outline the advantages and disadvantages of economic growth
- understand the importance of sustainable economic development and the steps we can take in order to achieve it.

Economic growth

- Two common ways of measuring economic output are:
  - **Gross Domestic Product:** The total value of all goods and services produced in Ireland in a year, whether by Irish or foreign-operated companies.
  - **Gross National Product:** The total value of all goods and services produced in a year by Irish-operated companies, whether located in Ireland or abroad.
- In most countries, these two measures give similar answers.
- However, since there are more foreign-owned transnationals operating in Ireland (e.g. Google) than there are Irish-owned transnationals operating abroad (e.g. Ryanair), our GDP is much higher than our GNP. The difference is called **net factor income from abroad**.
- Therefore, in the case of Ireland, GNP is often seen as a better measure of economic output, since much of our GDP goes abroad and not to us.

How economic growth is calculated

Economic growth is calculated by finding the percentage difference in economic output from one year to the next.

$$\frac{\text{GNP in Year 2} - \text{GNP in Year 1}}{\text{GNP in Year 1}} \times \frac{100}{1}$$

Example

- GNP in Year 1: €253Bn
- GNP in Year 2: €263Bn

$$\frac{\text{GNP in Year 2} - \text{GNP in Year 1}}{\text{GNP in Year 1}} \times \frac{100}{1}$$

$$= \frac{\text{€263Bn} - \text{€253Bn}}{\text{€253Bn}} \times \frac{100}{1}$$

$$= \quad 3.95\%$$

Conditions that encourage economic growth

- Low rates of taxation allow people to keep more of what they earn and therefore reward work and entrepreneurship.
- Stable prices (low inflation) and stable wage rates allow businesses to plan with greater confidence, thus encouraging investment.
- Investment in education enables people to realise their potential and also attracts foreign transnationals.
- Investment in infrastructure such as transport and high-speed broadband allows goods, services and labour to move freely around the country, as well as to and from other countries, while also attracting foreign transnationals.
- A stable political climate in which people work out their differences peacefully and respect one another.
- A spirit and a culture of enterprise, a feeling of confidence, a strong work ethic and a desire to do well.

Advantages of economic growth

- Better standard of living as people's incomes rise and they purchase more goods and services.
- More employment and opportunity as more businesses are set up and existing businesses expand.
- Emigrants have the chance to return home and fewer people are forced to emigrate.
- Higher government revenue to fund public services such as health and education and improvements in infrastructure.
- Less government spending on Jobseeker's Allowance.
- Reduced poverty, as more people are working and can afford the goods and services that they need.

top tip

Since countries have different populations, they are frequently compared by GDP per capita (per person). In recent years, Ireland routinely comes in the top 10 in the world.

Disadvantages of economic growth

- The benefits are not shared equally, widening the gap between rich and poor.
- A stressful, materialistic society: people spend longer commuting to and from work, have less time to spend with their families, and often judge themselves and other people based on financial success. Money makes many things possible, but it cannot buy happiness.
- A sense of community can be lost as more people move to cities for work and less people live in rural areas.
- This can drive up house prices and rents in overcrowded urban areas, leaving the countryside neglected and underpopulated.
- Damage to the environment:
  — More goods and services leads to more refuse and packaging waste.
  — Natural resources are used in the production of goods and services. Some of these are non-renewable, e.g. oil.

- More factories and vehicles result in more pollution.
- Expansion of cities and the building of roads reduce green space.
- A worsening of the effects of climate change such as extreme heatwaves.

The challenge is to reap the benefits of economic growth, while minimising its harmful effects.

Sustainable development

(See also Chapter 9.)

This involves engaging in economic activity and achieving economic growth without depleting natural resources for future generations. It means that we must try to satisfy our needs and wants today without preventing our children and grandchildren from satisfying their needs and wants in the future. This is a responsibility shared by individuals and businesses, not just governments and environmental activists.

Steps that governments can take to promote sustainable development

- Pay careful attention to the work of climate scientists and their projections regarding the dangers of climate change.
- Fund research into energy-saving technologies and ways of generating clean energy, e.g. more efficient solar panels.

The problem of sustainability could be a rich source of ideas for your CBA 1 project if you take the Economics Option (see Chapter 37).

- Encourage households and businesses to conserve energy, e.g. by turning off lights when not needed, cycling or walking to work where feasible.
- Tax or outlaw single-use coffee cups, plastic straws, bottles and plastic bags.
- Give grants to households to retrofit older houses in order to reduce energy bills, e.g. upgrading attic and wall insulation.
- Raise taxes on cars that run on fossil fuels, subsidise hybrid and electric cars, install recharging points in public places.
- Work to lighten school bags and improve road safety so that more young people can cycle to school.
- Sign up to and adhere to international accords such as the **Paris Agreement under the United Nations Framework Convention on Climate Change** and the **United States 2030 Agenda for Sustainable Development**.
- Develop initiatives such as the **Climate Action Plan to Tackle Climate Breakdown** to help to focus society on the seriousness of the problem and the need to take immediate action.
- Pass legislation such as the **Climate Action and Low Carbon Development Act 2015**.

exam Q

Question 10, Junior Cycle Sample Paper (SEC)
'The Irish economy is growing three times faster than any other European country.'

Adapted from *The Irish Times*, February 2018

State **two** ways in which economic growth can have a positive impact on a small town in rural Ireland.

Answer

- Economic growth enables investment in motorways and broadband, both of which enable more people to live and work in small towns.
- Economic growth brings jobs and spending power, reducing the need for young people to move to larger towns and cities or to emigrate.

33 International Trade and Globalisation

 Main Learning Outcome

3.7 Students should be able to debate the implications of globalisation of trade, including the benefits and challenges of international trade.

> **aims** By the end of this chapter you should:
> - be familiar with key trade terms and definitions
> - be able to outline the advantages and disadvantages of international trade
> - understand the advantages and disadvantages of the emergence of multinational companies
> - be able to discuss the advantages and disadvantages of globalisation
> - understand the barriers that exist to international trade and the role of the World Trade Organisation.

Key trade terms

- **Trade** occurs whenever people buy or sell goods or services, either in exchange for other goods or services or for money.
- **Barter** (or **counter-trade**) occurs when no money changes hands, but instead people swap goods or services with one another. Since it depends on a **double coincidence of wants**, i.e. each party has to want what the other party is offering, barter worked quite well in traditional societies. But as goods and services became more numerous and people's needs more varied, money was invented.
- **Domestic trade** refers to trade within a country, e.g. Majella from Limerick buys a top while in Galway.
- **International trade** refers to trade between countries, or to be exact, between individuals and businesses inside different countries, e.g. Richard from Wicklow goes on holiday to Florence.
- **Exporting:** selling goods or services to individuals or companies in other countries.
- **Importing:** buying goods or services from individuals or companies in other countries.
- **Visible exports:** goods sold to foreigners by Irish firms, e.g. crystal manufactured in Cavan sold to the U.S.
- **Invisible exports:** services sold to foreigners by Irish firms, e.g. a German tourist stays in a hotel in Wexford.

- **Visible imports:** goods bought by Irish people from foreign firms, e.g. a bunch of tulips grown in the Netherlands sold in Howth.
- **Invisible imports:** services bought by Irish people from foreign firms, e.g. an Australian pop singer gives a concert in the 3Arena.
- **Balance of trade:** Visible exports – visible imports.
  — If exports exceed imports, it is **favourable**.
  — If imports exceed exports, it is **unfavourable**.
- **Balance of payments:** (Visible + invisible exports) – (Visible + invisible imports).
  — If it is in deficit, it means more money is leaving the country than coming in, costing jobs. In the short run, this can be financed by borrowing.
  — However, in the long run, a country must pay for its imports by exporting – much like a household must work to pay for what it consumes.
- A deficit can be reduced by:
  — increasing exports, e.g. by paying subsidies
  — decreasing imports, using taxes and other barriers to trade
  — **import substitution**, producing goods and services at home that were previously imported.

Benefits of international trade

- **Wider choice of goods:** A small country such as Ireland can import goods, services and raw materials not available here, e.g. tropical fruit, mobile devices, Italian wines. Irish people have developed diverse tastes, fuelling a demand for many goods which can only be sourced outside of Ireland.

- **Larger markets:** The world is a lot bigger than Ireland, offering Irish companies a lot more consumers to sell to. The small Irish economy only provides limited opportunities for expansion.
- **Economies of scale:** By exporting, firms benefit from lower average costs as their output increases, allowing them to cut prices both at home and abroad. This boosts exports further while benefiting domestic consumers too, e.g. Ryanair.
- **Employment and investment:** Exporting creates jobs in the Irish economy. Firms invest in order to meet demand from abroad.
- **Standard of living:** Exports increase national income, thus improving our standard of living.
- **Foreign currency:** Exports earns the foreign currency needed to pay for imports. A balance of payments surplus in the eurozone also increases the value of the euro.

- **Competition:** Irish firms must lower prices if they are to stand up to international competition, again benefiting domestic consumers.
- **Lower costs:** Firms can spread production worldwide, again benefiting from economies of scale. Lower costs are passed on to consumers in the form of lower prices.
- **Market for excess output:** Once a country has provided for its own needs, it can export excess output to others who need it and vice versa, e.g. Ireland exports most of the beef produced here.

top tip

In Economics, if we say something is an advantage, it will not be so for everyone. We may source cheaper goods from low-cost countries, but at the cost of lost revenue for domestic producers.

- **Better international relations:** When countries trade, contact and mutual understanding is increased, and the potential for conflict is reduced.
- **Economic recovery:** Whenever the domestic economy is in recession, exports can help it to recover.

Disadvantages of international trade

- **Foreign competition:** Irish companies come under pressure from foreign firms locating here, often charging lower prices due to greater economies of scale, e.g. IKEA.
- **Lower wage countries:** Irish producers cannot always compete with firms from countries with cheaper labour, e.g. Bangladesh.
- **Cultural, language and legal variations:** When exporting, firms must adapt to the different needs and requirements of each market, e.g. reshooting television advertisements in several local languages.
- **Exchange rate risks:** When trading outside the eurozone, there is the risk of currencies rising and falling in value.
- **Collecting payment:** When trading with some countries, particularly outside the EU, there may not be the same legal remedies if a buyer does not pay on time.
- **Environmental impact:** Transporting goods and people around the world contributes greatly to pollution.
- **Ethical concerns:** Firms importing goods should be conscious of the working conditions and care of the environment in the country of origin.
- **Transport costs:** Unlike France or Germany, everything that is exported out of or imported into Ireland (except to and from Northern Ireland) must be moved by air or sea. This pushes up the cost and increases the risk of delay.

Transnational companies

Transnational companies, also called multinational companies (MNCs), are firms that operate in more than one country. They may produce or source parts of their product in several different countries, assemble them in another, carry out their research and development in yet another, and market and sell them all over the world.

A central part of Ireland's industrial policy has been to attract foreign companies to locate here, bringing jobs and investment with them. Ireland has several advantages as a location for foreign companies:

- Our **English-speaking labour force**, which appeals in particular to American companies.
- Our **corporation tax rate** of 12.5% is one of the lowest in the world.
- **Educated workforce:** a high percentage of our population holds a third-level qualification.
- **Good infrastructure:** Ireland has excellent international air access, has built up a good motorway network, and has high-speed internet in most – but not all – of the country.
- **Membership of the EU Single Market and the euro** means that a non-EU firm exporting from Ireland to the rest of the EU escapes tariffs on goods from outside the EU.
- Our **stable political environment** means that transnationals here do not have to fear a change of government or worry about the risk of political turmoil.
- Generally, our government follows **pro-enterprise government policies** and tries to make it as easy as possible to do business here.
- Transnationals tend to be reassured by the **presence of other transnationals** in the same industry, such as pharmaceuticals or technology.

Advantages of transnationals

- **Employment:** Transnationals directly employ over 225,000 people in Ireland.
- **Spin-off jobs:** Additional workers are employed by firms that supply or serve multinationals or their employees, e.g. local shops, security companies, etc.
- **Tax revenues:** Apart from the corporation tax they pay directly to the government, multinationals are also responsible for much of the income tax, PRSI, VAT, motor tax, etc. that the government collects each year.
- **Experience:** Ireland has learned a lot about how to attract and facilitate multinational companies, which helps us to attract still more.

Disadvantages of transnationals

- **Overdependence:** Many towns in Ireland are heavily reliant on the continued presence of one large foreign firm and therefore at risk if they choose to leave.
- **Pressure on governments:** If a country is overdependent on a foreign multinational, that multinational can demand changes in taxes or laws to enable it to make more money at the expense of its workers or the environment.
- **Ethics:** For some transnationals, exploiting cheap labour and damaging the environment does not upset their conscience.
- **Tax avoidance:** Many multinationals locate in Ireland largely or solely for tax reasons. Ireland has been accused of operating a 'tax haven'.
- **Exploitation of small local suppliers:** Small local firms that supply multinationals may have little choice but to accept low prices or late payment.

> **top tip**
>
> Many other EU countries are naturally jealous of our low rate of corporation tax of 12.5% and have tried to introduce a standard rate across the EU. So far Ireland has blocked this move.

Globalisation

(See also Chapter 10.)

Globalisation means that the economies – and societies – of different countries have increasingly merged and integrated into a single global economy and society. This is partly thanks to improvements in transport and information and communications technology, allowing for greater exchange of world views, products, services, ideas and other aspects of culture. More and more companies see themselves as global businesses rather than from one country, e.g. Coca Cola, Samsung, Toyota.

Advantages of globalisation

- Individuals, businesses and countries can **treat the whole world as their market**. They can buy raw materials and hire labour and also sell their products and services around the globe, e.g. Ford cars.
- Consumers have access to a **wider choice** of goods and services from all over the world, e.g. exotic cuisines.
- Companies develop **global brands**, recognisable everywhere in the world. This results in economies of scale in marketing and production, and enables them to introduce new products to more people more quickly, e.g. Apple.
- Individuals, businesses and countries gain by specialising in what they do best and trading with other individuals, businesses and countries anywhere in the world for their other needs. This is called **the theory of comparative advantage**.
- Increased trade leads to **more jobs and investment**.

Disadvantages of globalisation

- The emergence of **large transnationals** which wield huge power in the world market. This is not always good for workers, consumers or local communities.
- **Greater uniformity** of products, services and culture and a reduction in local diversity and difference as people are expected to think and act as global citizens.
- **Greater inequality** between rich and poor as large companies dominate smaller ones, and a small number of key companies earn huge profits, e.g. Google.
- Improvements in technology and the liberalisation of trade can lead to **reduced job security**, as jobs can be replaced by automation or firms can relocate to lower wage countries.
- The emergence of an **unregulated world economy** that cannot be controlled when it needs to be. An economic downturn in one part of the world can spark a global recession.
- **Environmental destruction** due to greater production of goods and services, and increased pollution due to increased levels of transport.

Barriers to trade

Despite the advantages of international trade, governments often **restrict** it. This is called **protectionism** and it happens for a number of reasons:

- To protect **employment**, e.g. the Irish government may block imports of goods that could be produced in Ireland, thus creating jobs here instead of abroad.
- To protect from competition from **low-wage countries.**
- **Balance of payments deficit:** If imports exceed exports, the government may wish to impose barriers in order to restore the balance.
- Protection against **dumping**, i.e. a foreign firm attempting to enter an export market by selling at below the price it charges at home.
- **Infant industries:** To allow small firms to gain economies of scale so that they can compete internationally.
- To allow the **phasing out** of an industry: If an industry is dying, rather than letting it collapse, the government may opt to phase out restrictions, giving workers time to find alternative employment.
- To reduce dependence on imports of **vital goods**. This avoids scarcity of important goods, e.g. food.
- For **political reasons**: Trade barriers are used as a means of political pressure e.g. UN sanctions against Syria.
- **Retaliation** against another country for imposing trade restrictions on your exports to that country.

Negative effects of barriers to trade

- They reduce the **gains from trade**.
- They restrict **consumer choice**.
- They increase the cost of imported **raw materials**.
- They protect **inefficient producers** from international competition.
- They create a **dependence on continued protection** that leaves producers even less prepared for when the barriers are eventually taken away.

Types of trade barriers

- **Tariffs:** taxes on imports, which force up their price and make them less competitive.
- **Quotas:** a limit on the amount that can be imported, leaving the rest of the market for domestic firms.
- **Subsidies:** government payments to domestic producers to allow them to reduce their prices.
- **Exchange controls:** Imports from a particular country are limited to a specified money value, e.g. €3 billion.
- **Administrative barriers:** paperwork, 'red tape', regulations, etc. that are created to discourage the importation of goods without the need for tariffs, e.g. time-consuming, costly and needless form-filling.
- **Embargoes:** banning imports from or exports to a particular country, or both, e.g. the U.S. embargo on Cuba. It can also mean banning a specified good regardless of its country of origin, e.g. illegal drugs.

The World Trade Organisation (WTO)

An international body with 164 member countries – including Ireland – which aims to reduce trade barriers and promote international trade.

- It provides a forum for negotiations (called 'rounds').
- Ireland is represented at these negotiations by the EU.
- It settles trade disputes.
- **'Most favoured nation' clause:** if you lift trade barriers for one country, you must lift them for all.
- The WTO have successfully negotiated dramatic falls in trade barriers and an expansion in world trade, but it still has more to do.

Question 2, Junior Cycle Examination 2019

Answer true or false to each of the following statements about globalisation.

		True	False
(i)	Companies have access to bigger markets.	✓	
(ii)	Consumers have less choice.		✓
(iii)	Increased trade leads to increased pollution.	✓	

Question 9, Junior Cycle Examination 2019

The figures for Ireland's exports and imports of goods are shown below.

> ### Ireland Exported €123 Billion
> ### and Imported €79 Billion of goods

(i) Using the above information calculate Ireland's balance of trade.

(ii) Give one reason why international trade is important for Ireland.

Answer

(i) **Balance of trade:**
  - Exports – Imports =
  - €123B – €79B =
  - **€44 Billion**

(ii) **Employment:** Exporting creates many jobs in the Irish economy, e.g. in the pharmaceutical industry.

34 Ireland and the EU

Main Learning Outcome

3.8 Students should be able to discuss the economic and social benefits and challenges of Ireland's membership of the EU.

aims By the end of this chapter you should:

- understand what the European Union is and the part played by each of its main institutions
- be able to outline the economic and social implications of Ireland's membership of the EU
- be able to describe the advantages and disadvantages of Ireland's membership of the euro
- understand the possible implications of Brexit for Ireland.

The **European Union** is an economic and political union of 28 countries and over 500 million citizens that cooperate closely on a range of economic, social and political issues. Ireland has been a member since 1973.

- Its member states are: Austria, Belgium, Bulgaria, Croatia, Cyprus, Czech Republic, Denmark, Estonia, Finland, France, Germany, Greece, Hungary, Ireland, Italy, Latvia, Lithuania, Luxembourg, Malta, Netherlands, Poland, Portugal, Romania, Slovakia, Slovenia, Spain, Sweden and the United Kingdom. (See page 251.)
- It has developed a **single market**, i.e. freedom of movement of goods, services, capital and labour.
- It has common policies on agriculture, fisheries, regional development and other issues.

Have adopted the euro
Have not adopted the euro

- Nineteen of its members share a common currency, called the euro. Together, these 19 countries are called the **eurozone**. Ireland adopted the euro at its introduction in 1999.

Main institutions of the European Union

European Parliament

The European Parliament sits in Strasbourg and Brussels. It is made up 751 **Members of the European Parliament (MEPs)** directly elected by the voters of the EU every five years. Ireland elects 11 MEPs.

- It shares legislative and budgetary authority with the Council of Ministers.
- It approves the appointment of the EU Commission and supervises its operation.
- It advises the Council of Ministers.
- It deals with issues that affect all states.

European Commission

The main body responsible for running the EU.

- It is the executive of the European Union and promotes its general interest.
- It has the sole power to propose new EU laws.
- It makes sure that EU treaties and laws are obeyed.
- It is independent of national governments.
- Each member state nominates one member to the commission for a period of five years. They must be approved by the Parliament.
- It manages the day-to-day business of the EU.
- It proposes the EU budget.
- It negotiates international trade agreements on behalf of the EU.
- It is answerable to the Parliament.

Council of the European Union (Council of Ministers)

Sets the political objectives of the EU and takes the final decision on all new laws.

- It is the main decision-making body of the EU.
- It shares legislative and budgetary power with the European Parliament. It enacts legislation through regulations, directives and decisions.
- It coordinates the policies of member states, including their broad economic policies, and resolves differences between them.
- Its meetings are attended by the 28 national ministers responsible for the topic under discussion, e.g. trade or education.
- Votes are taken either by majority or unanimity, with votes allocated according to population.
- Twice a year, the heads of government – making up the **Council of Europe** – meet in an EU summit. They are responsible for defining the general political direction and priorities of the Union.

Once a proposal is adopted by the Council of the European Union, it is implemented in one of three ways:

- **Regulations:** These apply immediately across the EU without the need for laws to be passed in each member state.
- **Directives:** These must be implemented in each country, but the way in which this is done is decided by country.
- **Decisions:** These can be addressed towards particular countries, individuals or companies, and are binding.

Court of Justice of the European Union (CJEU)

Ensures that EU law is observed in all 28 member states.

- It interprets EU law for member states, companies and EU citizens.
- Its rulings ensure that everyone has the same understanding of the EU treaties, regulations and directives.

Court of Auditors

Ensures that taxpayer funds from the budget of the European Union have been correctly spent.

- The auditors prepare an annual report.
- They provide Parliament and the Council with a statement of assurance certifying that the accounts are reliable, and that the operations to which they relate are legal and regular.
- They perform spot checks, and work to prevent fraud.
- They advise on how EU finances could be better managed and made more accountable to its citizens.
- The goal is to ensure that taxpayers get value for money.

European Central Bank (ECB)

Acts as the central bank for the 19 countries of the eurozone.

- It operates independently of the governments of both the eurozone and the EU.
- Its main goal is to maintain stable prices by adjusting the interest rate to control the amount of money in circulation and thus prevent inflation. This is called **monetary policy**.

- It maintains the value of the euro in relation to other currencies and manages the eurozone's foreign currency reserves.
- Oversees the issuing of euro notes and coins.
- Ensures that financial markets and institutions are well supervised, and that payment systems are working well.

Approximately 75% of all new laws that come into force in Ireland every year are EU laws. The EU plays an ever-growing role in how our country is shaped, and will always be a source of topical exam questions.

- Ensures the safety and soundness of the European banking system.

Economic and social implications of Ireland's EU membership

- **Freedom of movement** of goods, services, capital and labour across the EU (much like already happens across the USA). Irish people can live, work and study in other EU states; citizens of other EU states can do the same here. Passing between EU countries is much like travelling between counties within Ireland.
- **Larger market:** Irish companies can sell their products unhindered in any other EU member state. This has reduced Ireland's dependence on trade with the UK.
- **Foreign competition:** Any EU producer can market their goods and services in Ireland.
  - Increases the variety of goods available to Irish consumers, e.g. Lidl, Aldi.
  - Irish firms are forced to become more competitive, which in turn increases exports and employment.
  - Places small Irish producers under threat, e.g. the Irish fishing industry.
  - In addition, firms are free to relocate to lower wage countries within the EU.
- **EU Laws:** Most of our new laws every year originate not from Dublin but from Brussels. Many of our laws in relation to consumer rights, environmental protection, data protection, mobile phone roaming charges and employment rights are EU laws.
- **Loss of sovereignty:** Since joining the EU, Ireland has given up its currency and some of its ability to pass its own laws. The EU has been criticised for being bureaucratic and for ignoring the wishes of the people.
- **Economies of scale:** Firms make cost savings from trade, hopefully passing them on to consumers in the form of lower prices.
- **EU funds:** Since joining the EU, Ireland has received billions in grants from the EU for agriculture, infrastructure and other projects. This has helped to make Ireland one of the richest countries in the EU. However, as we have grown richer, we have had to become net contributors to the EU budget, i.e. we pay in more than we receive.
- **Public procurement:** Competition for government contracts is open to all firms in the EU and not just those of the member state concerned, e.g. the building of motorways.
- **Product standards:** States have negotiated common product standards and regulations, allowing them to be more easily traded across the EU, e.g. the CE mark. This process is continuing.
- **Recognition of qualifications:** This makes it easier for a citizen of any member state to work in any other member state. They also do not lose their rights to social welfare payments.
- **Single passport in banking and insurance:** This is intended to allow banks and insurance companies to operate in any member state, while still being controlled by the regulator in their home country.

- **Foreign Direct Investment (FDI):** In order to access the EU single market, many firms from outside the EU have chosen to locate in Ireland.
- **Peace and mutual understanding:** The history of Europe is marked by a long list of wars and conflicts, not least in the 20th century. The EU has contributed to a culture of peaceful cooperation, negotiation and communication.

- **Language and cultural differences:** Due to the diversity across its 28 member states, trade and communication within the EU will never be as smooth as in the United States or China. On the other hand, the cultures and languages of the EU, including the Irish language, are our greatest blessing.

The euro

Ireland joined the single currency in 1999. Notes and coins came into use at the beginning of 2002. This is referred to an **Economic and Monetary Union (EMU)**.

- 19 EU member states have adopted the euro as their currency: Austria, Belgium, Cyprus, Estonia, Finland, France, Germany, Greece, Ireland, Italy, Latvia, Lithuania, Luxembourg, Malta, the Netherlands, Portugal, Slovakia, Slovenia and Spain.
- In addition, the euro is officially used in Andorra, Monaco, San Marino, and in the Vatican City State. It is also used by Kosovo and Montenegro.

Advantages of Ireland's membership of the euro

- Exchange rate risk removed. Businesses can buy and sell on credit with greater confidence.
- It is easier to compare prices between member countries, thus encouraging competition and making travel and online shopping less confusing.
- A single currency for a single market makes sense.
- Currency speculation is eliminated.
- Transaction costs fall for both businesses and consumers.
- Increased trade between eurozone countries.
- Increased foreign investment, especially from US companies who want an English-speaking base in the eurozone.
- Support from the ECB if we fall into financial difficulty.

Disadvantages of Ireland's membership of the euro

- The UK – one of our biggest trading partners – chose to remain outside the euro. Since the UK voted in 2016 to leave the EU, the prospect of it joining the euro receded further.
- In a recession, we need low interest rates to assist recovery. In a boom, we need higher interest rates to dampen inflation. As part of the euro, however, Ireland gets the same interest rate as the rest of the eurozone – whether it suits us or not.

Impact of Brexit

Advantages for Ireland

top tip

- If the EU imposes taxes on imports from the UK, Irish exports will become more competitive within the EU.
- Ireland will gain jobs and investment if UK firms relocate here in order to maintain access to the EU market. As

> Regardless of whether Brexit happens or when it happens, the UK's relationship with the EU will continue to be topical for a long time to come, and it is therefore likely to be of interest to Ireland.

the only English-speaking country not just in the eurozone but in the EU, Ireland can attract other non-EU multinationals for the same reason.

Disadvantages for Ireland

- EU taxes on imports from the UK would make them more expensive for consumers here.
- If the UK imposes taxes on imports from Ireland, this will reduce our exports to the UK, costing Ireland jobs in the process.
- Given the Republic's border with Northern Ireland and the strong economic links between the two, our economy is additionally vulnerable.
- Any decline in the British economy resulting from Brexit would also hurt Irish exports to the UK, in turn affecting employment.
- To attract and maintain FDI the UK may cut its rate of corporation tax, drawing investment and jobs away from Ireland.
- Because the UK has been an important contributor to the budget of the EU, the Irish agriculture industry, as well as other recipients of EU spending, are likely to lose out.
- EU regulations will no longer apply in the UK. Differing standards would create barriers to trade and labour movement, e.g. goods ordered from the UK will no longer be covered by EU consumer law.
- Since no country has previously left the EU, no one knows exactly what its effects will be, and some even doubt that the UK will ultimately go through with Brexit. Such uncertainty causes investors to delay decisions, reducing trade, jobs and economic growth.
- An influx of UK firms to Ireland would add to residential and commercial property prices and rents, and increase traffic congestion and inflation.
- Brexit may encourage other countries to consider leaving the EU.

Question 8, Junior Cycle Examination 2019

Identify **two** benefits of membership of the European Union for Ireland.

Answer

- Freedom of movement. Irish people can live and work in any of the other 27 member states with most of the same rights they enjoy at home.
- Larger market for exports. Irish firms have access to a market of over 500 million people.

Question 18 (d), Junior Cycle Sample Paper (SEC)

A new poll suggests that 88% of Irish people think Ireland should remain in the European Union.

Explain one economic benefit and one social benefit of Ireland's membership of the EU.

Answer

- **Economic benefit:** Many people in Ireland are employed by transnational companies whose decision to locate in Ireland is partly based on the access doing so gives to the larger EU marketplace.
- **Social benefit:** EU membership enables young Irish people to avail of educational and travel opportunities in other EU countries, broadening their horizons and increasing their language proficiency in the process.

Question 18 (c), Junior Cycle Sample Paper (SEC)

The Pure Confectionery Company is planning to export to the UK market but is concerned about the effects of Brexit.

Outline two difficulties the company might face in selling to the UK market after the UK leaves the European Union.

Answer

- If the UK leaves the EU, there is the possibility of tariffs being imposed on goods from Ireland, making the Pure Confectionary Company's products less competitive in the UK.
- If the UK leaves, it will no longer have to follow EU product standards, meaning that the Pure Confectionary Company may have to adapt its product or packaging for the UK market, driving up its costs and again making it less competitive in the UK.

Using Skills For Business

35 The Chief Economic Indicators

 Main Learning Outcome

3.9 Students should be able to explain the relevance of economic indicators such as inflation, employment rates, interest rates, national income, economic growth and national debt for individuals and the economy.

 By the end of this chapter you should:

- understand each of the key economic indicators and their relevance for the Irish economy.

An **economic indicator** is a key economic statistic that can be used to assess the current state of the economy and to predict its future performance. The main economic indicators that we will examine are:

- inflation
- employment rates
- interest rates
- national income
- economic growth
- national debt.

top tip

You can find most of these indicators updated on a monthly basis on the website of the Central Statistics Office: www.cso.ie.

Inflation

- Inflation is defined as a rise in the general level of prices over time.
- In Ireland, the inflation rate is measured by the Central Statistics Office using the **Consumer Price Index (CPI)**.

Causes of inflation

- **Cost-push** inflation is caused when cost increases are passed on to consumers. This can be due to a rise in:
  — the cost of labour
  — the cost of raw materials
  — transport or energy costs.
- **Demand-pull** inflation happens when supply cannot keep up with an increase in demand. This can be due to:
  — an unexpected increase in consumer confidence
  — goods that cannot be imported or manufactured fast enough to meet new demand
  — firms taking advantage of the situation to raise prices and make more money.

- **Government-caused** inflation is a rise in prices as a result of some action by the government. This can be due to:
  — an increase in VAT or customs/excise duty
  — a decrease in PAYE, which can cause demand-pull inflation as people spend more
  — an increase in government expenditure
  — a rise in interest rates, driving up mortgage costs.

Relevance of inflation

- Inflation reduces the purchasing power of money. If prices rise but incomes do not, individuals can no longer buy as much as they could before.
- Inflation also reduces the value of savings.
- Low inflation leads to stable wages, as workers don't need to demand wage increases to compensate for price rises. This encourages investment and leads to greater employment.
- Low inflation also makes Irish exports more competitive abroad and helps to attract foreign investment and jobs.

Employment rate

The employment rate is the percentage of the labour force that is currently employed.

The labour force is the number of people between 16 and 65 who are available for work, i.e. either employed or looking for work. It does not include those who are in full-time education or are retired.

Relevance of the employment rate

- When more people are working, more money is earned and spent in the economy by individuals, increasing national income.
- Government revenue rises, and it can afford to provide more public services. Less money is needed for Jobseeker's Allowance.
- Wages may rise due to a shortage of labour, and more immigrants are attracted to the country.
- If the employment rate falls, people have less money to spend and the economy slows down, leading to further job losses.

Interest rates

The interest rate (see Chapter 5) is the percentage you earn by depositing money in a bank or the percentage you pay to borrow money from a bank.

- The interest rate paid to borrow money is higher than the rate earned on savings.
- Interest rates in the eurozone are set by the European Central Bank (ECB), based in Frankfurt.

Relevance of the interest rate

- When interest rates rise, more money is saved and less is borrowed and invested. Jobs are lost and the economy slows down. The cost of debt servicing rises.
- When interest rates fall, less money is saved and more is borrowed and invested. There are more jobs and the economy expands.
- The ECB raises the interest rate when it wants to reduce inflation. It lowers the interest rate when the economy needs help to make it grow.
- Since joining the euro, Ireland has no control over its interest rates.

National income

National income is the total value of all goods and services produced in a country in a year. It is measured in two ways:

- The **income method** measures the total income earned by the factors of production (wages, interest, rent and profit).
- The **expenditure method** measures all spending on goods and services plus exports minus imports.

Relevance of national income

- The higher the national income, the more goods and services there are to consume.
- More jobs are created, and the standard of living rises.
- Government revenue rises and more can be spent on public services and infrastructure.

Economic growth

Economic growth (see Chapter 32) is calculated by finding the percentage increase in national income from one year to the next.

Example

- National income in Year 1: €315Bn
- National income in Year 2: €298Bn

$$= \frac{€315Bn - €298Bn}{€298Bn} \times \frac{100}{1}$$

$$= 5.7\%$$

Relevance of economic growth

- Individuals have more money to spend, the standard of living rises, more jobs are created and the government has more revenue to spend on public services or paying off the national debt.

- Poverty is reduced and less money is needed for Jobseeker's Benefit.
- Emigrants have the chance to return home and more immigrants come into the country.
- The government can develop the country's infrastructure, leading to further economic growth.
- If the benefits are not shared by all, there will be an increase in inequality.
- Economic growth also leads to higher house prices, more traffic congestion and more damage to the environment.

National debt

The national debt is the total amount of money borrowed by the Irish government.

- It does not include money borrowed by Irish people or businesses (e.g. credit cards, mortgages), it only includes money borrowed by the government.
- It is divided into domestic debt (borrowed from Irish banks) and foreign debt (borrowed from banks abroad).
- If the government has a budget deficit (when expenditure exceeds revenue), the money that is borrowed is added to the national debt.
- Ireland's national debt is managed by the National Treasury Management Agency (NTMA).

top tip

The national debt as a percentage of national income is more important than the size of the national debt by itself. To understand why, imagine two people each owe €50,000. One earns €30,000 a year, the other earns €100,000 a year. Clearly, one is in more trouble than the other even though their debts are the same size.

Relevance of the national debt

- The higher the national debt, the more the government must pay in interest. This is called **debt servicing**.
- This, in turn, requires higher taxes or cuts in other areas of government expenditure.

- A lower national debt reduces the interest bill and means that taxes can be cut or more can be spent in other areas.
- Borrowing to invest in education or infrastructure makes sense if it leads to greater economic opportunity in the future.

Question 18 (c), Junior Cycle Examination 2019

On the graph below, the economic indicators for unemployment and economic growth are shown for Ireland for 2017 and 2018.

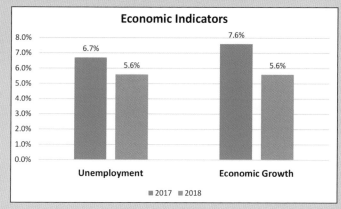

(i) Indicate in each case whether the change in the indicators is a good or bad trend for the Irish Economy. Tick (✓) the correct box below.

Economic Indicator	Good Trend	Bad Trend
Unemployment	✓	
Economic growth		✓

(ii) Explain the impact of the above trend in unemployment on individuals and on the economy.

Answer

Impact on individuals:

When an individual finds a job, they experience an immediate increase in income and an improvement in their standard of living. They also experience an improvement in self-worth and don't have to worry as much about the future and how they will make ends meet.

Impact on the economy:

For the economy in general, a fall in unemployment means that more people are earning and therefore spending, which increases economic activity, improving the standard of living and creating more jobs. It can also mean that less taxation is required to pay for Jobseeker's Allowance.

Question 2, Junior Cycle Sample Paper (SEC)

The rate of inflation in a country over four years is shown in the graph below.

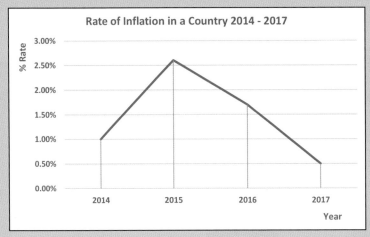

Using the above information answer the following questions.

(a) Which year has the highest rate of inflation?

(b) State one way in which a large increase in the rate of inflation may affect consumers in an economy.

Answer

(a) 2015

(b) Inflation reduces the purchasing power of your money. What €100 bought you last year will not be enough to buy you the same amount of goods and services this year.

3.10 Students should be able to use their knowledge, and information from a range of media sources, to discuss current economic issues and present an informed view.

3.11 Students should be able to evaluate the benefits and costs of a government economic policy and assess who enjoys the benefits and who bears the costs.

> **aims** By the end of this chapter you should:
> - understand the main economic policies available to the government
> - be able to outline how each can be used to achieve the various economic aims of the government
> - understand how conflicts can arise between various economic policies.

Economic policies

- An **economic policy** is any action the government takes that is intended to influence or control the economy of the country for the better and to address the economic issues faced by its people.

- An **economic issue** is any economic problem currently facing the country or its citizens, e.g. unemployment, rising prices or lack of opportunity. Even in good times, there are always economic issues that need to be addressed. Economic policy is the means by which this is achieved.

exam focus

The economic issues that come up in your exam will depend on the year. It could be house prices, the minimum wage, Brexit or emigration. It would be good to discuss from time to time the issues of the day at home or at school and how they affect you or may do in the future.

In order to address economic issues, the government can use the following economic policies.

Fiscal policy

Refers to any increase or decrease in any area of either government revenue or expenditure. It is the most powerful tool the Irish government has. It can be used to:

- encourage investment in certain industries or regions, e.g. by cutting corporation tax
- redistribute wealth through taxation and social protection payments, e.g. raising Jobseeker's Benefit

- fund vital services, e.g. education, health, etc.
- invest in infrastructure projects, e.g. airports and motorways.

Monetary policy

This means controlling the money supply by means of the interest rate, with the objective of controlling inflation and encouraging economic growth. Because Ireland is a member of the euro, our monetary policy is controlled by the ECB. It has, however, a major impact on Ireland.

- When the ECB raises interest rates, it costs more to borrow money and it makes more sense to save. Demand for goods and services goes down, and inflation in turn is reduced.
- When the ECB lowers interest rates, it costs less to borrow money and it makes less sense to save. Demand for goods and services goes up, hopefully leading to economic growth.
- The ECB tries to strike a balance between low inflation and economic growth.
- Because Ireland is only one of 19 countries in the eurozone, we don't always get the monetary policy that we would prefer.

Legislation

This involves the government passing laws to try to achieve its economic objectives. It can pass laws to:

- set a minimum wage, e.g. €9.80 an hour
- impose maximum or minimum **price controls**, e.g. to keep rents under control or to restrict access to cheap alcohol
- open up markets to more competition, e.g. the insurance industry or the legal profession
- protect the right of consumers, e.g. the Consumer Protection Act 2007
- ban the use of fossil fuels or restrict the use of diesel cars
- regulate how industries work, e.g. ban discrimination in the workplace
- make the country more inclusive for workers and consumers, e.g. mandatory wheelchair accessibility.

Market intervention

This means that the government becomes a competitor or even the sole producer in an industry. Many socially desirable but unprofitable goods and services would not be provided unless the government intervened. Examples include:

- RTÉ
- Irish Water
- Iarnród Éireann.

Economic aims

Now that we know the economic policies that are available, we can examine the various aims of government and which policies can be used to achieve them.

Economic growth

An increase in output per person in the economy. When output per person rises, more goods and services can be consumed, and the standard of living increases.

Policies

- Cut the interest rate to make it easier to borrow and hence to invest.
- Increase government spending, which injects more money into the economy.
- Reduce corporation tax to encourage companies to invest and expand.
- Reduce PAYE, PRSI, USC, VAT, customs and excise duties in order to encourage consumer spending.

Managing the public finances

If government spending exceeds revenue, the result is a budget deficit.

Policies

- Cut government spending, e.g. reduce public sector pay.
- Increase tax rates in order to increase revenue, e.g. raise the rates of PAYE, USC, PRSI or VAT.
- Borrow. However, the higher the national debt, the higher the cost of interest payments for future taxpayers. Borrowing cannot continue indefinitely.

Infrastructure

Our country needs good roads, rail, broadband, water, sewage systems, harbours, airports, etc.

Policies

- Direct government spending on infrastructure, e.g. new rail stations.
- Public-private partnerships, e.g. the government shares the cost of building a new motorway with a private firm, then allows that firm to collect the tolls for a set period of time.

Low inflation

Inflation erodes the competitiveness of our exports and reduces consumer's purchasing power. Low inflation leads to stable wages, which encourages investment and economic growth while keeping exports competitive.

Policies

- Impose a wage freeze, i.e. ban pay increases in the public sector.
- Impose price controls, e.g. to prevent increases in the price of electricity.

- Increase interest rates, making saving more attractive and borrowing less attractive. Only the ECB can do this.
- Increase direct taxes to cut consumer spending.
- Reduce VAT, thereby cutting prices and hence inflation.
- Reduce government spending.
- Pass laws to restrict lending by banks.

Full employment

Full employment occurs when everyone who is available for work at the present wage rate is employed. The government wants the maximum possible number of people in employment.

Policies

- Increase public sector employment, e.g. take on more nurses and Gardaí.
- Train and upskill the unemployed.
- Use grants and a low corporation tax rate to attract multinational companies to Ireland.
- Reduce PAYE, PRSI and USC to encourage workers to take up jobs.
- Reduce VAT to encourage spending and hence create jobs.
- Cut interest rates, increasing the availability of loans for business expansion. Again, only the ECB can implement this.

Equilibrium in the balance of payments

This occurs when imports and exports are roughly equal. If imports exceed exports, money and jobs leave the country and money must be borrowed to pay for the deficit. If exports exceed imports, more money is flowing into the country than out, and this can contribute to inflation. It also drives up the value of the euro and reduces the competitiveness of our exports.

Policies

- Devalue the euro to make exports cheaper abroad and imports more expensive at home. Only the ECB can devalue the euro.
- Increase taxes on imports to make them less attractive.
- Pay subsidies to exporting firms to help them to compete abroad.

Social fairness

It is widely felt that the government should provide basic services to all citizens, regardless of economic status, e.g. free education, and should also try to reduce inequality by redistributing income from the rich who can afford it to the poor who depend on it.

Policies

- Increase PAYE, PRSI and USC for higher earners.
- Cut VAT on essential items, increase VAT on luxury goods.
- Provide adequate social protection payments.
- Fund services and supports for those with disabilities.
- Give education grants to the less well off.

Regional development

Economic development tends to be concentrated in big cities where the largest markets are located, e.g. in the greater Dublin area. The government tries to redirect some of this activity to other parts of the country that are neglected. Doing so also eases traffic congestion and house price increases in Dublin.

Policies

- Tax cuts or grants for firms that locate in the BMW region (Border, Midlands and the West).
- Investment in broadband, motorways and regional airports, e.g. Knock Airport.
- **Decentralisation:** relocate some of the government outside Dublin, e.g. the State Examinations Commission in Athlone, Co. Westmeath.
- Encourage tourists – both Irish and foreign – to travel outside of Dublin, e.g. the Wild Atlantic Way.

Environmental sustainability

We must be careful to make use of our resources in a way that ensures that there are adequate resources for future generations. Sustainability has therefore become a vital part of the government's economic policy (see Chapter 9).

Policies

- Lower motor tax on hybrid and electric cars, raise tax on petrol and diesel cars.
- Grants for housing insulation, solar panels, etc.
- Investment in bicycle lanes, windfarms and public transport.
- Laws banning single-use plastic straws, coffee cups, etc.

Conflicts between economic policies

There are many examples of how an economic policy intended to achieve one objective can negatively impact on another objective:

- Increased government spending and lower interest rates are good for employment, but they also lead to inflation. Attempts to cut inflation can also cost jobs.

- Increased government spending creates jobs, but if the increase in income creates a demand for imports, it worsens the balance of payments.

> At times, some people form the false impression that the government can 'just fix it', and some politicians are happy to let people believe things are that simple. But the reality is that just as households face opportunity costs, governments do too. Nobody can do everything they want to do.

- Social fairness requires higher taxes on the rich, but this can discourage investment and hence cost jobs and reduce economic growth.

- On the other hand, policies that encourage economic growth, while good for most people, also increase inequality.

- Borrowing can make sense if it creates jobs, stimulates demand and finances infrastructure, but it also adds to the national debt and drives up inflation.

Question 17, NCCA Sample Questions

Population By Age Group

Children	Pre-school	Primary	Secondary
	331,515	548,693	371,588
	↓ down 7.0%	↑ up 8.8%	↑ up 7.7%

Adults	19-24 years	25-64 years	Over 65 years
	331,208	2,541,294	637,567
	↓ down 6.5%	↑ up 1.9%	↑ up 19.1%

Figure: Sourced from CSO.ie, August 2017

With reference to the data above, explain **two** ways in which this data may impact on government **spending** in the future.

Answer

- Because of the rising numbers of children at primary and secondary school, the government will need to hire more teachers and special needs assistants, and invest in the building of more schools.
- Due to the climb in the number of people over 65, the government may need to raise the retirement age and raise taxes in order to pay for a higher pensions bill in the future.

Question 22, NCCA Sample Questions

Governments have many objectives when they change tax policy. Here are three of the objectives:

- The objective to raise government revenue
- The objective to be fair to taxpayers
- The objective to influence taxpayers' behaviour.

Choose **one** of the government's objectives. Do you think the government has achieved this objective with the Sugar Tax? Give **two** reasons for your answer.

Answer

Yes, I think the government has achieved the objective of being fair to taxpayers because:

- The Sugar Tax makes people less likely to consume drinks containing sugar, which is a good thing for public health.
- The Sugar Tax also raises money for the government to spend on the health system to deal with the problems caused by overconsumption of sugar.

37 Guide to the Exam, the Classroom-Based Assessments and the Assessment Task

Your assessment in Junior Cycle Business Studies consists of four elements:

- **The Exam**
- **Classroom-Based Assessment 1 (CBA 1): Business in Action**
- **Classroom-Based Assessment 2 (CBA 2): Presentation**
- **The Assessment Task**

The Exam

- A two-hour long common level paper (no Higher or Ordinary levels).
- It is worth 90% of your overall grade in Junior Cycle Business Studies.
- There are two sections:
  - **Section A: 15 short questions worth 6 marks each (90 marks).**
    - o The questions will be drawn from all three strands of the course.
    - o You should spend approximately three minutes on each of the 15 short questions.
  - **Section B: 3 long questions worth 60 marks each (180 marks).**

    - o Again, the questions can come from all three strands.
    - o Sections of a question may come from different strands.
    - o You should spend approximately 25 minutes on each of the three long questions.
- You must answer all questions.
- Write your answers in blue or black pen. You may use only use a pencil for graphs and diagrams.
- It is important to write your answers only in the spaces provided, because the answer booklet will be scanned for the examiner to view on computer, and anything that you write outside the answer areas may not be marked.

- Show all workings. You may still get partial marks even if your final answer is incorrect.
- Calculators may be used. You must enter the make and model in the space provided in the answer booklet.

Classroom-Based Assessment 1 (CBA 1): Business in Action

- CBA 1 is a **written group project** of up to 1,500 words in length.
- It must be based on one of the three following options:
  — Enterprise in action
  — Economics in action
  — Finance in action
- Ideally, each group in a class will follow the same option. Students and their teacher can work together in choosing which one. They must still, however, choose a separate topic within that option, e.g. each group must organise an event, but no two groups can organise the same event.
- The project is completed in Second Year over a maximum of four weeks. Your teacher will inform you of the dates in advance and will offer guidance and support throughout.
- In addition to the group project, each individual student must also submit:
  — a Student Research form.
  — a Student Reflection form.
- Not every member of a group is entitled to the same descriptor.

Option 1: Enterprise in Action

If you choose this option, you are required to:

- Develop a product or service **or** organise an event or activity:
  — The product or service can be a new idea with a potential market, or one that already exists but with the potential to expand its market.
  — The event or activity can be for-profit or not-for-profit; it can be once-off or over a longer time period; and it can be for economic, social or cultural purposes.
- Carry out research to assess the feasibility of your idea and evaluate your findings.
- Submit a business plan describing the marketing mix and detailing the finances of the enterprise.
- Produce and market your product or service or hold your event or activity, where possible.
- Record the inputs and outputs of your enterprise, where possible.

Option 2: Economics in Action

If you choose this option, you are required to:

- Explore an economic trend, development, change or policy that is affecting the Irish economy and society either positively or negatively.
- Research your chosen issue and evaluate the findings in terms of the economic, social and environmental benefits and costs.
- Make use of relevant economic indicators and graphs to support your findings.
- Submit an action plan recommending a suitable change to economic policy.

Option 3: Finance in Action

If you choose this option, you are required to:

- Identify and research a financial challenge either for a consumer or a for-profit or a not-for-profit organisation.
- Evaluate your research findings in terms of the causes of the financial challenge, its costs and its impact on income and expenditure.
- Support your analysis with tables and graphs.
- Submit an action plan to address the financial challenge.

CBA 1 is made up of four stages:

1. Conducting research

- You and your fellow group members should brainstorm to decide the topic of your group project.
- You should then assign an area for each individual member to research.
- You can undertake field (primary) research or desk (secondary) research or both, for example:
  — go on a field visit
  — conduct an interview
  — carry out a survey
  — engage in online research
  — consult newspapers and magazines.
- You should keep a record of any sources used in order to assess their reliability and quality, and so that you can reference them in your project.

2. Evaluating information

- Each individual student should examine the information they have collected and appraise their findings.
- Your group should then examine all the information it has gathered and appraise each member's findings together.

Enterprise option

If following **the enterprise option**, you will need to assess the feasibility of your enterprise. Some issues to be addressed:

- Based on your findings, do you need to change your idea?
- Is there a market for your product/service?
- How much will it cost?
- Will you earn a profit?

Economics option

If following the **economics option**, you will need to assess the benefits and costs of your economic issue. Some issues to be addressed:

- What are the economic, social and environmental costs and benefits to the various stakeholders?
- Does your data support your analysis?

Finance option

If following the **finance option**, you will need to assess the financial position of a consumer or organisation. Some issues to be addressed:

- How does the issue affect revenue and expenditure?
- Is the problem short, medium or long term?
- Does your data support your analysis?

3. Developing action plans

- Working together in active and meaningful collaboration, your group must develop its action plan.
- All judgements made must be supported by evidence and must address the challenges posed by your project.

Enterprise option

If following **the enterprise option**:

- Your group must develop a business plan describing the marketing mix and detailing the finances of your enterprise.
- You should also try to produce and market your product or service or hold your event or activity, where possible.

Economics option

If following the **economics option**: Your group must develop an action plan recommending a suitable change to economic policy that will address the issue you studied.

Finance option

If following the **finance option**:

- Your group must develop an action plan that addresses the financial challenge and will improve the financial position of the individual or organisation you studied.
- You should use tables and graphs in support of your plan.

4. Reporting findings

- Your group should select the information you feel is most relevant, reliable and of good quality to be included as evidence in your completed project.
- Your project should include the following:
  — an introduction to the project
  — a **Student Research** form for each group member (see template)
  — an action plan for implementing the findings of your research
  — conclusion and recommendations
  — a **Student Reflection** form for each group member (see template)
- Your project should also include support materials such as:
  — prototypes or artefacts
  — graphic representations
  — financial accounts
  — surveys
  — interview questions
- images and photographs
- storyboard and infographics.

The Student Research form

The Student Research form is your evidence that you conducted and evaluated your research and that you submitted it to your group. You should answer honestly and try to fill the spaces provided.

Business in Action: Template for Student Research

Project option:		
Enterprise in Action	☐	
Economics in Action	☐	
Finance in Action	☐	
Title of your project	Student name	
Method of research	Field (primary) research	☐
	Desk (secondary) research	☐

1.1 Introduction: Outline briefly the purpose of your research.

1.2 Method of research: Explain briefly why you have chosen your method of research.

1.3 Sources: List your source(s) of information.

1.4 Summary: Give a brief summary of what you found out as a result of your research.

1.5 Evaluation of findings: Think critically about the following questions and write a short response.
(a) Were you surprised by your findings? Give a reason for your answer.

(continued on the next page)

(b) Is the source of your research reliable? Give a reason for your answer.

(c) Is the information one-sided or biased? Give a reason for your answer.

1.6 Conclusion: Based on your findings what is the key message you will share with your team?

1.7 Decision-making: How do you think your findings will affect your team's action plan?

1.8 Recording your sources: Provide some evidence of your research e.g. interview questions, questionnaire, photocopies, images, notes, graphic organisers.

The Student Reflection form

The Student Reflection form is your specific declaration of the part you played in the group project. Again, you should answer honestly and try to fill the spaces provided.

Business in Action: Template for Student Reflection

Project option: Enterprise in Action ☐ Economics in Action ☐ Finance in Action ☐	
Title of your project	Student name
1.1 Introduction: Provide a brief outline of your project.	
1.2 Roles and responsibilities: Describe your key role and your main responsibilities.	
1.3 Summary: Give a brief summary of how you contributed to your project during the following activities: (a) How I contributed to researching the project. (b) How I contributed to analysing the research information.	

(continued on the next page)

(c) How I contributed to developing the action plan.

(d) How I contributed to compiling the project.

1.4 Review: Describe how you got on as a team and any difficulties you overcame while working as a team, or Describe the advantages and challenges of working on this group project from your individual perspective.

1.5 Teacher feedback

Awarding your descriptor

After you have submitted your work, your teacher will award you a descriptor based on the following **features of quality**.

Exceptional

- Highly effective research method used, high level of analysis of findings.
- Evaluation of collective findings is of excellent quality, different points of view and credibility of sources considered.
- Action Plan shows ambition and creativity, based on a sound, evidence-based judgement of all information.
- Of a very high standard, very comprehensive, information presented in a variety of formats, very little room for improvement.
- Individual Student Reflection describes clearly and in detail how you engaged at an exceptional level in all stages, presents a meaningful reflection on your experience of group work.

Above expectations

- Effective research method used, good analysis of findings.
- Evaluation of the collective findings of very good quality, some consideration of other points of view and credibility of sources.
- Action Plan shows an evidence-based judgement of the information.
- Completed to a high standard, clear and organised, some scope for improvement.
- Individual Student Reflection shows you engaged fully in all stages, presents some reflection on your experience of group work.

In line with expectations

- Acceptable research method used, analysis lacks depth.
- Evaluation of the collective findings is sufficient, limited consideration of other points of view and credibility of sources.
- Action plan of a good standard, reasonably sound judgement of the evidence.
- Has some omissions but overall is complete, presented in an organised manner.
- Individual Student Reflection shows some evidence of how you engaged at some stages of the project, reflections on your experience of group work are limited.

Yet to meet expectations

- Ineffective research method used, analysis of findings is cursory (basic).
- Evaluation of the collective findings is poor, little consideration of other points of view or credibility of sources.
- Action plan shows judgement of the evidence, evidence flawed in places.
- Very basic summary of information, omits important elements, lacks clarity.
- Individual Student Reflection shows limited engagement in the project, reflection on your experience of group work very narrow.

If it is unclear which descriptor to apply, your teacher selects the one that best matches on balance. Your work is only judged against the features of quality and not other students' work.

- Your teacher then takes part in a **Subject Learning and Assessment Review (SLAR)** meeting, at which each teacher brings examples of student work and compares their judgements with their colleagues. Following the SLAR, your teacher may change your descriptor.
- Your CBA 1 descriptor will appear on your **Junior Cycle Profile of Achievement (JCPA)**.
- Your teacher will also give you feedback on the strengths of your work and areas for improvement.

Classroom-Based Assessment 2 (CBA 2): Presentation

- Unlike CBA 1, CBA 2 is an **individual presentation** in front of your class, based on an investigation of a business-related topic.
  - It should be no longer than three minutes, including time for engagement with the audience.
  - Questions or interventions from your teacher may form part of the presentation.
  - You can speak with or without notes and you may read from a prepared script.
  - You are encouraged to use digital technology, handouts, tables, graphs, posters, storyboards, etc.
- CBA 2 is prepared in Third Year over a maximum of three weeks before being presented. Your teacher will inform you of the dates in advance and will offer guidance and support throughout.
- You may collaborate with classmates in researching and practising for your presentation, but the presentation itself must be your own work.

CBA 2 is made up of three stages:

1. Investigating

Before you present, you must choose a topic and investigate it.

- Your topic can be directly related to a specific part of the Junior Cycle Business Studies course.
- It can be an issue of personal or local relevance, as long as it is related to the business environment.
- Examples:
  - field visit to a local enterprise
  - investigation of a business-related story in the media
  - Irish business leaders
  - investigation of the impact of an organisation on the community
  - some aspect of consumerism
  - a current economic issue
  - any career in business.
- As part of your investigation, you should gather information from both primary and secondary sources.
- Given the length of the presentation, you should ensure that you focus on a narrow enough aspect of the topic.
- You should make a note of all the sources of the information you gather.
- You should be conscious of differing viewpoints on the topic.
- You may **not** investigate the same topic you studied in CBA 1.

2. Reflecting on learning

After completing your investigation, you should be able to:

- evaluate what you have learned
- reflect on whether and how your view of the topic has changed and how you see the world differently
- reflect on whether and how your behaviour has been changed
- explain different opinions related to the topic, express your own opinion and back it up with evidence
- explore the importance of the topic from personal, local, social or environmental perspectives.

3. Communicating

- You must give an oral presentation on what you have learned, showing an understanding of the knowledge and ideas relevant to your chosen topic.
- You must show evidence of learning and an ability to express an opinion.
- You should practise both at home and in collaboration with classmates at school. This will build your confidence and help you to demonstrate the development of your presentation and communication skills.
- Your presentation should be structured as follows:
  — Give a brief overview of your topic.
  — Explain your interest in the topic.
  — Evaluate what you have learned about the business environment.
  — Reflect on whether and how you see the world differently and how your behaviour has changed.

Awarding your descriptor

After you have submitted your work, your teacher will award you a descriptor based on the following **features of quality**.

Exceptional
• Communicates eloquently and very confidently, very comprehensive knowledge of topic, very well structured.
• Support material shows creativity, used very effectively to captivate audience.
• Your reflections are of excellent quality, showing how your point of view has developed or evolved over time.
Above expectations
• Communicates clearly, competently and with confidence, very good knowledge of topic, well structured.
• Support material well chosen to interest audience, displaying some creativity.
• Your reflections are of very good quality.
In line with expectations
• Communicates well, good knowledge of topic, lacks some confidence, unclear in places.
• Support material appropriate, not used to full potential.
• You showed an ability to reflect on your own perspective of the topic.
Yet to meet expectations
• Does not communicate clearly or confidently, very limited knowledge of topic, lacks structure.
• Support material used in a basic manner.
• Your reflections are narrow, of poor quality.

- As with CBA 1, if it is unclear which descriptor to apply, your teacher selects the one that best matches on balance. Again, your work is not judged against other student's work.
- Your teacher will then take part in a second **Subject Learning and Assessment Review (SLAR)** meeting, following which they may change your descriptor.
- Your CBA 2 descriptor will appear on your **Junior Cycle Profile of Achievement (JCPA)**.
- Once again, your teacher will also give you feedback.

Assessment Task

- This consists of a focused **written reflection** on CBA 2 and takes place after CBA 2.
- You will be provided with a booklet in which to complete it.
- It assesses your:
  - ability to evaluate new knowledge or understanding gained from CBA 2
  - capacity to reflect on the skills developed during CBA 2
  - ability to reflect on how your value system was influenced by CBA 2.
- It is worth 10% of your overall grade in Junior Cycle Business Studies.
- The assessment task is completed in **two stages** over a double class or over two separate single class periods (total of 80 minutes).

First stage: Discussion and reflection (40 minutes)

Discussion (20 minutes)

- Your teacher will display the features of quality on the board.
- You should have your individual presentation notes, support materials and student self-reflection sheet with you.
- You are then asked to discuss the features with your classmates in relation to your individual presentations and give feedback to one another.

- This can happen in pairs, in small groups or as a class.
- Some questions to stimulate the discussion:
  - What are the strengths of your communication skills?
  - What would like to improve about them?
  - How did you structure your presentation?
  - Why did you apply this structure?
  - How effective did you find it?
  - What did you learn about your topic?
  - Why is what you learned important?
  - What support materials did you use?
  - Why did you choose them?
  - How effective were they?

Reflection (20 minutes)

- This is a time for quiet, critical reflection on the features of quality and the discussion from your own perspective, based on your individual presentation.
- You can make note of any points arising from the discussion on the features of quality and you can also refer to the student self-reflection sheet if you choose.
- Some questions to help you reflect:
  - What were the strengths and weaknesses of your presentation?
  - Has your opinion about your topic changed?
  - How would you improve your presentation if you did it again?

Second stage: Completion of booklet and submission (40 minutes)

Completion of the assessment task booklet (35 minutes)

- Now you fill in the booklet. As you do so, you can still have your presentation notes, presentation support materials and student self-reflection sheet in front of you.
- You complete the booklet on your own, much like a normal exam.

Submission (5 minutes)

- Clearly label your answer booklet.
- Your teacher will send it away to the State Examinations Commission for correction.

Acknowledgements

For Beata Krystyna Krygiołka-Wasik-Kozdroń